God's Englishman

CROSSCURRENTS IN WORLD HISTORY
Norman F. Cantor, Editor

God's Englishman

Oliver Cromwell and the English Revolution

Christopher Hill

'God is decreeing to begin some new and great period . . .
What does he then but reveal himself . . . as his manner is, first
to his Englishmen?'
John Milton, *Areopagitica* (1644)

'We are English, that is one good fact.'
Oliver Cromwell to Parliament, 17 September 1656

HARPER TORCHBOOKS
Harper & Row, Publishers
New York, Evanston, San Francisco, London

Published by arrangement with The Dial Press.

GOD'S ENGLISHMAN: OLIVER CROMWELL AND THE ENGLISH REVOLUTION

First TORCHBOOK edition published 1972

STANDARD BOOK NUMBER: 06-131666-0

The author and publishers would like to thank the following for supplying photographs for this book: the City Museum and Art Gallery, Birmingham, plate 1 and the jacket; the Cromwell Museum, Huntingdon, plate 2 (photo Edward Leigh); Philip Dickinson, plate 3; Radio Times Hulton Picture Library, plates 4, 5, 6, 8, 9, 10, 11, 12, 13, 14, 16, 17; The Headmaster, Kimbolton School, Huntingdonshire, plate 7; the British Museum, plate 15 (photo John Freeman).

Contents

List of Illustrations

Is it not really a bit silly to speak of the 'failure' of men who fought and wrote and committed themselves as the great English revolutionaries did? What more is possible in life than defiance of known evil and the courage to create and fight for new illusions? Cromwell's generation was no failure.

C. H. GEORGE, *Revolution* (New York, 1962), p. 319

Preface

In 1958 I wrote a pamphlet for the Historical Association, to celebrate the tercentenary of Oliver Cromwell's death. (*Oliver Cromwell, 1658–1958*). Inevitably I have had to use in this book some of the ideas put forward there, and I am grateful to the Publications Committee of the Historical Association for permission to do so: but I have tried not merely to expand that pamphlet. The reader may feel that I have referred too often to other writings of my own. The object was to avoid having to recapitulate arguments which are available elsewhere if anyone is interested in pursuing them. In order not to overburden this little book with footnotes, I have not usually given references for quotations from Cromwell, all of which (unless otherwise indicated) can be found in W. C. Abbott's monumental *Writings and Speeches of Oliver Cromwell* (see Bibliography); nor have I always annotated quotations from familiar seventeenth-century sources when there should be no difficulty in identifying them. Spelling, capitalization and punctuation have been modernized in all quotations except titles of books. I have always assumed, as contemporaries did not, that the year began on 1 January.

The governing body of Balliol College gave me a term's sabbatical leave in the summer of 1968, during which I finished writing this book: I am most grateful to them. As a teacher of English history I have been arguing about

Oliver Cromwell for some thirty years now. I have tried to make acknowledgements whenever I am conscious of having picked the brains of my pupils (or of anyone else): but I cannot always have succeeded. In writing this book I have received generous help in various ways from Professor Gerald Aylmer, Mr Peter Brown, Dr Robin Clifton, Mr Mervyn James, Mr Raphael Samuel, Professors Lawrence Stone and Austin Woolrych. None of these however is responsible for what I have written. Miss Pat Lloyd most kindly read the proofs. I wish I could find a new way of expressing gratitude to Bridget, who helped most of all.

Christopher Hill

I

OLIVER CROMWELL AND THE ENGLISH REVOLUTION

When I read the book, the biography famous,
And is this then (said I) what the author calls a man's life?
And so will some one when I am dead and gone write my life?
(As if any man really knew aught of my life,
Why even I myself I often think know little or nothing of my
    real life,
Only a few hints, a few diffused faint clews and indirections
I seek for my own use to trace out here).

WALT WHITMAN, Leaves of Grass, 1871

How many books are still written and published about Charles
the First and his times! Such is the fresh and enduring interest
of that grand crisis of morals, religion and government! But
these books are none of them works of any genius or imagination; not one of these authors seems to be able to throw himself back into that age; if they did, there would be less praise
and less blame bestowed on both sides.

COLERIDGE, Table Talk, 9 November 1833

I

Oliver Cromwell lived from 1599 to 1658. During the first forty years of his life a tangled knot of problems was forming which was only to be unravelled, or cut through, in the revolutionary decades 1640–60. It may help our understanding of his life's work if we take a preview of these inter-related problems.[1]

The seventeenth is the decisive century in English history, the epoch in which the Middle Ages ended. England's problems were not peculiar to her. The whole of Europe faced a crisis in the mid-seventeenth century, which expressed itself in a series of breakdowns, revolts and civil wars.[2] The sixteenth century had seen the opening up of America and of new trade routes to the Far East; a sudden growth of population all over Europe, and a monetary inflation which was also all-European. These phenomena are related (both as effect and as cause) to the rise of capitalist relations within feudal society and a consequent regrouping of social classes. Governments tried in different ways to limit, control or profit by these changes, and with varying results. The republic of the United Provinces, where a burgher oligarchy had taken power during the sixteenth-century revolt against Spain, was best adapted to weather the crisis and enjoyed its greatest prosperity in the seventeenth century. But with a population of only some 2–2½ millions and meagre natural resources, its predominance could not last once its larger rivals had won through to a more appropriate political organization.

Germany and Italy failed to establish national states based
on a single national market during this period, and
slipped behind in the race: so too did Spain, where the
power of landed interests and the church counter-acted
the flying start which the conquest of South America
appeared to have given. In France, after a series of
convulsions in the first half of the century, national
unity was secured under the monarchy with the
acquiescence of the commercial classes, who accepted a
recognized but subordinate place in the country's power
structure.[3] Only in England was a decisive break-through
made in the seventeenth century, which ensured that
henceforth governments would give great weight to commercial considerations. Decisions taken during this
century enabled England to become the first industrial-
ized imperialist great power, and ensured that it should
be ruled by a representative assembly. Within the seventeenth century the decisive decades are those between
1640 and 1660. In these decades the decisive figure is
Oliver Cromwell. Any study of Cromwell is therefore not
merely the personal biography of a great man. It must
incorporate the major events of his lifetime which proved
so crucial for the later development of England and its
empire. I hope in this study to suggest some of the overtones which reverberate from his actions.

First, there are the political and constitutional problems,
arising mainly from the relationship between the executive and the men of property who regarded themselves
as the natural rulers of the counties and cities. In the
course of the sixteenth century the great feudal lords
had been disarmed and tamed, the church had lost its
international connections, much of its property and many
of its immunities. The residuary legatees were the crown,
and the gentry and merchant oligarchies who ran local
affairs. So long as there was any danger of revolt by
over-mighty subjects, or of peasant revolt, or of foreign-

supported Catholic revolt, the alliance between crown and 'natural rulers', though tacit, was firm. There was no need to define it, especially during the last half of the century when the sovereigns of England were successively a minor and two women. But before Oliver had reached his tenth year all these things had changed. The defeat of the Spanish Armada in 1588, the failure of Essex's rebellion in 1601, of Gunpowder Plot in 1605 and of the Midlands peasant rising in 1607, the peaceful and uneventful succession of James ɪ on Elizabeth's death in 1603, all these showed the stability of protestant England. It was now possible to fall out over the distribution of authority between the victors.

In James's reign Parliament, representing the men of property, was quite clearly arrogating more power to itself – over taxation, over commercial policy, over foreign policy – and asserting its own 'liberties', its independent status in the constitution. James ɪ, an experienced and successful King of Scotland for thirty-six years, retaliated by enunciating the theory of Divine Right of Kings and stressing the royal prerogative, the independent power of the executive. Elizabeth also had probably believed in the Divine Right of Queens, but she had been too prudent to thrust her views down her subjects' throats. James proved more circumspect in practice than in theory, and genuinely sought compromise with his powerful subjects. But his son Charles ɪ was less wise. By arbitrary arrest and imprisonment he enforced his claim to tax without Parliamentary consent; he tried to rule without Parliament by a quite novel use of the prerogative courts as executive organs to enforce government policy. Elizabeth, Professor Elton tells us, had always shown 'reluctance to assert the central authority against local interests'.[4] The first two Stuarts interfered increasingly with these interests, and in the 1630s there was a concerted campaign to drive local government, to force

unpopular government policies on the sheriffs, deputy-
lieutenants and justices of the peace who were used to
being little sovereigns in their own areas. In the 1620s
billeting of troops and the use of martial law had seemed
to be a preparation for military rule, over-riding the
authority of justices of the peace; in the thirties Sir
Thomas Wentworth was believed to be building up an
army in Ireland with which to subdue England and
Scotland. Thanks to control of the judges Charles seemed
likely to establish Ship Money as an annual tax, over
which Parliament had no control. He seemed on the
way to establishing an absolute monarchy of the continental type.

These political and constitutional quarrels concealed,
or were mingled with, deeper issues. Disputes over
customs and impositions in James's reign raised the question of whether the King alone or the King in Parliament
should control commercial policy. Disputes over foreign
policy included questions affecting Anglo-Dutch rivalry
for the trade of the world, British imperial policy in
India, North America and the West Indies. On all these
questions the governments of the first two Stuarts gave
little satisfaction to commercial interests (which included
many gentlemen investors). Indeed, they seemed by their
passivity in the Thirty Years' War (due to shortage of
money, itself the result of the taxpayers' lack of confidence), by Charles 1's provocation of protestant Scotland
and his concessions to papists in Ireland, to be endanger-
ing England's national security and independence.
Government regulation and control of the economy
contradicted the views of those who thought that freer
trade and industrial production would maximize output
as well as enriching the producers. The military basis of
feudalism had vanished, but fiscal feudalism remained.
If a tenant-in-chief of the crown – and this category included most great landowners – died before his heir had

reached the age of 21, the latter became a ward of the crown. The management of the ward's estates, and the right to arrange his marriage, were taken over by the Court of Wards; often the wardship would be handed on to a courtier, who made what profit he could from the estate during the minority, and no doubt married the heir or heiress to some needy relative of his own. A minority might thus gravely impair the family estate. Under James and Charles revenue from the Court of Wards rose rapidly.[5] In 1610 Parliament had tried to buy the abolition of this court and the feudal tenures of landlords: the theme will recur.

The problem of agricultural production was crucial. England's population was growing, and it was increasingly concentrated in urban or rural industrial centres, which were not self-sufficient. If this population was to be fed, a vast increase in production was necessary. In the sixteenth century starvation had been the inevitable consequence of a series of bad harvests, the worst of which occurred just before Oliver was born, from 1593 to 1597. More food could be produced if the vast areas reserved as royal forests were thrown open to cultivation; if commons and waste lands were ploughed up; if fens and marshes were drained. But each of these three solutions posed problems which were social as well as technical: who was to control and profit by the extension of cultivation? Smaller occupiers, squatters, cottagers and all those with common rights would lose valuable perquisites if forests, fens and commons were enclosed and taken into private ownership: the right to pasture their own beasts, to hunt game, to gather fuel. For exactly this reason Francis Bacon advised James I to retain control over royal wastes and commons, as potential sources of wealth if they were enclosed and improved. Throughout the first half of the century enclosing landlords fought cottagers and squatters claiming rights in commons and fens; the crown fought those who encroached on royal forests. The government sporadically fined enclosers, but did little to protect the victims of enclosure: it was itself an enclosing landlord.[6]

The interregnum saw a widespread movement against enclosure and for the rights of copyholders, which in 1649–50 culminated in the Digger or True Leveller movement. The Diggers demanded that all crown lands and forests, all commons and wastes, should be cultivated by the poor in communal ownership, and that buying and selling land should be forbidden by law. 'Do not all strive to enjoy the land?' asked their leader Gerrard Winstanley. 'The gentry strive for land, the clergy strive for land, the common people strive for land, and buying and selling is an art whereby people endeavour to cheat one another of the land.'[7] The expansion of food production waited on solution of the questions of landownership, of common rights, of security of tenure for copyholders, and a host of connected problems.

Many protestants had hoped that just as Henry viii's breach with Rome had been followed by more radical changes in Edward vi's reign, so the accession of Elizabeth would lead to a resumption of the policy of continuous reformation. They were disappointed, and a stalemate ensued. So long as England's national independence was in the balance the government needed Puritan support against papist enemies at home and abroad, and Puritans had no wish to overthrow Elizabeth to the advantage of Mary Queen of Scots and Spain. But the victories of the 1590s and the succession of James i brought questions of church government to a head. The bishops went over to the offensive against their critics, and harried sectaries out of the land.[8] Through the High Commission the independent authority of the episcopal hierarchy grew, and Parliament and common lawyers alike wished to control it. Especially under William Laud, Archbishop of Canterbury from 1633, but in effective control of ecclesiastical affairs from 1628, the claims of the clergy extended. Church courts were used impartially against members of the gentry and professions as well as against lower-class sectaries. But the independence of thought, the dissidence of dissent, which was rooted in a century of Bible-reading, could not so easily be crushed. Already some Baptists were suggesting the possibility of tolerating more than one brand of religious worship in a state.

As Winstanley suggested, ecclesiastical questions were also in part economic. The Laudian attempt to increase tithe payments (which had declined in real value during the inflationary century before 1640) would in effect have meant increased taxation of the laity without Parliament's consent. Laud's expressed desire to recover impropriated tithes for the church threatened the property rights of all who had succeeded to the estates of the dissolved monasteries.[9] Laud's attempt to suppress lecturers similarly challenged the right of richer members of congregations, and of town corporations, to have the kind of preaching they liked if they were prepared to pay for it. As society was progressively commercialized and as the common-law courts adapted themselves to the needs of this business society, so the jurisdiction of church courts, backed up by the power of the High Commission, was more and more resented. Their excommunications, their prohibition of labour on saints' days, their enforcement of tithe claims, their putting men on oath to incriminate themselves or their neighbours[10] – all these were increasingly out of tune with the wishes of the educated, propertied laity, who were also critical of ecclesiastical control of education and the censorship. The Laudians rejected the Calvinist doctrine of predestination, and doubted whether the Pope was Antichrist. This 'Arminian' theology, and the Laudian attempt to

elevate the power and social status of the clergy, seemed
to many protestants to be abandoning basic tenets of the
reformation.

In London at least the ideas of modern science were
beginning to spread. The earth had ceased to be the
centre of the universe, and men were less inclined to
believe in the day-to-day intervention of the diety or
the devil in the lives of ordinary men and women. In
Roman Catholic countries a miraculous transformation of
bread and wine was believed to be a daily occurrence;
in England this belief was regularly denounced from
the pulpit as superstitious, in terms which sometimes
encouraged a critical rationalism. Some men were
questioning the existence of witches. The last Englishman was burnt for heresy when Oliver was 13 years old.
Some brave spirits were beginning to ask how an
omnipotent and beneficent God could condemn the
majority of human beings to an eternity of torture
because of their distant ancestor's transgression. These
were only the first beginnings of an intellectual and moral
revolution, which was to be enormously stimulated
by the exciting events of the revolutionary decades:
but the new spirit was there, and it was already con-
tributing to the asking of new questions about government in church and state.[11]

At first glance, many of these disputes seem remote
from the life and interests of the Huntingdonshire
gentleman who became general of the Parliamentary
army in the civil war. But, as we shall see, he was deeply
involved in some of them even before 1640, and the
central position in the complex web of English life which
he later attained meant that Oliver's actions and decisions had a crucial bearing on most of the great turning
points of the century. In the pages which follow we shall
be looking more narrowly at Oliver's life, but we must

never forget the wider issues which were shaking his society. I shall return to them in my final chapter.

II

When Oliver Cromwell was born, the reign of Elizabeth was nearing its close. The great achievements of the reign were in the past. Protestantism had been re-established; religious wars had been avoided; the nobility had been disarmed; there was no longer any danger of feudal revolt. England's national independence had been secured by victory over the Spanish Armada, and by the establishment of friendly relations with Scotland. In 1603 'our cousin of Scotland' was to succeed Elizabeth peaceably. Though the war with Spain dragged on until 1604, the international situation finally precluded the Spanish preponderance which had seemed probable a dozen years earlier. Henri IV was securely on the throne of France, whence Spain had tried to drive him; the independence of the Dutch republic was also consolidated, though their war with Spain was to continue until 1609. The great age of what we call Elizabethan literature had just begun, and was to extend into James I's reign. In 1599 Spenser died, Shakespeare's *As You Like It, Henry V* and *Julius Caesar* appeared on the stage, together with plays by Dekker, Jonson and Marston. Poems by Daniel, Drayton and Greene were published, as were James VI's *Basilikon Doron*, Gilbert's *De Magnete* and Perkins's *Golden Chain*; Chapman and Middleton were beginning to write.

Yet, glorious though the Elizabethan age was to seem in retrospect, men had other thoughts in 1599. There was great war weariness, expressed by Shakespeare in *Troilus and Cressida,* perhaps written in that year. A series of bad harvests had brought famine and near-

revolt in 1596–7. At court there were fierce faction
fights as men prepared for the death of Elizabeth
and tried to take up positions of strength. These culminated in the revolt of the Earl of Essex in 1601, whose
easy suppression demonstrated the power of the monarchical idea, but led to something more like the dominance of a single faction than had been known for forty
years. Following his triumph over Essex, Robert Cecil
allied with the Howards and Sir Walter Ralegh to bring
James in as king: then Cecil overthrew Ralegh on a
trumped-up charge in 1604. At court many thought that
corruption had increased. These things are difficult to measure. It may be simply that there was more government,
and that civil servants and courtiers were less well paid
owing to inflation, and so sought more eagerly for perquisites. The struggle to build up a following of clients
may have caused an increase in demand for jobs,
pensions, monopolies, etc.[12] In the Parliament of 1601
there was an outcry against monopolies, and Elizabeth in
her 'golden speech' abolished many of them. This preserved her popularity, but did not eliminate the problem. Monopolies revived under James.

In another way, perhaps more seriously, national unity
had been impaired. The apocalyptic hopes of protestants
in 1558 had not been realized. In the compromise
ecclesiastical settlement of 1559, Elizabeth had been
forced to yield more than she would have wished.
Ever since there had been a party which hoped for still
further reform of the Church of England in a radical
protestant direction. These men, who became known as
'Puritans', wished to see the power of bishops abolished
or restricted. The clerical wing of the reformers hoped
to see a presbyterian system established within the
church (with or without a modified episcopacy). They
obtained support from a section of the gentry, which
was inspired both by strong protestant sentiments and

by a desire for parochial independence. Since the reformation, gentlemen had collected tithes and enjoyed
rights of patronage in nearly half the parishes of the
kingdom. At the same time their control over their
parishes had been vastly increased by a relative decline
in the power of the feudal nobility and the elevation of
JPs. The abolition of episcopacy, or a significant reduction in the powers of bishops, would add to the independence of the central authority enjoyed by the little
islands of sovereignty over which the gentry ruled.

But under Archbishop Whitgift (1583–1604) the
authority of bishops had climbed to greater heights
than had been known in England since Henry viii's
Reformation. The High Commission was used as a central
inquisition to pick off the clerical leaders of the Puritan
movement, and to overbear the protection of the
Puritan gentry. In 1588 Richard Bancroft, who was to
succeed Whitgift as Archbishop of Canterbury (1604–
10), proclaimed the divine right of episcopacy. Bancroft
was no theologian; but in the 1590s men more skilled
than he underpinned his assertion with theological arguments. Until the 1590s the government had feared to go
too far against the Puritan opposition, since from the
nature of the case Puritans were the most uncompromis-
ingly anti-Catholic and so the most staunchly anti-
Spanish of all the Queen's subjects. But in 1588 the
Armada was defeated. England was in no danger of
Spanish conquest. This at one stroke removed the government's fear both of papists and of Puritans. The bishops
mounted a counter-attack on the latter; the theologians
took arguments from the armoury of the former.

The Puritans themselves were split. Finally convinced
of the impossibility of reform through Parliament and
Queen, Robert Browne and his followers in the 1580s proclaimed reformation without tarrying for the magistrate.
They rejected the national church and formed themselves

into separatist congregations, which could function only
as illegal underground organizations or in exile. In 1587
John Field declared that 'seeing we cannot compass'
our reformist purposes 'by suit nor dispute', it is 'the
multitude and people that must bring the discipline
to pass which we desire.'[13] This was followed in 1588–9
by a series of bawdy and witty pamphlets (the Marprelate Tracts) holding the bishops up to ridicule.
Both separatism and the appeal to the people, let
alone the muck-raking of Marprelate, were going faster
and further than the respectable among the godly
wished, whether clerical like the Presbyterian Thomas
Cartwright or lay like Puritan MPs. The bishops
seized the opportunity to proclaim that those who criticized the wealth of bishops now would soon attack the
property of the gentry and aristocracy – a line of argument which Oliver Cromwell was to encounter in the
House of Commons in 1641. They were helped by an
attempt by three lunatics to establish the rule of God in
1591. In Cambridge Baro and Barrett began to teach
an anti-Calvinist theology which prefigured the Arminianism of Laud, and Hooker produced the first satisfactory
theoretical justification of an Anglican church which
pursued a *via media* between Catholicism and Puritanism. Some sectaries were executed, others were driven
into exile; the underground Presbyterian movement
was broken up, and in the last two Parliaments of
Elizabeth's reign (1597 and 1601) there was no vocal
Puritan opposition, though there was plenty of opposition to government economic policies.

The snake was scotched, not killed. For the fundamental fact of the gentry's wish to be free to control
their parishes and their parsons without supervision from
bishops or High Commission was matched by the inner
logic of protestantism: its exaltation of preaching and
the study of the Bible was continually training con-

sciences which would stand out against any attempt to regiment them or dictate to them. After their defeat in the 1590s the Puritan clergy put more emphasis on preaching, character-forming, morale-building, less on forms of church organization and discipline. In the long run they forged a better weapon, which in 1640 was too strong to be broken as it had been in the 1590s. Just because, in the last resort, a large section of the gentry and the urban merchant classes sympathized (for whatever reason) with Puritanism, the government was increasingly forced into dependence on the Catholic and crypto-Catholic sectors of the gentry and aristocracy.[14] This is shown by the attempts of James I and Charles I to ally with Spain, England's old enemy, even in the 1620s, when the Habsburgs again seemed to be aiming at a hegemony in Europe which would bring with it a triumph of the Counter-Reformation; and it was shown by the rise of Arminianism in the Church of England, culminating in the 1630s in the rule of Laud. Laud was offered a cardinal's hat by the Pope, and was profoundly embarrassed by the Calvinist theology of his predecessor Whitgift, who had suppressed the Puritan movement but did not move far from it in theology. Yet since church and state were one, in the eyes of all contemporaries, Laud was only carrying to its logical conclusion the disruption of national unity by Whitgift and Bancroft, which had already been accomplished when Cromwell was born in 1599. One aspect of the latter's life's work was to be the attempt to re-establish a national church which should have room for most brands of protestantism, and whose government should not interfere with the local supremacy of the gentry and urban oligarchies.

So when Oliver was born, the spacious days of Good Queen Bess were already perhaps in the past. But as he grew up, there soon grew up with him a legend of an

Elizabethan golden age, in which Parliament and crown worked in harmony, in which the church was resolutely protestant, in which bishops were subordinated to the secular power, and protestant sea-dogs brought gold and glory back from the Spanish main. This legend, promoted by aged courtiers like Sir Fulke Greville and Sir Robert Naunton and clearly formulated in Shakespeare's last play, *Henry VIII,* owed more to a criticism of what was happening (or not happening) under the Stuarts than to anything that had really existed under Elizabeth: but it was no less potent for that. 'Queen Elizabeth of famous memory' always meant a great deal to Oliver Cromwell.[15] His mother, his wife and his favourite daughter were all called Elizabeth.

The behaviour of James and Charles I made men look back nostalgically to Elizabeth. James had his financial problems: inflation was continuing, he had an expensive wife and three children to maintain. He was surrounded by mendicant courtiers, English and Scots, and (unlike Elizabeth) he refused to subsidize them at the expense of the church. Nevertheless, when all has been said in James's favour, his financial extravagance cannot be gainsaid; and what there is to be said on his behalf is clearer to historians than it was to contemporaries. They saw merely that James's government appeared to spend as much in peace as Elizabeth's had done in war. It was sensible to put an end to the Spanish and Irish wars in 1604, and trade flourished during the next decade in consequence. But the militant anti-Spanish party, of which Sir Walter Ralegh was the spokesman, was dissatisfied. 'It is true, King James made a peace', Oliver was to say in 1656; 'but whether this nation, or any interest of all the protestant Christians, suffered not more by that peace than ever by his [Spain's] hostility, I refer it to your consideration'.

Lenience to Catholics at home and a pro-papist foreign policy were the logical consequences of Elizabeth's break with the Puritans. The latter had hoped that the accession of the King of presbyterian Scotland would lead to a reversal of this policy, and James before 1603 had encouraged all groups to expect his favour. But the Hampton Court Conference of 1604 confirmed that the King would not change Elizabeth's policy. Gunpowder Plot (1605) was followed by a pamphlet warfare, in which James himself attacked papal claims and tried to alert European monarchs, whether protestant or Catholic, to Jesuit theories of the lawfulness of tyrannicide. But the severe anti-Catholic laws which Parliament passed were not enforced. When the Thirty Years War broke out in 1618 James's agitated search for agreement with Spain intensified, and with it the concern of the Puritan gentry. In 1618 Sir Walter Ralegh was executed, at the demand of the Spanish Ambassador, who seemed the most powerful figure at the English court. James refused to assist his son-in-law the Elector Palatine, when the latter's rash acceptance of the Bohemian crown involved him in disaster and started the Thirty Years' War. As the protestant cause on the continent languished, England, the leading protestant power, continued to negotiate with Spain. James, the contemporary joke ran, promised to send to the assistance of the stricken German protestants 100,000 . . . ambassadors! How natural it was to look back to the golden days of Good Queen Bess, staunchly patriotic and anti-Spanish.

James's economic policy was as conspicuously unsuccessful. An attempt to raise customs rates to meet inflation led to an outcry in the House of Commons of 1610. Negotiations in the same year, aimed at securing a regular income of £200,000 a year from Parliament in return for the abolition of the hated Court of Wards, failed. This episode showed that the prerogative could be up for sale, and had whetted Parliamentary appetites. (The Court of Wards was abolished in 1646 after

Parliament had won the civil war.) The ten years' prosperity which followed the peace with Spain was broken
by rash royal action in abolishing the monopoly of the
Merchant Adventurers (the principal cloth exporters)
and transferring their privileges to a new company of
King's Merchant Adventurers. The latter promised to dye
and dress cloths in England, instead of exporting white
cloths, as the Merchant Adventurers had done. The promise was fair; but the performance failed to live up to it.
The new company was unable to organize the dyeing and
dressing, or to find export markets. A crisis of over-
production resulted.

Since the cloth industry was England's major industry,
this was a very serious matter: there was mass unem-
ployment in the clothing counties. James climbed down
ignominiously, and restored the Merchant Adventurers
to their privileged position. The economy was just beginning to recover when it was hit by a greater crisis, the
result of a collapse of central and eastern European
markets. When Parliament met in 1621 it attacked the
economic and foreign policies of the government. There
had been no effective session of Parliament since 1610;
that of 1614 had been dissolved after five weeks of wrang-
ling over alleged government attempts to manage it
through 'undertakers'. The 1621 Parliament impeached
Lord Chancellor Bacon and some of the economic para-
sites protected by the favourite, George Villiers, Marquis
(later Duke) of Buckingham. While insisting that James
should reverse his foreign policy and intervene on the
protestant side in the Thirty Years' War, Parliament
voted derisory sums for this purpose. It was dissolved in
an atmosphere of frustration. A large section of the
gentry and merchants was already totally out of sympathy with the government.

When Parliament met again in 1624 it seemed for a
brief time that the Elizabethan national unity might be

recovered. For in the intervening period Buckingham and Prince Charles had visited Spain to woo the
Infanta, whose marriage to the Prince of Wales James
had regarded as the solution to all the problems of
Europe. They learned on the spot (at the cost of over
£100,000 to the Exchequer) what had been obvious
to most observers for a long time: that Spain was not
seriously interested in an English alliance. With characteristic frivolity Charles and Buckingham switched
horses, clamoured for war with Spain, and put themselves at the head of the 1624 Parliament to force this
policy on a reluctant James. When Lord Treasurer
Middlesex pointed out that England could not afford
war, the House of Commons was encouraged to impeach
him. James presciently but vainly pointed out to Buckingham that he was making a rod for his own back. In
one of the most remarkable statutes in English history,
Parliament voted money to the King explicitly in return
for his reversing his foreign policy at their request. Yet
they had so little confidence in the court that they
insisted on the money being paid in to treasurers appointed by themselves, and expended only with their
approbation. Buckingham and Prince Charles had taught
the Commons that it was possible to coerce the government provided the formal decencies were observed; that
unpopular ministers could be impeached and disgraced,
even without the blessing of the King; and that financial
control could be used to force a change of foreign policy.
The Commons did not forget.

Charles and Buckingham did, however. Their foreign
policy for the next four years more than justified the
lack of confidence which the House of Commons had
shown. In 1625 James died. By then England was at
war with Spain in alliance with France. In 1627, because
Buckingham had quarrelled with the French court in
another of his disastrous wooing expeditions, England

was at war with both France and Spain. These military undertakings were uniformly unsuccessful. They did nothing to help German protestantism, which by 1628 was in grave danger of extinction. In that year England helped the Catholic King of France to deprive his protestant subjects of the privileges which Queen Elizabeth had helped them to win in the Edict of Nantes (1598). When Buckingham was assassinated in 1628 England's international reputation was at its nadir. The assassin, Felton, was the most popular man in England.

In other ways unity between King and Parliament was broken. Parliament refused to vote taxes for this impossible foreign policy, and Charles resorted to forced loans. In 1627 five knights refused to pay, and were imprisoned. When Parliament met in 1628 the Petition of Right declared both unparliamentary taxation and arbitrary imprisonment illegal. Meanwhile William Laud had come into favour at court. He and his supporters in the church, the Arminian or anti-Calvinist party, provided a theoretical defence of arbitrary government. In 1625 Parliament had attacked Richard Montague's *New Gag for an Old Goose* and *Appello Caesarem* because they were alleged to favour popery: Charles made him a bishop. Parliament attacked the sycophantic royal chaplain Roger Mainwaring for justifying unparliamentary taxation: Charles promoted him to what Cromwell described as 'a rich living'. 'If these be the steps to preferment', he continued in what was probably his maiden speech (February 1629), 'what may we not expect?' Before Parliament was dissolved in 1629 two MPs held the Speaker down in his chair while resolutions were passed against unlawful taxation and Arminianism. Already some men's minds were so 'incensed' that the possibility was contemplated of deposing Charles in favour of his daughter Elizabeth, Queen of Bohemia. But this was 'likely to be merely the conceit of the multitude'.[16]

Parliament was not to meet again for eleven years. In retrospect we can see that 1629 was an even more important turning-point than the 1590s. For now the victims of the government's attack were not merely the Puritan clergy but the protestant gentry. The Rev. John Penry was executed as a traitor in 1593; Sir John Eliot died in the Tower in 1633. Just as many of the Puritan clergy accepted defeat in the 1590s and concentrated on saving souls, so in the 1630s many of the Parliamentarians gave up the struggle. Sir Thomas Wentworth and William Noy accepted prominent positions in the government, and made it more efficient than it would otherwise have been. Noy's antiquarian researches led to a quite novel extension of the old tax of Ship Money from the ports to the inland towns: a tax had been discovered which might have balanced the country's budget so long as Charles abdicated from foreign affairs. In Ireland Wentworth actually made the colony pay for its own subjection, and started to build up an army whose sinister possibilities were not lost on Englishmen. But there was no fundamental reform. In Professor Tawney's famous phrase in *The Agrarian Problem in the Sixteenth Century,* the government's good intentions were 'smeared with the trail of finance'. Monopolies proliferated. The profits of wardship increased. Fines for encroachments on the royal forests, for enclosures, for refusing to be knighted (at a price),[17] still further alienated the gentry, already outraged by unparliamentary taxation. The government's alliance with a ring of big London capitalists, who produced loans in return for baronetcies and privileges like farming the customs, alienated London citizens outside the favoured circle, and this alliance gave the government a sense of financial security which was wholly illusory. In 1640 some branches of the customs revenue had been anticipated for years ahead. Bankruptcy was concealed, but it was bankruptcy all right.[18]

Laud's religious policy carried the re-catholicizing tendencies started in the 1590s to their logical conclusion. Arminians held all the best bishoprics and deaneries. Lecturers in market towns were suppressed: Laud forced the Feofees for Impropriations (a group of Puritan merchants, lawyers and divines) to stop buying in impropriated tithes in order to use them to finance preaching. In each case the result of Laud's attempt to prevent Puritan preaching was to get no preaching at all. Laud's own ritualistic tendencies, plus favour to Catholics at court, where Henrietta Maria had succeeded Buckingham as the chief influence on Charles, gave plausibility to allegations that Laud was a secret papist. In 1637 a papal agent was admitted to England for the first time since Mary's reign. In so far as Charles had a foreign policy, it was pro-Spanish. Cooperation with papists in Ireland, pressure on Presbyterians in Scotland: it all seemed to fit into a picture.

The Scottish troubles were the last straw. Threats to resume church lands held by the aristocracy there were followed by revisions in the prayer book in a Catholic direction. The result was a national explosion with which the English government was totally unable to cope. In the 1590s Puritans and near-Puritans had hoped that their fortunes might be transformed by the succession of James. In the 1630s Puritans and Parliamentarians again hoped for salvation from the North, and our brethren of Scotland proved a stronger support than our cousin of Scotland had been. Knox, the rebellion of whose presbyterian supporters Elizabeth had hated having to finance, had proclaimed that the gospel of Christ would unite England and Scotland; the execution of Mary Queen of Scots in 1587 (which Elizabeth had also hated having to agree to) set a precedent for sitting in judgment on the Lord's Anointed.[19] The Scottish army which entered England in 1640, singing metrical

psalms, brought home to roost the policy which Elizabeth had so reluctantly adopted. Charles tried in the
Short Parliament of 1640 to appeal to traditional anti-
Scottish feeling, and failed miserably. Ideological bonds
and material interests were too strong.

But we have looked too far ahead. In the early 1630s
all was confusion and disarray among those who had
opposed the government. Some merchants refused to
pay customs, in accordance with the House of Commons
resolution of March 1629; but after the London merchant
Richard Chambers had gone to jail for saying that 'merchants were screwed up in England more than in Turkey',
most succumbed. Chambers, who did not, stayed in prison
for six years, and was soon back again for opposing Ship
Money. It was probably in the 1630s that Cromwell experienced the spiritual crisis that led to his conversion;[20] and
he was not alone. Puritan emigration to New England
reached a peak in the 1630s: Oliver thought of going,
and his friend of later years, Sir Henry Vane, actually
went. Returning New Englanders were to play a prominent part in the revolutionary movement of the forties:
Cromwell was said especially to favour them in his
regiment.[21] In the 1630s the opposition group organized
its activity around the Providence Island Company, a
trading company of which John Pym was Treasurer
and many of Oliver's cousins members. Providence
Island lay just off the mainland of Spanish America, cutting the route for the silver galleons: its occupation would
make sense only as part of an aggressive anti-Spanish
policy – the policy which Cromwell took up in the
1650s. The Providence Island group organized Hampden's symbolic opposition to Ship Money.

The judgment in 1637, that Hampden must pay,
shocked the propertied class. For if Ship Money was legal,
non-Parliamentary government had come to stay. The
situation was saved only by the Scottish war, which made

resistance possible. In 1636 3½% of Ship Money was unpaid, in 1638 61%. The Providence Island group were in touch with the Scottish leaders, and in 1640 concerted their policies with them. The Short Parliament which Charles was compelled to call in April 1640 insisted on peace with the Scots. Charles dissolved it and tried to fight on, but could get no support. Peace was concluded at Ripon in October 1640 on terms which forced the summoning of another Parliament. This (the Long Parliament) was to sit for more than the eleven years for which Charles's personal government had lasted. In both the Short and the Long Parliament Oliver Cromwell represented the borough of Cambridge.

II

FROM COUNTRY GENTLEMAN TO LORD OF THE FENS: 1599-1640

I was by birth a gentleman, living neither in any considerable height, nor yet in obscurity.

CROMWELL, Speech to Parliament, 12 September 1654

Oliver Cromwell was born on 25 April 1599 in Huntingdon. His father was Robert Cromwell, gentleman, younger son of Sir Henry Cromwell, the Golden Knight of Hinchinbrooke. His mother was Elizabeth Steward. On both sides the fortunes of the family had been founded on the spoliation of the church. At the Reformation Elizabeth Steward's great-uncle Robert had been the last Prior of Ely and its first protestant Dean. Her father William and after him her only brother Sir Thomas farmed the lands of Ely Cathedral. The connection between the two families went back two generations: for the man who persuaded Prior Robert Steward to throw his lot in with the Reformation was Sir Richard Cromwell.

Richard Cromwell was born Richard Williams, grandson of a Welshman said to have accompanied Henry VII when he came to England in 1485. The grandfather settled at Putney, and married his son Morgan to the daughter of the local blacksmith, Walter Cromwell. Her brother was the great Thomas Cromwell, Henry VIII's minister, the hammer of the monks, the architect of the English Reformation, who was created Earl of Essex just before his fall and execution in 1540.

Richard Williams took the name of his famous uncle, and acted as his agent in the suppression of the monasteries. He had his reward. Three abbeys, two priories and the nunnery of Hinchinbrooke, worth perhaps £2500 a year, came into his possession; and he married the daughter of a Lord Mayor of London. His son Sir Henry

built a magnificent mansion out of the ruins of Hinchinbrooke, fit to entertain royalty, and a summer residence
on the site of Ramsey Abbey. In the year of the Armada,
1588, he ordered all his copyhold tenants in the manor of
Ramsey to be ready to attend him at an hour's notice.
He too married the daughter of a Lord Mayor of London,
represented his county in the House of Commons and was
four times sheriff of Cambridgeshire and Huntingdonshire.
His son Sir Oliver, also knight of the shire and high
sheriff, married first the daughter of a Lord Chancellor,
then the widow of a government financier, Sir Horatio
Palavicino. He was the uncle of our Oliver.

But notwithstanding these prudent marriages, old Sir
Oliver managed in a life of nearly 100 years to dis-
sipate the family fortunes. He entertained James I at
Hinchinbrooke in the most lavish way, when the King
was on progress from Scotland in 1603 and on many
later occasions. Apparently Sir Oliver got very little in
return. He is a classical example of a man who ruined
himself by unsuccessful investment in the court. He had
to sell the great house at Hinchinbrooke to the Montagu
family, of whom we shall hear again.

Oliver's father Robert, as a younger son, inherited little
of this great patrimony; but what he had was also former
church property. Oliver was born in a house which had
been part of the hospital of St John in Huntingdon. His
father occupied property which had formerly belonged
to the Austin friars, and farmed the tithes of the nearby
parish of Hartford; from his maternal uncle Sir Thomas
Steward, Oliver was later to inherit extensive leases from
the Dean and Chapter of Ely. So if ever the protestant
vested interest meant anything, it meant that Oliver
would grow up strongly anti-Catholic. But he must also
have grown up conscious of the fact that he was a poor
relation. He visited the splendours of Hinchinbrooke from
time to time; but his father's £300 or so a year was

less than Sir Oliver would spend on a fleeting visit from
King James. Young Oliver had many rich and important
relations, but his own upbringing was modest.

Robert Cromwell died when Oliver was just 18, and in
any case seems to have had a less powerful personality
than his wife, who brought up Oliver and his seven sisters
in Huntingdon. We may speculate on the effects of this
petticoat environment; by all accounts (some of them not
very reliable) he grew up to be a rough, boisterous,
practical-joking boy, with no effeminate characteristics.
More important, or at all events better documented than
Oliver's father as an influence, was his schoolmaster
Thomas Beard. When Oliver was nearly five Beard was
appointed by the town of Huntingdon to its free school,
the school which Oliver attended. Beard also became
rector of Oliver's parish church, St John's. The young
Puritan minister wrote and produced plays, in which
Oliver is said to have acted. Beard had already published
in 1597 a famous book, *The Theatre of Gods Judgments,
translated from the French and augmented with over
300 examples.* He became a friend of the Cromwell family
– he witnessed Robert Cromwell's will – and a leading
figure in local politics. Oliver would almost certainly read
Beard's book, and in any case he would no doubt hear
as sermons the many additional passages which were inserted in the later editions published in 1612 and 1631.
This latter edition was dedicated to the mayor, aldermen
and burgesses of Huntingdon.[1] At Huntingdon Beard also
wrote a book, published in 1625, proving that the Pope
was Antichrist. His *Theatre* is in the tradition of John
Foxe's *Acts and Monuments.* It pictures the whole of
existence as a struggle between God and the powers of
darkness, in which the elect fight for God and are certain
of victory in so far as they obey his laws. One chapter
is given up to showing 'how rare . . . good princes have
been at all times', and God's destructive power is invoked

against the 'mighty, puissant and fearful'. Another chapter
shows 'that the greatest and mightiest princes are not
exempt from punishment for their iniquities'. God is no
respecter of persons: he intervenes to help the poor and
humble. Princes, Beard assured his readers, are subject to
civil laws, provided these are founded upon equity and
right. 'It is unlawful both by the law of God and man' for
kings to tax 'above measure'. Private property is sacred
even against kings.[2] The lessons were not wasted on the
young Oliver.

Beard prepared Oliver for entrance to Cambridge University. Cromwell did not go to his father's college,
Queen's, nor to Beard's college, Jesus, but to a new foundation more Puritan than either of them, Sidney Sussex
College. The Montagu family (shortly to purchase Hinchinbrooke from old Sir Oliver) were benefactors of and
closely connected with the newly-endowed college, whose
first Master had been a Montagu. The Master of the College
from 1610 to 1643 was Samuel Ward, a well-known Cambridge Calvinist, to whom the most famous of all Puritan
divines, William Perkins, had entrusted the publication of
one of his attacks on Catholicism. Ward represented England at the Synod of Dort and was Lady Margaret Professor of Divinity at Cambridge. Laud described Sidney
Sussex under him as 'a hotbed of Puritanism', and the
College managed to avoid having its chapel consecrated
throughout Laud's period of ascendancy. Cromwell was
a gentleman-commoner, and so would dine with the Fellows. He presented a piece of silver to the college on
admission. But he was at Cambridge for one year only,
before he was called home by his father's death. There is
little evidence that he received much intellectual stimu-
lation from university life. He apparently preferred 'the
mathematics, wherein he excelled' to the humanities and
civil law which his parents had expected him to read.
The evidence is not very strong, but it receives some

confirmation from the fact that mathematics was a speciality of Sidney Sussex and of its Calvinist Master; and that Oliver later recommended history, mathematics and cosmography to his son Richard.[3]

When Robert Cromwell died in June 1617, the Court of Wards tried to have Oliver declared a royal ward, which might have proved very expensive for the family estate: but he escaped. We are ignorant of what he was doing in the next three years. He may have gone back to Cambridge for a time, though he took no degree there: he may have proceeded to one of the Inns of Court in London (Lincoln's Inn is most likely) to pick up the smattering of legal knowledge that befitted a landowner. But there is no record of his presence at any of them. He may even have fought for the protestant cause in Germany, though again this is mere conjecture based on his later military prowess: no evidence exists. The next hard fact that has survived is that on 22 August 1620, four months after attaining his majority, Oliver Cromwell married Elizabeth Bourchier at St Giles's, Cripplegate. His wife was the daughter of a London merchant, a fur-dealer and leather dresser, who had done well enough to be knighted and buy a country estate in Essex. Sir John Bourchier was a neighbour and distant relation of the Barringtons, Oliver's powerful Essex cousins, and a neighbour of the Earl of Warwick. So the marriage, in addition to its no doubt considerable financial advantages, brought him closer to the heart of the powerful group which was to lead the Parliamentary opposition.

This is the time to emphasize that though Oliver was a poor relation of the great house of Hinchinbrooke, yet he was no ordinary country gentleman. He was connected with some of the most powerful families in England, and this 'cousinry' linked a number of men who were subsequently to be of the first importance in the struggle against Charles I. In addition to the Barringtons, Oliver

B*

was related (now or later) to the Hampdens, the St Johns, the Wallers, the Whalleys, the Goffes, the Trevors, the Hammonds, the Hobarts, the Gerrards, the Waltons, the Pyes, the Knightleys, the Mashams, the Ingoldsbys, the Flemings, the Dunches, the Brownes. Six of his cousins were imprisoned for refusing to subscribe to the forced loan of 1627, and Sir Edmund Hampden was one of the defendants in the Five Knights' Case arising out of this opposition. When Oliver was first elected to the House of Commons in 1628 he found nine cousins there. Four of his cousins were Adventurers of the Providence Island Company,[4] whose head was the Earl of Warwick. When the group associated with this company decided to test the legality of Ship Money in 1637, Oliver's cousin John Hampden was defended by another cousin, Oliver St John. Oliver had eleven cousins and six more distant relatives in the Long Parliament; six more cousins and three other relations joined him there later.

The next fact that we know about Oliver Cromwell is probably to be explained by this political connection. In November 1620 his name followed those of the two bailiffs of the town of Huntingdon, and headed those of fifteen citizens who witnessed the indenture of the election of two MPs for what was to be the 1621 Parliament. The MPs were Sir Henry St John (a cousin) and Sir Miles Sandys, brother of Sir Edwin, a leader both of the opposition party in Parliament and of the colonizing activities associated with the Virginia Company and the Earl of Warwick. (Sir Oliver Cromwell had shares in the Virginia Company too.) It was from the estate of another Sandys brother, Scrooby in Nottinghamshire, that the Pilgrim Fathers had been driven into exile in 1608. Oliver's influence was not the only one brought to bear in this election. The sheriff of Huntingdonshire was yet another St John, brother of the Huntingdon MP. The young Oliver was already part of a connection which aspired to influence government policy through Parliament. When Cromwell himself first entered the House of Commons in 1628 it was as burgess for Huntingdon, in company with James Montagu, third son of the Earl of Manchester. The Montagus' influence in the county was increasing as that of Sir Oliver was declining, and this election may represent a compromise between the two families.

For eleven years after 1620 Oliver Cromwell and his wife lived at Huntingdon. There is some near-contemporary evidence, apart from royalist propaganda, that he carried on the trade of a brewer there.[5] But his main occupation, then as later, would be farming, in this dull, flat country of the south-east Midlands. We first hear of enclosure and engrossment of lands in Huntingdonshire in 1607, when Oliver was eight years old. Twenty years later we are told that many citizens of London had bought land in the county, which they sub-let. The presence of these speculative purchasers may have stimulated enclosure.[6] It may also have strengthened links between the county gentry and the capital. Here Oliver had five children – Robert (born 1621), Oliver (1623), Bridget (1624), Richard (1626), Henry (1628). Others born later were Elizabeth (1629), Mary (1637) and Frances (1638). In 1628 Oliver's childless uncle Richard Cromwell died, leaving his property to his nephew.

For a brief period in 1628–9 Oliver Cromwell ceased to be an obscure cadet of a great family: his life became momentarily part of the history of England. In his first recorded speech, to the Commons' Committee on Religion in February 1629, Oliver joined in complaints that Roger Mainwaring, though censured by Parliament, had been given preferment by the King. Oliver then described how Dr Beard had been 'exceedingly rated' by the Laudian Bishop Neile of Winchester for having preached against 'one Dr Alabaster', who in a sermon at Paul's Cross, had preached flat popery.[7] The House resolved to send

for Beard for further questioning, and Neile was censured
along with Laud as one of 'those near about the King
who are suspected to be Arminians, and . . . unsound in
their opinions that way'.

Cromwell was already playing a prominent part in local
politics; and because Huntingdon was a Parliamentary
borough, control of its corporation was of national importance. In 1627 Cromwell and Beard had worked together against the barrister and local political boss Robert
Bernard on behalf of a Puritan and less oligarchical
group. But in 1630, taking advantage of the changed
political atmosphere following the dissolution of 1629 and
the beginning of the 11 years' personal government, the
ruling group called in the central government to its assistance. The government was carrying on a campaign to
purge corporations, with a view to being one day able
to face elections for a new Parliament; and gladly intervened to transform the government of Huntingdon into
a close oligarchy. In place of two bailiffs and a common
council of twenty-four, freely elected each year, the new
charter of 1630 laid down that Huntingdon was to be
governed by twelve aldermen and a recorder chosen for
life, and a mayor chosen each year by and from the
aldermen. Just to make quite sure, the first mayor and
aldermen were named in the charter. Apparently as a sop
to the defeated party, Cromwell and Beard were named
JPs for the borough, together with Robert Bernard. But
within a matter of months, Oliver and the postmaster of
the town were accused of 'disgraceful speeches' against
Bernard and the mayor, and of an attempt 'to gain many
of the burgesses against this new corporation'. Among
other things, it was apparently feared that the new
charter threatened the right of the inhabitants in the
common lands. Oliver and his colleague were hauled
before the Privy Council, who referred the matter to the
Lord Privy Seal. The latter, by a remarkable coincidence,

was the Earl of Manchester, and so presumably a highly interested party. Hardly surprisingly, he reported in favour of Bernard and his cronies. 'Those supposed fears of prejudice that might be to the said town by their late-altered charter' were, he decided, 'causeless and ill-grounded.' Cromwell was declared to have spoken ill words against Bernard and the mayor, 'in heat and passion'. Pressure was brought to bear upon him, and he went through a formal reconciliation with the leaders of the oligarchy. But a few months later he sold nearly all his Huntingdon property and moved to St Ives, in the same county. Manchester's power extended there too, for he was lord of the manor and enjoyed the tolls of the town.

Oliver's move looks like recognition of political defeat. It was obvious that he could never be returned to Parliament again for Huntingdon. At St Ives he rented grazing land from Henry Lawrence, lord of the adjacent manor of Slepe, who just over twenty years later was to be President of the Lord Protector's Council. Oliver may also have been in financial difficulties. There are unconfirmed stories of extravagance and mismanagement in his early days, of the sort that tend to gather round men who are later to be famous. But the Huntingdon dispute may well have involved him in expense, and at almost exactly the same time (April 1631) he was fined £10 for refusing to purchase a knighthood. Knighthood had been debased by being put up to auction by James I,[8] and many gentlemen were reluctant to accept what had once been an honour. Charles I tried to exploit this situation by fining those who refused – one of the many fiscal devices used to raise revenue in the absence of Parliament. Oliver and six others from his neighbourhood appeared before royal commissioners (including the Earl of Manchester again) for repeated refusal to pay; he was the last to submit. The sale of his Huntingdon property may also be con-

nected with the unconfirmed story that he intended to
emigrate to New England, which from 1630 onwards was
regarded as at least a temporary refuge by many religious and political malcontents.

The years spent farming at St Ives were a period of
lowered status. Oliver was no longer a justice of the
peace, nor even a freeholder. So he continued until 1636.
In that year his maternal uncle, Sir Thomas Steward, died
childless leaving most of his considerable estate to Oliver.
This property consisted largely of land leased from the
Dean and Chapter of Ely, and Oliver and his family
moved to Ely in the same year. He was now suddenly a
man of considerable wealth. Some have associated the
humble years at St Ives with a period of religious
melancholia ending with conversion: but for this evidence is lacking. In 1628, while attending Parliament in
London, Oliver had consulted the well-known physician
Sir Theodore Mayerne, who kept a note describing Oliver
as 'extremely melancholy'. Cromwell's own doctor at
Huntingdon, John Symcotts, confirmed the melancholia,
and suggested that he was also at this time hypochond-
riac.[9] In a letter of October 1638 Oliver put his conversion
in the recent past. 'Oh, I lived in and loved darkness,
and hated the light. I was a chief, the chief of sinners
... Oh the riches of his mercy.' In the Calvinist scheme
of conversion, which Oliver accepted, grace always came
from without after one's own works had failed and one
had sunk to the depths. But whether there was any connection between the riches of uncle Thomas Steward and
the riches of God's mercy we shall probably never know.

Parallel with the attempt of Charles's personal government to purge corporations in Parliamentary boroughs,
and confine the franchise in the hands of an easily-
influenced oligarchy, was Archbishop Laud's campaign
against lecturers. In many parishes of England the
maintenance available for the minister was woefully small,

and this was especially true of towns.[10] The exiguous stipends offered very little attraction to learned men, and the incumbent of many a parish, especially in towns, was a 'dumb dog', unable to preach. Yet the whole emphasis of protestantism had been on the importance of preaching, as opposed to the sacramental and ceremonial elements in religion. Urban congregations, becoming more educated and more sophisticated as well as richer in the century before 1640, made higher demands on their ministers; and as, in the seventeenth century, government and hierarchy began to lose the confidence of the solid middle class in the towns, the latter began to demand preaching of a special sort, which the parochial clergy rarely supplied. In most parishes the advowson (the right to nominate the minister) was in the hands of a local gentleman, or of the crown, or of a bishop or dean and chapter. In a few cases the advowson belonged to the town corporation, or the patron might be a Puritan gentleman; but in the vast majority of urban parishes even where the minister was licensed to preach he was not very likely to preach the kind of sermons his congregation wanted to hear.

It was to meet this situation that lecturers arose. A congregation might subscribe funds to maintain a lecturer, and would give the money to the incumbent of their parish if they liked his theology. (Such voluntary contributions could be withdrawn if his successor was less popular.) Or a lecturer from outside might be brought in, with or without the goodwill of the incumbent of the parish. In many towns the lecturer was nominated (and paid) by the corporation. Or groups of merchants in London, as a pious work, might subscribe to maintain a lecturer in their own county, or in one of the 'dark' outlying regions of the kingdom. Because of the way in which lecturers were chosen and paid, the hierarchy disliked them. They were accused of 'popularity', of preaching sedition. There were few corporate towns in the

1630s which were not having a quarrel with their bishop over such lecturers. Puritans were often accused of making an especial drive to buy patronage rights and endow lectureships in Parliamentary boroughs, in order to influence elections. Laud conducted a regular campaign against lecturers, and succeeded in suppressing a great number of them.

Thomas Beard died two years after Cromwell had left Huntingdon, and Laud at once suppressed his lectureship. Upon this the Mercers' Company of London set up a new lectureship in the town, reserving to themselves, said Laud indignantly, the right to dismiss the lecturer 'upon any dislike they may have of him', without reference to a bishop. Laud appealed to the King 'that no layman whatsoever, and least of all companies or corporations may . . . have power to put in or put out any lecturer or other minister.' Charles agreed, and the Puritan lecturer at Huntingdon was dismissed in 1634. Whereupon the Mercers appointed him to a vacant vicarage in the same town.[11] A year later (January 1635) we find Oliver Cromwell writing about another London-endowed lectureship to 'Mr Storie, at the sign of the Dog in the Royal Exchange'. Cromwell urged the citizens who had endowed the lecture – it is not quite clear where – not to let it fail for lack of financial support 'in these times wherein we see they are suppressed with too much haste and violence by the enemies of God his truth'. (By this phrase I fear Oliver must have referred to the bishops.) The lecturer, if he is correctly identified as Dr Samuel Wells, was subsequently a chaplain in the Parliamentarian army.

In the internal political conflicts of Huntingdon, then, in the quarrels over lectureships, Oliver Cromwell was serving his political apprenticeship. It is in this context that we must discuss his more famous activities as 'Lord of the Fens'. As we saw,[12] one of the crucial economic problems of the seventeenth century was to extend the cultivated area so as to feed the growing population. But to whose benefit? In the 1630s Charles's government, its actions as always 'smeared with the trail of finance', tried to raise money by fining those who encroached on the royal forests (in order to cultivate them) or who made depopulating enclosures: and it attempted to share the profits anticipated from large-scale Fen drainage. But the crown and big landowners were not the only interested parties. Popular movements of protest against loss of rights, in Wiltshire and the Forest of Dean in 1629-31, in the Fens in the later 1630s, and enclosure riots all over England in 1640–43, expressed the views of the smaller cultivators.

Cromwell was involved in disputes over the Fens at various periods. One story has him presenting a petition against Fen drainage to James I in 1623.[13] Certainly Sir Thomas Steward had resisted the draining of the Fens in James's reign, in the interests of the poor commoners and Fen dwellers: Oliver may have inherited this attitude with his uncle's lands. It is also worth recalling that in the famine year before Oliver was born his grandfather and uncle had prevented food riots by rounding up grain speculators. In 1638 it was 'commonly reported by the commoners in Ely Fens adjoining that Mr Cromwell of Ely had undertaken, they paying him a groat for every cow they had upon common, to hold the drainers in suit for five years and in the meantime they should enjoy every foot of their common'. With this encouragement, men and women 'armed with scythes and pitchforks uttered threatening words against anyone that should drive' their cattle off the Fens. When the King decided to take the whole project into his own hands, Oliver 'was especially made choice of by those who ever endeavoured the undermining of regal authority, to be their orator at Huntingdon unto the ... King's Commissioners of Sewers there, in opposition to his Majesty's most commendable design'.[14]

When we add to this that Cromwell was alleged to be
'a great stickler against Ship Money', and to have spoken
in favour of the Scots, we can understand that he won a
considerable local reputation among those opposed to
Charles's government. It is worth recapitulating. Though
himself a poor relation, he was connected both by birth
and by his City marriage with some of the most important
families in the land, and with a group of men who were
organizing opposition. He himself had played a part, in
Parliamentary elections at Huntingdon, by his own parti-
cipation in the 1628 Parliament and by his battle against
the corporation over the new charter which imposed an
oligarchy on the town. He had been defeated by the
power of the royal government (symbolized for him by
the Earl of Manchester, the head of the great local rivals
who were buying out the Cromwells and succeeding to
their political influence in the county). He had also been
in trouble with the government for his stubborn refusal
either to take a knighthood or to pay for not doing so,
and surrendered only at the last possible moment. In
effect driven out of Huntingdon, he had continued from
the rural obscurity of St Ives to interest himself in the
maintenance of Dr Wells as a lecturer, entering for this
purpose into correspondence with the London merchants
who financed him. He was also related to many of the
Virginia Company and Providence Island Company Adventurers, and there are stories that in the 1630s he
thought of emigrating to New England himself. He opposed Ship Money and favoured the Scottish cause. In
the dispute over Fen drainage he won more than local
notoriety as leader and organizer of the commoners' opposition. In this as in his attack on the Huntingdon
oligarchy he made himself the spokesman of humbler and
less articulate persons.

In all this we must recall his own position – a member

of the cadet branch of a family which had risen to influence in the county on the spoils of the monasteries but whose elder branch was declining and yielding place to the courtier Montagus, with whom at many points Oliver came into conflict. His own economic position, however, was moderately affluent after the death of Sir Thomas Steward in 1636. Oliver's hereditary protestantism had been reinforced by his schoolmaster and friend Thomas Beard, by his education at the very Puritan College of Sidney Sussex, by his own conversion, and by reaction against the Catholicism fashionable at Charles I's court. It would not diminish his distaste that one of the leading figures round Henrietta Maria was the Catholic priest Wat Montagu (son of the Earl of Manchester), who before his ordination had supplanted old Sir Oliver as Ranger of the Forest of Weybridge.[15] Wat Montagu had been two years Oliver's junior at Sidney Sussex.

It is thus not surprising that when in 1640 Charles finally decided to summon another Parliament Oliver Cromwell was a candidate. Huntingdon was impossible, but Cambridge was within 20 miles of Ely, St Ives and Huntingdon; and he was invited to stand for the town. On January 7 he was made a freeman (a necessary precondition), and ten weeks later he was elected one of its two burgesses. His fellow-burgess was Thomas Meautys, Clerk of the Privy Council, a nominee of Lord Keeper Finch. The Short Parliament lasted only three weeks; but at the end of October, in a hard-fought election, Meautys was replaced as Cromwell's partner by a man more acceptable to the opposition. This was John Lowry, chandler of the town, later a colonel in the Parliamentary Army, who was nominated as one of Charles I's judges in 1649, though he did not serve. If Oliver's political enemies thought they had eliminated him from national politics when they drove him from Huntingdon, they had been proved wrong. Cambridge satisfactorily avenged the loss of his Huntingdon seat. But at forty-one years of age the farmer of St Ives was only at the beginning of a political career which was to contain many surprises.

III

FROM CAPTAIN
TO LIEUTENANT-GENERAL:
1640-46

My nation was subjected to your Lords.
It was the force of conquest: force with force
Is well ejected when the conquered can ...
     Samson, in JOHN MILTON, *Samson Agonistes*

I profess I could never satisfy myself of the justness of this
war but from the authority of the Parliament to maintain
itself in its rights; and in this cause I hope to approve myself
an honest man and single-hearted.
     CROMWELL to Colonel Walton, 5 September 1644

A goodly hotch-potch: when vile russetings
Are matched with monarchs and with mighty kings.
     JOSEPH HALL, *Virgidemiarum* (1597)

I

Most of the lasting achievements of the English Revolution came during the first two hundred days of the Long Parliament's existence. There was a great deal of agreement among men who were later to fight on opposing sides in the civil war that the old régime must be dismantled. At this optimistic stage even a future royalist like Edward Hyde hoped for 'the dawning of a fair and lasting day of happiness to this kingdom', in which 'the dejected broken people of this island' would be restored 'to their former joy and security'.[1] The prerogative courts – Star Chamber, High Commission, Council in the North – were abolished. All taxation without consent of Parliament was declared illegal. The Earl of Strafford (Sir Thomas Wentworth) was executed, Archbishop Laud imprisoned in the Tower (executed 1645), other ministers and judges were impeached, many fled overseas. Bishops were excluded from the House of Lords. Triennial Parliaments were agreed to, and the Long Parliament was declared indissoluble except with its own consent.

Yet already some of these actions were dividing the Houses. Bishops found defenders in the Commons as well as in the Lords, on the ground that they had as good a property in their offices as any landowner in his land. The indefinite prolongation of the life of Parliament was clearly an infringement of the royal prerogative, a revolutionary step. Yet how else were the initial achievements to be secured? Charles would certainly feel it to be his conscientious duty to reverse them at the first possible opportunity, whatever promises might be extorted from him. So there was continuous pressure to carry the Revolution further, in order to consolidate what had already been attained.

There was, moreover, much pressure from outside Parliament from men who had few of the traditional inhibitions of MPs belonging to the propertied class. There were quite genuine popular fears of popish plots, which expressed themselves in the disarming of papists, uncovering caches of arms and so on, not always with the strictest respect for property rights. Laudian ceremonial innovations were reversed, altar rails removed, communion tables replaced in the centre of the church, again not always peaceably. Crowds of Londoners came to Westminster to lobby, often with menaces, for popular measures to be passed – for instance against bishops and for the execution of Strafford. Initially the leaders of the Commons did little to discourage these popular movements. In May 1641, between the condemnation and execution of Strafford, Parliament agreed to a Protestation that they would defend the true protestant religion, and the power and privileges of Parliament, against all enemies. Two months later they ordered all their supporters to sign this Protestation – an appeal to the people outside Parliament. But when the breakdown of the repressive organs of church and state allowed public worship by hitherto proscribed sectarian congregations, when riots against enclosure and Fen drainage began to spread in the countryside, above all when demonstrators began to put forward their own demands, many MPs began to be seriously alarmed. Every gesture towards the lower-class radicals outside Parliament lost some support from the gentry. But if it was to come to a fight, the numbers of the former would be decisive. For some this seemed an argument for avoiding a fight at all costs.

But it was not so easy to call a halt. As some members

of the propertied class rallied to the King, the keystone of the social arch, so he made it increasingly clear that he would exact vengeance. The outbreak of a national rebellion in Ireland in October 1641 forced the issue: who was to command the army which, all agreed, was necessary to suppress the revolt? Pym, Hampden and their colleagues in the House of Commons used the unity recreated by the news from Ireland to demand that the King should dismiss his 'evil councillors' and 'take such as might be approved by Parliament'. They brought before the House the Grand Remonstrance, a long and comprehensive list of all the charges which could be brought against Charles's government over the past decade. And having got it accepted, they forced through another vote ordering it to be printed. This unprecedented step, a deliberate appeal to support outside the charmed circle of the political nation, split Parliament and the country in two. ('If the Remonstrance had been rejected', Oliver told Lord Falkland, 'I would have sold all I had the next morning, and never seen England more.') Swords were drawn in the House on the night of 22 November. Six weeks later the King tried, in a botched military coup, to arrest the leaders of the Parliament. They fled to the safety of the City of London; Charles left the capital to look for support in Scotland and in the North and West of England. After a propaganda conflict lasting seven months, in which each side sought to win support by branding the other as an unconstitutional aggressor, war broke out in August 1642.

Parliament's main backing came from London and the Home Counties, the ports, the clothing counties of the south-west and East Anglia, and the clothing areas of Yorkshire and Lancashire. These were the richest areas in the country, so that in a long war Parliament was certain to win. As Professor Stone pointed out in *The Crisis of the Aristocracy, 1558–1641*, the King's weakness was that the

Tudors had been so successful in establishing a monopoly of force within the country that the English aristocracy had forgotten how to fight. Since the accession of Elizabeth eighty years earlier very few Englishmen had seen any land fighting. Some soldiers of fortune and gentlemen had served in the Dutch forces and in the Thirty Years War, including the Earl of Essex, Sir Thomas Fairfax, Philip Skippon, George Monck, Sir John Hothan, Alexander Leslie and many of the officers of the Scottish army. In the early days of the civil war 'none was thought worthy' of the name of soldier, wrote the historian of the Royal Society in 1667, 'but he that could show his wounds, and talk about his exploits in the Low Countries'. But this did not last long: 'the whole business of fighting was afterwards chiefly performed by untravelled gentlemen, raw citizens, and generals that had scarce ever before seen a battle.' Sprat was too tactful to point out that this had been much more true on the Parliamentary side than on the King's. He used the argument to suggest that in war as in natural philosophy 'greater things are produced by the *free* way than the *formal*'.[2] Cromwell is the outstanding proponent of the free way in war, as his brother-in-law John Wilkins was of the free way in natural science. Professional soldiers were however perhaps as disappointing to the royalists as to the Parliamentarians, since they were apt not only to leave the battlefield in search of plunder at crucial moments, but also to surrender positions they thought untenable, whereas an amateur like Robert Blake held Taunton and Lyme Regis for Parliament for months, contrary to all the rules. In a civil war morale is in the last resort more important than professional skill. General Monck cheerfully changed from the King's side to Parliament's as soon as the latter was clearly winning; with equal lack of principle he changed back again in 1660 when Parliament in its turn was going under.

The vast majority of English merchants and gentle-

men did not want a war at all. 'No reformation is worth
the charge of a civil war', Lord Clarendon wrote after
the event: he was one of those who supported reformation down to the end of 1641. 'The cause was too good
to have been fought for', said Andrew Marvell, referring
to Parliament's cause. He served the republic in the 1650s,
but had taken no part in the civil war. James Harrington
and Thomas Hobbes also thought civil war unnecessary,
because the balance of property would have made a
victory for Parliament inevitable in the long run, war or
no war. Many Parliamentarians, like Richard Baxter and
Edmund Ludlow, were astonished that anyone was prepared to fight for the King in 1642. Large numbers of
gentlemen tried to remain neutral for as long as possible,
and were more likely to take up arms or pay taxes in
order to save their estates from confiscation by the locally
dominant forces than from any ideological conviction.[3]
After the King's failure to win swift victory, many of the
Parliamentarian leaders hoped to force him to a negotiated peace.

When Charles's obstinacy frustrated this, the question
was which side could most effectively draw on its reserves.
Parliament's first-line reserve was the Scottish army, its
second-line the political and religious radicals in England.
The enthusiastic supporters of Parliament were the
humbler folk, with less to lose and more to win. That is
why it was thought so important to give positions of
command to all the aristocrats who could be persuaded
to declare for Parliament. 'Had Essex refused to be
general', the astrologer William Lilly said, 'our cause in
all likelihood had sunk in the beginning, we having never
a nobleman at that time either willing or capable of that
honour and preferment, indeed scarce any of them were
fit to be trusted'.[4] Too great reliance on the radicals was
socially dangerous. They were yeomen, merchants and
artisans, and if they played too big a part they might

aspire to too great a say in the determination of peace terms. But ultimately, when the win-the-war party came to realize that they were in a minority in Parliament, they – like the Jacobins in the French Revolution – called upon first one, then the other of these reserves, though each of them alienated a further section of the gentry, and to that extent built up at least sentimental support for the King.

But Charles was even less able to deploy his reserves, which consisted first of the papist Irish and Highlanders of Scotland, and secondly of foreign continental support. Just as the Tudor pacification of England meant that the English aristocracy had forgotten how to fight, so the other great triumph of the monarchy, the protestantization of England, meant that a victory won by preponderantly popish support would be unacceptable to the English political nation, so many of whom had inherited monastic lands. A victory for Charles won by Irish support would have been no less a revolution than a victory won for Parliament by lower-class sectaries: and none of Charles's supporters were revolutionaries, while some of Parliament's were. Charles never dared fully to utilize Irish armies, but he flirted with the idea dangerously, and then allowed his correspondence to be captured after the battle of Naseby, just in time to counteract the social anxieties which the victory of the radicals on Parliament's side must have aroused among its more conservative supporters.

Naseby (14 June 1645) was Oliver Cromwell's victory, and Cromwell was one of those Parliamentarian leaders who had no inhibitions about using the loyalty and enthusiasm of the lower-class radicals.

II

We should be wrong to think of Cromwell simply as the military leader on Parliament's side. He was that, of course, but he also played an important role as a political leader before, during and after the civil war. In Chapter II we saw how his political connections and loyalties had been formed long before Parliament met in November 1640. When it did meet, he at once assumed a prominent role in its deliberations – not in the very first rank, but far from the back benches.

He moved the second reading of the bill for annual Parliaments. He took the lead in calling for reform of the Exchequer. He was on innumerable committees, including one for impeaching Matthew Wren, Bishop of Ely, and others for ecclesiastical reform. He had the pleasure on 8 September 1641 of successfully moving a resolution to permit the parishioners of any parish to elect a lecturer. Thus Laud's short-lived victory was annulled.[5] Cromwell attracted considerable notice by his obstreperous behaviour in defence of the poor commoners of Somersham, near St Ives. Their waste land had been enclosed without their consent and sold to the Earl of Manchester. Like many of their fellows all over England, the commoners took advantage of the political disturbances and resorted to direct action, 'in a riotous and warlike manner' to destroy the enclosure. Years after, when the Earl of Clarendon came to write his *Autobiography*, he still remembered Oliver's tempestuous carriage and insolent behaviour in defence of the commoners. Thanks to his pertinacity a clause about taking 'common and several grounds ... from the subject' was included in the Grand Remonstrance.

Cromwell was frequently asked to carry messages to the

House of Lords, as well as to present petitions from out-
siders to the lower House. He was deeply concerned in
Irish matters from 3 May 1641, when he moved unsuc-
cessfully 'that we might take some course to turn the
papists out of Dublin'. He was sent several times to ask
the Lords to expedite the ordinance for raising troops to
go to Ireland. He was also concerned with the raising of
money for Ireland. He himself subscribed £500 towards
its reconquest, receiving in return a promise of nearly
1000 acres in Leinster. He was in sufficient contact with
the City to be able to assure the House on 1 June that
'there were certain merchants' prepared to furnish arms
and food for forces in Ireland on six months' credit. As
soon as military preparations for England itself were imminent, Cromwell was in the middle of them. On 3 May
1641 it was 'upon Mr Cromwell's motion' that the Lords
were asked to pass an ordinance giving the Earl of Essex
power to assemble the trained bands south of Trent, on
the sole authority of Parliament. On 14 January 1642 he
asked for, and got, a committee 'to consider of means to
put the kingdom in a posture of defence'. He carried a
motion in the Commons instructing the Company of
Armourers to report weekly to the House what saddles,
arms and muskets were being made and who bought them.
He took an order from the Commons to the Lords for
supplying the defensive needs of Hull. He subscribed
another £500 to 'the defence of the realm'.

Oliver's contemporaries later liked to emphasize the
contrast between the simple country gentleman, the back-
bencher of 1640–2, and the uncrowned king of 1654–8.
'A very mean figure of a man in the beginning of this
Parliament', Sir Philip Warwick called him, going on to
describe in an oft-quoted set piece Oliver's 'plain cloth
suit, which seemed to have been made by an ill country
tailor' ('we courtiers valued ourselves much upon our
good clothes').[8] But, whatever Cromwell's sartorial defects,

we should not allow ourselves to be deceived as to his standing in the House. The man who between 11 and 21 July 1642 was ordered to bring in instructions for a committee to go into Wiltshire, to manage a conference with the Lords on foreign policy and on the impeachment of the Lord Mayor of London; who was put on one committee to deal with the affairs of Munster, and another about money for volunteers in Shrewsbury and Hertfordshire; who was ordered to prepare a letter to the Lords Justices of Ireland, which was approved next day and sent to the Lords with Cromwell as its bearer; who successfully moved that Cambridge be allowed to raise troops – the man who did all this was no obscure back-bencher. He was the trusted colleague of John Pym and John Hampden, the leaders of the Commons. When he was put on to the Committee of Both Kingdoms at its initiation in February 1644, this was a recognition of his importance as a politician no less than as a soldier. The political skill with which in the winter of 1644–5 he piloted through the Self-Denying Ordinance and the ordinance setting up the New Model Army was not suddenly and mysteriously acquired; it was the slow accumulation of years of detailed work in committees of the House and conferences with the Lords.

III

It was of course primarily as a soldier and military organizer that Cromwell won the remarkable position he had attained by 1645. He was early put on a committee for disarming recusants. He was a channel through which protestants in the counties (e.g. in Monmouthshire, March 1642) asked for their local papists to be disarmed. In August 1642, on receipt of rumours that plate was being despatched from Cambridge colleges to the King,

Cromwell, apparently on his own initiative, together with his brothers-in-law, John Desborough and Valentine Walton, seized the magazine of Cambridge castle and forcibly detained the plate. In East Anglia and the east Midlands, the official historian of the Long Parliament tells us, 'a great and considerable number of the gentry, and those of highest rank among them, were disaffected to the Parliament, and were not sparing in their utmost endeavours to promote the King's cause and assist his force, ... which might have thrown those counties (if not wholly carried them to the other side) into as much distraction and sad calamity as any other part of the land had felt ... if those gentlemen had not been curbed and suppressed by that timely care which the Parliament took, and more particularly by the successful services of one gentleman, Master Oliver Cromwell of Huntingdon'.[7]

In August the King had raised his standard at Nottingham, and Oliver Cromwell started to raise a troop of horse at Huntingdon, which by March 1643 had become a regiment, later the famous 'Ironsides'. Many years afterwards Thomas Tany remembered Oliver 'at Huntingdon in the market-house, myself there present' promising 'to stand with us for the liberty of the gospel and the law of the land'.[8] All accounts agree that Oliver's troops were carefully picked men, 'most of them freeholders and freeholders' sons, who upon a matter of conscience engaged in this quarrel'.[9] This was deliberate policy. Cromwell much later recorded a conversation he had had with John Hampden, probably after Parliament's failure to win the Battle of Edgehill in October 1642. 'Your troopers', Cromwell told his cousin, 'are most of them old decayed serving men and tapsters and such kind of fellows: and ... their [the royalists'] troopers are gentlemen's sons, younger sons, persons of quality. Do you think that the spirits of such base and mean fellows will be ever able to encounter gentlemen that have honour, courage and resolution in them? . . . You must get men of a spirit . . . that is likely to go on as far as a gentleman will go, or else I am sure you will be beaten still.'[10] Hampden was sceptical, but Oliver proceeded methodically to collect men of middling rank who, 'being well armed within by the satisfaction of their conscience, and without by good iron arms, they would as one man stand firmly and charge desperately'.[11] From the start Oliver's men kept their powder dry as well as trusting in God. A less friendly account makes almost the same point about the Ironsides: 'having been industrious and active in their former callings and professions, . . . afterwards finding the sweet of good pay, and of opulant plunder and of preferment, suitable to activity and merit, the lucrative part made gain seem to them a natural member of godliness.'[12] But Richard Baxter, no friend either, said 'these men were of greater understanding than common soldiers . . . and making not money but that which they took for public felicity to be their end, they were the more engaged to be valiant'.

A corollary of picking men with care was that Cromwell imposed strict discipline on his regiment. When in April 1643 two troopers tried to desert, he 'caused them to be whipped at the market place in Huntingdon'. 'No man swears', said a newspaper in May 1643, 'but he pays his twelvepence; if he be drunk he is set in the stocks, or worse; if one calls the other "Roundhead" he is cashiered; insomuch that the counties where they come leap for joy of them, and come in and join with them. How happy were it if all the forces were thus disciplined!' We need not believe all the journalist's claims, but we can accept that Cromwell's troops were far better behaved than most.

It was in his selection of officers, however, that Oliver most remarkably and portentously departed from tradition. He chose, wrote the hostile second Earl of Manchester in 1645, 'not such as were soldiers or men of

estates, but such as were common men, poor and of mean
parentage, only he would give them the title of godly,
precious men'. Manchester emphasized Cromwell's hostility towards professional soldiers, quoting him as saying
'oftentimes ... that it must not be soldiers nor Scots that
must do this work, but it must be the godly'. From the
start Cromwell adhered to 'the *free* way' and not 'the
formal'.[13] In June 1643 John Hotham complained that
'Colonel Cromwell had employed an Anabaptist against
him, and that one Captain White had been employed
against him, who was lately but a yeoman'. (Since the
word Anabaptist also implied low social rank, the aristocratic Hotham was making one point, not two.) Some
months before this Hotham had entered into correspondence with the royalists, since he feared that if the war
continued 'the necessitous people of the whole kingdom
will presently rise in mighty numbers', and ultimately
'set up for themselves, to the utter ruin of all the nobility
and gentry'.[14]

But such views were not confined to royalists and those
about to join them. It is important to remember how subversive Cromwell's attitude must have seemed to contemporaries, who took a hierarchically graded society for
granted. Oliver's officers, said another account, were 'not
such as were soldiers or men of estate', but 'common men,
poor and of mean parentage', 'such as have filled dung
carts both before they were captains and since'. 'Honest
gentlemen' he cashiered.[15] The Parliamentary Committee
in Suffolk objected that Ralph Margery, who had raised
a troop of horse for the Parliament's service, was not a
gentleman, and therefore was ineligible for such a command. Cromwell incorporated Margery's troop in his own
regiment. It was apropos Margery that in August 1643
Cromwell expressed his principles in their most quotable
form. 'It may be it provokes some spirits to see such plain
men made captains of horse. It had been well that men

of honour and birth had entered into these employments, but why do they not appear? Who would have hindered them? But since it was necessary the work must go on, better plain men than none.' The reserves had to be drawn upon.[16] He made the social point in a phrase that has become famous. 'I had rather have a plain russet-coated captain that knows what he fights for and loves what he knows than what you call a gentleman and is nothing else. I honour a gentleman that is so indeed.'[17] Cromwell gave a utilitarian explanation. 'If you choose godly honest men to be captains of horse, honest men will follow them. . . . A few honest men are better than numbers'. So officers as well as men in Cromwell's regiment tended to be of the middling sort.

At the very beginning of the war Charles I had tried to smear all the supporters of Parliament as Congregationalist followers of Robert Browne or Anabaptists – the seventeenth-century equivalent of 'Reds'. 'You shall meet no enemy but traitors', he told his troops, 'and most of them Brownists, Anabaptists and atheists, such as desire to destroy both church and state.' Even Cromwell felt he had to defend himself on this score. 'I have a lovely company', he wrote, in a confidential appeal for help to his cousin Oliver St John in September 1643; 'they are no Anabaptists, they are honest, sober Christians: they expect to be used as men.'[18]

But if there were no Anabaptists in Oliver's regiment, he soon had them under his command. In January 1644 Cromwell was promoted to Lieutenant-General, and two months later he was involved in a quarrel with the Scottish Major-General Crawford, a professional soldier. Crawford had cashiered a Lieutenant-Colonel for refusing to accept the test of Presbyterian orthodoxy, the Solemn League and Covenant, and accused him of being an Anabaptist. 'Are you sure of that?' Cromwell retorted. 'Admit he be, shall that render him incapable to serve the public?'

Cromwell then laid down his own principle, the modern principle which then appeared terribly revolutionary. 'Sir, the state in choosing men to serve them takes no notice of their opinions; if they be willing faithfully to serve them, that satisfies.' By this date, in proclaiming such principles, Cromwell was speaking not merely as a regimental commander or even as an MP, but as the second-in-command of the army of the Eastern Association, one of the three great armies under Parliament's command. More important, he was coming forward as the leader of a nation-wide trend.

I suggested that among Parliament's reserves were the energy and enthusiasm of religious and political radicals. The course of the war had inevitably drawn such men into greater prominence. Cromwell is particularly well-documented, and we see him in the early months of the war rounding up all pockets of royalist resistance in his area ('It's happy', he wrote, 'to resist such beginnings betimes'); seizing arms, raising and training troops, calling for money. His demands must have been a continual source of irritation to the slow-moving, cautious, conservative committee-men with whom he often had to deal. One of them was his old enemy Robert Bernard of Huntingdon, who was finally denounced as a delinquent and ran to the Earl of Manchester for protection against sequestration. Cromwell's victory over Manchester enabled him to settle two old scores at once.

The curt commands in Cromwell's letters of August 1643, though justified by a royalist incursion, cannot have endeared him to the Cambridge Committee and the Essex Deputy Lieutenants. To the former he wrote: 'It's no longer disputing, but out instantly all you can. Raise all your bands; send them to Huntingdon; get up what volunteers you can; hasten your horses.... You must act lively; do it without distraction.' The activists naturally gravitated towards Cromwell as their leader. Captain Margery was not only no gentleman, he also annoyed the Suffolk Committee by commandeering horses from alleged royalists. Oliver hinted pretty freely that he thought some of the Suffolk authorities were protecting delinquents.

There were similar conflicts in other counties on Parliament's side. The traditional rulers of the counties, who originally manned the committees, were for the most part anxious to avoid an all-out conflict, to protect friends and relations who had chosen the other side, to arrive at a compromise peace as quickly as possible, to avoid unleashing dangerous social forces. 'No man that hath any reasonable share in the commonwealth can desire that either side should be absolute conquerors', wrote John Hotham. 'It is too great a temptation to counsels of will and violence.'[19] On the other hand were men of strong religious and political principles, often not gentlemen at all, who were prepared to run risks and make sacrifices, and who thought there was no point in fighting a war unless there was a determination to win it.

In Staffordshire, Kent, Suffolk, Buckinghamshire, Devon, Warwickshire, Oxfordshire, the Isle of Wight and other counties, the greater gentry were squeezed out of controlling positions on the county committees (or resigned) and were replaced by men of lesser rank. Military efficiency brought men of the lower classes to the fore. 'Tinker' Fox of Walsall raised a troop among Birmingham small craftsmen and rose to the rank of colonel. The gentleman governor of Stafford had to be replaced by a more efficient and enthusiastic merchant.[20] In the garrison at Newport Pagnell a silk-weaver captain incurred the wrath of Sir Samuel Luke by refusing to take the Covenant. As Professor Underdown put it, writing of the period after 1645: 'In effect the committees supplanted the JPs, and as many of their members came from origins less elevated than those of the substantial gentry who made up the Commission of the Peace, they were often unpopular with the leading men of the county, even those of nominally Parliamentarian persuasion. The moderates, peace-party men, Presbyterians (call them what you will) thus wished to curb the powers of the County Committees; the radicals, war-party men, pro-Army Independents, wished just as passionately to maintain them'.[21]

The issue on which local quarrels often turned was finance. The original local committee members were anxious to protect their friends and relations, to keep money and troops inside the county, not to be compelled to pay for military activities which did not directly affect their interests. The radicals who gradually replaced them were less county-minded (not being themselves of 'the county' in the social sense which the word still retains), more outward-looking, less worried about property rights. In the early days it was thought (on both sides) that the war could be financed by voluntary subscriptions or loans: Oliver contributed £1000 in this way, with Irish lands as security for £500 of it. But as it became clear that loans were inadequate, an excise was introduced (on the Dutch model), and an assessment or land tax. In addition the rents from sequestrated property of royalists were used for military purposes. Inevitably tension developed between the local sequestration committees, originally often dominated by men with narrowly local views, and London, to which the radicals more and more looked for a national lead as well as for finance. Winning the war became a matter of financial as well as military organization. The New Model Army was financed by a policy of 'compounding' with delinquents, i.e. allowing them to buy back their sequestrated estates for a fine calculated according to the degree of their delinquency. This was a compromise, falling short of the confiscation which the radicals wanted: but in 1646 bishops' lands were sold outright. The military revolution necessitated a financial revolution.

IV

When Oliver Cromwell emerged as the leader of the win-the-war party, linking up the radicals in many localities, it was natural that there should be social overtones. 'A company of Brownists, Anabaptists, factious inferior persons' was how the Hothams described their enemies.[22] Before the war started Cromwell had successfully protested against interference by a peer in a Parliamentary borough election. He was alleged – long after the event – to have told his men 'that if the King chanced to be in the body of the enemy that he was to charge, he would as soon discharge his pistol upon him as at any other private person'. If he really said it, this was no doubt his blunt protest against Parliament's claim to be fighting 'to secure His Majesty's person ... out of the hands of those desperate persons', his evil councillors.[23] In January 1643 Cromwell successfully opposed Hampden in the Commons with a call for greater severity against royalists. In July of the next year Oliver intervened to rescue John Lilburne, later the Leveller leader, when his commanding officer the second Earl of Manchester had threatened to hang him for seizing a royalist castle in defiance of orders. The Earl repeated gossip which said that Cromwell hoped to 'live to see never a nobleman in England', and loved some persons the better 'because they did not love lords'. Cromwell's remark 'it would not be well until Manchester was but Mr Montagu' may have related to the family quarrel between the Cromwells and the Montagus as much as to the peerage as such; but others report him as saying 'God would have no lording over his people'.[24]

On winning the war the issues between the two men and the two parties were clear-cut. 'If we beat the King 99 times, yet he is King still', said Manchester; 'but if the

King beat us once, we shall all be hanged.' 'My Lord,
if this be so', Cromwell replied with irrefutable logic,
'why did we take up arms at first? This is against fighting ever hereafter.' 'I had a great deal of reason,' Cromwell told the House of Commons soberly, 'to think that
his Lordship's miscarriage in these particulars was neither
through accidents (which could not be helped) nor
through his improvidence only, but through his backwardness to all action; and had some reason to conceive
that that backwardness was not (merely) from dullness or
indisposedness to engagement, but (withal) from some
principle of unwillingness in his Lordship to have this
war prosecuted unto full victory', but rather to end it
'on some such terms to which it might be disadvantageous
to bring the King too low.' Manchester, on the contrary,
alleged that Cromwell had admitted to packing the Army
of the Eastern Association with men of his own principles,
'so that in case there should be propositions for peace, or
any conclusion of a peace, such as might not stand with
those ends that honest men should aim at, this Army
might prevent such a mischief'. Cromwell did not deny
the charge. The Earl of Essex was complaining at about
the same time (December 1644): 'Posterity will say that
to deliver them from the yoke of the King we have sub-
jugated them to that of the common people', whose
'audacity' he declared that he would henceforth 'devote
his life to redressing'.[25]

Cromwell had built up a virtually impregnable position
for himself before he struck at Manchester and all he
stood for. Not only was he 'a person of great favour and
interest with the House of Commons', as a hostile fellow-
MP put it. By sheer hard work and military efficiency he
had become the outstanding figure in the Eastern Association, which after London was the main centre of support
for Parliament. In June 1644 his leadership had been
decisive at the battle of Marston Moor, the first really

crushing victory the Parliamentarians had won. He had remained in the background when the London radicals had tried to build up Sir William Waller as a rival commander to the Earl of Essex, and so had not suffered their discomfiture when 'William the Conqueror' was routed by Prince Rupert at Roundway Down in July 1643. Oliver's speech to the Commons on 9 December 1644 is evidence of his consummate skill as a Parliamentary tactician:

> It is now a time to speak, or forever hold the tongue.[26] The important occasion now is no less than to save a nation out of a bleeding, nay, almost dying condition, which the long continuance of this war hath already brought it into; so that without a more speedy, vigorous and effectual prosecution of the war – casting off all lingering proceedings like [those of] soldiers of fortune beyond sea, to spin out a war – we shall make the kingdom weary of us, and hate the name of a Parliament.
>
> For what do the enemy say? Nay, what do many say that were friends at the beginning of the Parliament? Even this, that the members of both Houses have got great places and commands, and the sword, into their hands; and, what by interest in the Parliament, what by power in the Army, will perpetually continue themselves in grandeur, and not permit the war speedily to end, lest their own power should determine with it. This I speak here to our own faces is but what others do utter abroad behind our backs. I am far from reflecting on any. I know the worth of those commanders, members of both Houses, who are yet in power: but if I may speak my conscience without reflection upon any, I do conceive if the Army be not put into another method, and the war more vigorously prosecuted, the people can bear the war no longer, and will enforce you to a dishonourable peace.

He was speaking to a report from a committee which had been set up to inquire into the quarrel between himself and Manchester; but he succeeded in elevating the dispute to one of principle. And he had clearly prepared the ground well behind the scenes. For immediately after

Oliver's speech Zouch Tate (the chairman of the committee, a Presbyterian and therefore a political opponent of
Cromwell) moved 'that during the time of this war no
member of either House shall have or execute any office
or command, military or civil, granted or conferred by
both or either of the Houses'. Oliver's close colleague,
Sir Henry Vane, seconded the motion, offering to lay
down his commission as co-Treasurer of the Navy, and
Cromwell at once offered to resign his own military command.

This was the germ of the Self-Denying Ordinance,
adopted by the Commons ten days later, and (in a revised
form) by the Lords on 3 April. His enemies no doubt saw
the ordinance as a means of getting rid of Cromwell; he
and his friends saw the broader problem of removing
peers and all those who owed their military commands to
social rank, not ability. It was a logical extension of
Oliver's policy of promoting by merit in his own regiment.
The New Model Army, Baxter tells us, was 'partly the
envy and partly the scorn of the nobility'.[27] It could be
argued that the southern Netherlands had been lost to
the United Provinces seventy years earlier because no
way was found to take leadership away from the greater
nobility and entrust it to lesser nobles and townsmen.

In assessing Cromwell's statesmanship here we suffer
from hindsight. We know that he (and one or two other
MPs) in fact retained their commands, whilst the Self-
Denying Ordinance got rid of Essex, Manchester and
others of Cromwell's bugbears. But it was by no means
clear in advance that this would be the outcome. Tate's
original resolution said that 'during the time of this war,
no member of either House' should hold a military command. Oliver played a leading part in the whole plan of
operations which led from the Self-Denying Ordinance to
the New Model Army, and in getting Sir Thomas Fairfax
appointed Commander-in-Chief of the new force (January

1645). Despite reports of a mutiny in his regiment at the prospect of being put under another colonel,[28] Cromwell was actually at Windsor, paying his respects to Fairfax before laying down his commission, when he was ordered by the Committee of Both Kingdoms to prevent a junction between the King and Prince Rupert prior to a march northwards. On the very eve of the Battle of Naseby Fairfax was still without a Lieutenant-General to command his cavalry, and his Council of War joined the City of London in petitioning for Cromwell to be appointed. The lower House agreed, four days before Naseby; the Lords reluctantly concurred only after that overwhelming victory in which Cromwell played so decisive a part, and only to the extent of prolonging his commission for three months. Had the outcome of the battle been otherwise they would undoubtedly have put up more resistance. When the three months came to an end, the rise of a neutralist third party, the Clubmen in south-western England, Montrose's victories in Scotland and the likelihood of his coming to the rescue of Charles's shattered forces, again made it impossible to dismiss the Lieutenant-General: and on 12 August his commission was extended for yet another four months. By the end of this period the Army's successes in the south-west were such that it was inevitable that Cromwell's commission should again be renewed (for six months, on 23 January 1646). Though no doubt Cromwell's supporters hoped from the start that he would survive the Self-Denying Ordinance, the issue was in doubt for at least six months. Cromwell's political tactics were superb, but they included the calculated risk that he might have to pay the price of political eclipse himself. The fact that he survived should not blind us to the chances he took. And after July 1646 he was a civilian again.

V

The political radicals whose leader Oliver Cromwell had become were very often also the religious radicals; and with them he was in obvious agreement. In February 1641 he was in trouble in the House of Commons for attacking the great revenues of bishops, and denying that their abolition ('parity in the church') would lead to a parity in the commonwealth. In May he was one of the principal draftsmen of the Root and Branch Bill, proposing the extirpation of episcopal government; and in August he moved the ejection of bishops from the House of Lords – which the Commons had already accepted but over which the Lords procrastinated for another six months. In September he spoke against the Prayer Book and sponsored a motion authorizing the parishioners of any parish where there was a non-preaching minister to set up a lectureship at their own cost – a reversal of Laud's policy from which Cromwell had suffered.[29] His troops from the start enthusiastically carried out the Commons' policy of destroying stained glass and images in churches, for which Oliver has wrongly received personal blame.[30] At Ely in January 1644 he warned Canon Hitch 'lest the soldiers should in any tumultuary or disorderly way attempt the reformation of your cathedral church, I require you to forbear altogether your choir service, so unedifying and offensive, and this as you will answer it, if any disorder should arise therefrom'. When Hitch ignored the warning Cromwell emphasized that he was 'a man under authority, . . . commanded to dismiss this assembly' before bidding Mr Hitch 'leave off his fooling and come down'.

Under authority they may have been, but there can be little doubt that Cromwell and his troopers were in especial sympathy with this part of their duties. At the beginning of the war his officers had 'purposed to make their troop a gathered church', whose pastor they invited Richard Baxter to become.[31] Cromwell's protection of religious radicals under his command[32] won him respect among all who feared a Scottish-imposed Presbyterian discipline. Oliver was reported as saying to Manchester of the Scots 'in the way they now carry themselves, pressing for their discipline, I could as soon draw my sword against them as against any in the King's army'. (As early as February 1641 Cromwell had been enquiring through a London merchant about 'the reasons of the Scots to enforce their discipline of uniformity in religion'.) On one of his rare visits to the House of Commons in September 1644 Cromwell suggested to Oliver St John the wording of a successful motion that asked – failing substantial agreement in the Assembly of Divines – 'to endeavour the finding out some way, how far tender consciences, who cannot in all things submit to the common rule which shall be established, may be borne with according to the Word and as may stand with the public peace'. But religious toleration was secured not by votes in Parliament but by the victories of the New Model Army. A year later, after the successful siege of Bristol had virtually ended the war, Cromwell wrote to Speaker Lenthall on similar lines, but with a sharper note:

Presbyterians, Independents, all had here the same spirit of faith and prayer. . . . They agree here, know no names of difference; pity it is it should be otherwise anywhere. All that believe have the real unity, which is most glorious because inward and spiritual . . . As for being united in forms, commonly called uniformity, every Christian will for peace sake study and do as far as conscience will permit; and from brethren, in things of the mind, we look for no compulsion but that of light and reason. In other things God hath put the sword into the Parliament's hand, for the terror of evildoers and the praise of them that do well.[33]

Religious toleration, for those with the root of the matter
in them, Cromwell certainly believed in; and on principle,
not merely because it was an asset to fighting morale –
though it was that too. 'Truly, I think he that prays best
will fight best', he declared in 1650. 'I had rather that
Mahometanism were permitted amongst us than that one
of God's children should be persecuted.'[34] In such beliefs
he was with the radicals, and we must never forget how
very subversive these beliefs appeared to his contemporaries – not only to royalists but also to conservative
Parliamentarians.[35]

How far Oliver went with the radicals in other matters
at this time is less clear. His first recorded speech in the
Long Parliament was on behalf of John Lilburne, and
we have seen him protecting Lilburne against Manchester at a later date.[36] Lilburne was one of Cromwell's
witnesses against the Earl (their commanding officer). In
July Cromwell wrote to support Lilburne's request for
payment of the money voted him in compensation for
his Star Chamber punishment. But in none of these in-
stances was Cromwell associating himself with Lilburne's
democratic views, and it may not be quite irrelevant that
in 1628 a William Lilburne had been a fellow-burgess of
Oliver's at Huntingdon.[37] In August 1641 Cromwell had
however supported petitions from poor prisoners, and
more than one contemporary accused him of associating
himself with the radical demand for the abolition of
tithes. He disliked capital punishment for any offence less
than murder.[38]

But the overall impression of Cromwell at this time is
of a military and political leader anxious at all costs to
maintain unity among those who were prepared to fight.
This comes out again and again in his actions. In May
1641 he was in favour of an 'Oath of Association' to make
the Parliamentary Protestation of that month more effective. 'Combination carries strength with it,' he wrote to

his constituents in sending down the Protestation for signature. 'It's dreadful to adversaries; especially when it's in order to the duty we owe to God, to the loyalty we owe to our King and sovereign, and to the affection due to our country and liberties.' This passion for unity later determined his attitude to disputes within the Army.

VI

As a soldier Cromwell's greatness lay in that he adapted the military revolution which had started in the Dutch republic fifty or sixty years earlier[39] to English conditions, equally revolutionary. The essence of this military revolution was its reliance on 'the free way' as against 'the formal'; a recognition of the fact that free men consciously motivated by a belief in their cause could get the better of mere professionals simply by superior morale and discipline. Cromwell's troopers, originally, were picked men, well-drilled, well-equipped, well-horsed, well-paid. All these factors enabled him to use the cavalry charge as a battering ram instead of as a mobile infantry lightly armed with pistols. Prince Rupert's cavalry charged once, often with devastating effect, but then lost its cohesion in the search for plunder and destroying enemy stragglers. As Clarendon put it, 'though the King's troops prevailed in the charge and routed those they charged, they never rallied themselves again in order, nor could be brought to make a second charge again the same day; . . . whereas Cromwell's troops, if they prevailed, or thought they were beaten and presently routed, rallied again and stood in good order till they received new orders'. This, Clarendon added, 'was only under him, and had never been notorious under Essex or Waller'.[40] At Marston Moor it was the repeated charges of Cromwell's horse that turned apparent Parliamentary defeat into complete vic-

tory. At Naseby Cromwell won the battle while Rupert
was off the field pursuing Ireton's broken horse. Naseby-
Fight, Wither claimed, was where God first was plainly
seen on Parliament's side.[41] He was helping those who had
shown they could help themselves.

The other, prosaic point to make about Cromwell's
battles is that one reason for his always being victorious
was that he and his general, Sir Thomas Fairfax, rarely
engaged unless they enjoyed superiority in numbers. At
Naseby this superiority was nearly two to one. The New
Model's organization, commissariat and ordnance were
normally far superior to those of its enemies. Their lieutenants were organization men – Desborough, Ireton,
Fleetwood. In addition to this better discipline and
morale, the New Model Army had behind it better business methods, better supplies, better artillery.[42] Once the
was extended into its third year, the greater resources of
Parliament in money and trained business personnel inevitably began to tell. Charles I too tried to reorganize his
army and his finances on a national as opposed to a county
basis, but lacked both the financial resources and suitable
administrative personnel.[43]

Naseby was the decisive battle. Following it, the Army
turned to the south-west and scattered the Clubman
movement, which had had dangerous possibilities of forming the nucleus of a third, neutralist party. But the well-
disciplined, well-paid, victorious New Model could now
offer freedom from plundering and free quarter, if not
from taxation; and so persuaded the peasantry to disperse.
The final symbolic acts of the war were the surrender
and demolition of the great fortified houses of the aristocracy – the Catholic Marquis of Winchester's Basing
House, whose vast wealth Cromwell allowed his men to
plunder, and which was then burnt, so that it could never
again form a Catholic rallying-point; the Earl of Derby's
Lathom House; and Langford House, whose surrender

from Sir Bartholomew Bell was symbolically received by Lieutenant-Colonel Hewson and Major Thomas Kelsey, originally, so it was said, a cobbler and a button-maker respectively. The Marquis of Worcester's Raglan Castle survived until 19 August 1646. The King fled northwards to seek the protection of the Scottish army.

It now remained to be seen whether the country gentlemen and townsmen of the New Model Army could agree on an alternative system of government for an England so long dominated by its landed aristocracy. 'Oh for self-denying Cromwell home again,' John Lilburne cried in October 1645.

IV

FROM SOLDIER
TO POLITICIAN:
1647-49

It is our conquest, not the Army's: the Army being considered
as the people's power, chosen by the people, paid by the
people, entrusted with the people's welfare and defence,
acting all – as hitherto they have done and we hope shall –
for the good, liberty and freedom of the people. By 'people'
is meant the sound, well-affected part, the rest are the conquered subdued part, who can challenge no right in that free
election, which is the fruit of conquest. It would be frivolous
to dispute *de jure* and *de facto* when necessity calls for force
to preserve the whole: which force prevailing must always
be presumed to have right.

ANON., *The Extent of the Sword* (1653–4)

It matters not who is our Commander-in-Chief if God be so.
CROMWELL, Speech to Council of Officers, 23 March 1649

I

The conclusion of the civil war brought a period which may have seemed less of an anti-climax to Cromwell than it does to the historian, but which must in the end have become very frustrating. After the mopping-up operations, Oliver's commission was not renewed when it lapsed in July 1646. When he was called back to the Army eleven months later it was in full revolt against the civil power, against Parliament. For the months in between Cromwell was an MP who, although very active in the House and on committees, no longer enjoyed the influence which his rank of Lieutenant-General had hitherto given him. From the end of January to the middle of April 1647 he did not attend the House at all. This was said to be due to an 'impostume in the head'; but whether the illness was genuine, diplomatic or psycho-somatic is unclear. He was at least toying with the idea of leaving England to fight for the German protestants in the Thirty Years' War. These were the months in which those conservative MPs, whom we call 'Presbyterians' reasserted their control of the House of Commons, men 'who have so much malice against the Army as besots them', as Cromwell put it to Fairfax on 11 March. Parliament had resolved on 18 February to disband the Army without making any provision for payment of arrears or pensions for widows and orphans of those killed in Parliament's service, or even for indemnity for illegal actions committed under orders during the fighting. The troops might be permitted to re-enlist for service in Ireland. Even for Ireland there would

be no officers save Fairfax with a rank higher than
colonel; and all officers must take the Covenant. No MP
was to be permitted to hold a military command in
England.

The rank and file of the Army were at once up in arms.
During March the cavalry regiments organized themselves and appointed Agitators or delegates to represent
them. Although, as the Agitators themselves later put it,
'those resolutions to stand for freedom and justice began
among the soldiers only', many of the officers sympathized
with their demands for arrears. Others were chased out
of the Army by their own rank and file. By the end of
April mutiny threatened, and the House of Commons at
last grudgingly voted six weeks' arrears of pay to men
who disbanded without going to Ireland. It was too little
and too late. By now the infantry had followed the
cavalry's example in electing Agitators, who met in a
representative assembly, an Army soviet as it might be
called in the twentieth century. To complete the analogy,
the Agitators were already being influenced by the democratic political theories of the civilian party of the
Levellers.

In May the Commons sent Cromwell with three other
MPs down to Essex in an attempt to restore the Army to
obedience by offering further concessions – another fortnight's arrears and the promise of an indemnity. 'We
found . . . the common soldiers much unsettled,' the Commissioners reported to the Commons on 17 May, with
some understatement. Three days later, in a remarkable
document, the four Commissioners reported that officers
and other ranks were united in their demands, and that
the Commissioners associated themselves with them
('upon a kind of necessity as Providence hath cast it for
preventing worse'). Moreover, 'the officers thus joining
with the soldiers in a regular way to make known and give
vent to their grievances hath contributed much to allay

precedent distempers, to bring off the soldiers much from their late ways of corresponding and actings amongst themselves, and reduce them again towards a right order and regard to their officers in what they do'. In short, the strike was solid, and those who had been sent down to suppress it had associated themselves with it: so was discipline restored!

This was a turning point in Oliver Cromwell's career, and controversy has raged over it then and ever since. His enemies alleged that he egged Parliament on to provoke the Army by false assurances that it would obey, while secretly fomenting discontent among the troops. This is surely far too subtle. The Presbyterian MPs needed no encouragement, and their treatment of the Army was so outrageous that the troops' reaction is self-explained. What probably is true is that Oliver, as so often in moments of crisis, waited on events until he felt that inaction was no longer possible. By the middle of May a breach between the mutinous Army and Parliament could not be prevented: if Cromwell had opposed the demands of the rank and file, supported by most of the officers, he would have lost all influence with the Army which he had done so much to create. The troops would have fallen still further under Leveller influence, and so would have alienated many of the officers: the Army would cease to be a united force capable of playing a decisive role in politics. If the Army were crushed or disbanded – as the majority in Parliament wanted – or if through its own dissensions it lost its political unity, many of the causes to which Cromwell attached the greatest importance would have been immediately endangered. He had a natural sympathy with the professional demands of men who had served under his command. To this he might add the political calculation that if Army unity was broken, no force would remain capable of withstanding the intolerance of Parliament and the Presbyterian clergy. The Army might fall under the control of Levellers whose political radicalism Oliver distrusted, and internecine strife between Parliament and Army might ensue, from which only the royalists would benefit. Any of these results would mean the political eclipse of Oliver Cromwell. Whereas if he could keep the Army united and under his influence he could hope to work with it for the lowest common multiple of political objectives on which all ranks were agreed, to save the country from the anarchy of a new civil war or social revolution; and – no doubt incidentally – to enhance his own political position.

It would have needed a Machiavellian of genius to have worked all that out in advance. But the policy of waiting on events – or on the Lord – was temperamentally and theologically suited to Cromwell.[1] If he had any doubts, his hand was forced by the House of Commons now losing its head. On 25 May they proposed to go back on their promises by dividing the Army, disbanding the regiments separately, and giving the soldiers the mere alternatives of enlisting for Ireland or immediate dismissal without arrears. The Army decided to defy these orders and rendezvous at Newmarket.

At the same time a decision was taken to seize the King, hitherto a prisoner in the hands of Commissioners of Parliament. For the Presbyterians were proposing to send Charles to Scotland, in the hope that he would return at the head of a Scottish army to crush the New Model. That Cromwell knew of the plot to seize the King we can be reasonably certain; but it is more difficult to decide whether his was the master mind behind it, or whether he fell in with a plan the initiative for which came from the Agitators. Cromwell had returned to London when on 29 May the Army's decision to rendezvous was taken at Bury St Edmunds. Cornet Joyce, who seized the King, arrived in Oxford en route for Holmby House on 1 June. He saw Cromwell in London on 31

May, and clearly at least told him what was afoot; but it seems hardly likely that the decision to seize Charles could have been taken as late as that. Joyce told the Parliamentary Commissioners that he had come 'with authority from the soldiers'. When Charles asked to see his commission, Joyce at first prevaricated, and then pointed to the troops drawn up behind him.[2] Moreover Joyce – a cornet, the holder of the lowest commissioned rank in the army – was not the sort of person to whom a lieutenant-general (even if not then holding a commission) would have entrusted the command of 500 men. As soon as a horrified Fairfax heard of Joyce's seizure of the King, he sent a colonel down to take control of the situation. But Fairfax could get no action taken against Joyce.

It would fit in with our whole previous analysis of Cromwell waiting on events if his hand was forced by Joyce and the Agitators. Fairfax invited Oliver to join the Army at the end of May, but the latter did not leave London to throw his lot finally in with them until 4 June, the day after he knew that Joyce's *coup* had been successful.[3] According to Sir Gilbert Pickering in 1656 Oliver only joined 'that violent and rash part of the Army' after 'the third letter came to you [Cromwell] from them, wherein they peremptorily told you that if you would not forthwith, nay presently, come and head them, they would go their own way without you'.[4] On this assumption, Cromwell would be faced with unpleasant alternatives, but as always he chose the course most likely to hold the Army together as a political force. Even Major Robert Huntington, Cromwell's severest critic at this stage, says no more than that Oliver and Ireton *advised* the seizure of the King by the private soldiery.[5] The Levellers were later to attribute Cromwell's delay in committing himself to the fact that 'the House of Commons bribed you with a vote of £2500 [a year] to betray and destroy' the Army.[6] This had in fact been voted as long ago as 23 January 1646 in principle, but had not been ascertained: it may be significant that it was on 5 May 1647 that a decisive step forward was taken by an order for a survey of the lands of the Marquis of Worcester which were to be given to Cromwell. Denzil Holles, a Presbyterian, also alleged that Cromwell did 'privily convey his goods' from London before leaving for the Army.[7]

Those who regard Oliver as the contriver of the whole scheme adopt a naïve conspiracy theory of history ('strikes are always fomented by agitators') and underestimate the strength and self-confidence of the rank-and-file organization in the New Model Army. If my analysis is correct, it was precisely this strength which forced Cromwell's hand. The rank and file needed his prestige to give respectability to a course of action they were determined to follow. 'After Cromwell quitted the Parliament', Sir John Berkeley said, 'his chief dependence was on the Army, which he endeavoured by all means to keep in unity, and if he could not bring it to his sense, he, rather than suffer any division in it, went over himself and carried his friends with him into that way which the Army did choose.' He was their leader: he followed them. In June 1647 he was just in time to escape arrest: events would no longer be waited on. The providences were now clear to him. A thoroughly alarmed House of Commons voted full arrears for the Army. But it was too late.

At the Agitators' insistence, the Army rendezvoused at Newmarket on 4 and 5 June, and accepted a *Humble Representation,* in which officers and men agreed not to disband or divide until their grievances had been redressed. An Army Council was set up consisting of the generals plus two commissioned officers and two privates from each regiment. The unity of the Army had been given organizational form. The Army then began to advance on London, assuring the City Fathers that 'although you may suppose that a rich city may seem an enticing bait to poor hungry soldiers', they would not plunder the City unless they were opposed by its militia. This dubious reassurance was followed by a *Declaration* calling for a purge of Parliament, and arrangements for its dissolution and election of a new House of Commons. Eleven leading Presbyterians were accused of treason. The Army was claiming in effect to be more truly representative of the people of England than the House of Commons.

But though the Army had thus decisively intervened in politics as though it were a united force, in fact a struggle for power was already going on within its ranks. Cromwell, now resuming his post as Lieutenant-General, soon began to want to restore 'normal' military discipline; it was the Agitators and Levellers who continued to emphasize the words of the Army's *Declaration* of 14 June, that they were 'not a mere mercenary Army', but civilians in uniform, 'called forth and conjured by the several declarations of Parliament to the defence of our own and the people's just rights and liberties', which they would 'assert and vindicate ... against all arbitrary power'.[8]

When the northern Army mutinied against its general, Sydenham Poyntz, elected Agitators and declared its support for the southern Army, Fairfax at once ordered Poyntz's release. The first instinct of the generals, once they had broken with Parliament, was to turn to the King – now their prisoner – so as to use him and his supporters as a makeweight against the social revolutionary demands of their rank and file. In a letter which Cromwell is alleged to have written to one of the King's advisers in July, he declared that it was 'not only a most wicked, but a very difficult if not an impossible design for a few men, not of the greatest quality, to introduce a popular government against the King and his party, against the Presbyterians, against the nobility and gentry, against the laws established, both civil and ecclesiastical, and against the whole genius of the nation, that had been accustomed, for so many ages, to a monarchical government'. Cromwell believed that a restoration of monarchy was essential to the stability of property and the social order. ('No man could enjoy their lives and estates quietly without the King had his rights.') He threw himself into negotiations with such enthusiasm that his cousin and friend Oliver St John had to warn him that he was doing the King's business too fast. The effect was indeed only to make Charles more obstinately confident. 'You cannot do without me,' he said; 'you will fall to ruin if I do not sustain you.' Ireton had to say to Charles's face, 'Sir, you have an intention to be the arbitrator between the Parliament and us; and we mean to be it between your Majesty and the Parliament'. They deadlocked. The King had already written to one of his supporters that his hope was 'to draw either the Presbyterians or the Independents to side with me for extirpating one the other', and then he would 'be really King again'. How could one negotiate with such a man?

II

The Army's advance on London had been halted for a month while these negotiations went on, and Parliament showed no signs of surrendering. Fearing a renewal of civil war, the Agitators became understandably restive. On 16–17 July a General Council of the Army was called, including the Agitators, 'who now in prudence we admit to debate', as a newsletter revealingly put it. The writer (probably John Rushworth) continued: 'It is not more than necessary they should be [admitted] considering the influence they have upon the soldiers ... It is the singularest part of wisdom in the General and the officers so to carry themselves considering the present temper of the Army so as to be unanimous in the Councils, including the new persons into their number. It keeps a good accord, and obtains ready obedience. . . . If a man consider the alterations of officers that are now admitted, and interests of officers that are gone,[9] it is the greatest wonder that there is unanimity still.'

At this Army Council the Agitators demanded an immediate march on London. Cromwell pleaded at length against this step, urging that instead pressure should be brought to bear to strengthen the hands of the minority of the Commons which shared the Army's political views. They were, he said, 'upon the gaining hand; . . . that [which] we and they gain in a free way, it is better than twice so much in a forced, and will be more truly ours and our posterity's. . . Really, really, have what you will have, that [which] you have by force I look upon it as nothing. . . . Though you be in the right and I in the wrong, if we be divided I doubt we shall all be in the wrong'. The dispute, however, was only about whether to occupy London: the generals had to agree to an advance nearer the capital. This began on 19 July, and the 11 Presbyterian members withdrew from Parliament.

The Presbyterians in desperation called the London mob to their assistance. Disbanded soldiers, apprentices (to whom the House of Commons had recently voted a monthly holiday) and watermen declared their allegiance to the Covenant and demanded the restoration of the King. They invaded the House of Commons to force its compliance, and the City militia was called out. (This first appearance of 'church and king' mobs deserves further study: they became a permanent feature of English political life after the revolution of 1688 had imposed a political settlement in many ways very similar to that which the Independents advocated in 1647.) Nine peers and fifty-seven MPs fled to the Army, which proceeded to occupy the capital on 6 August. The Agitators had won the tactical battle, but they were still to be out-generalled.

Deeper divisions lurked behind these tactical disputes. To Cromwell's insistence on unity, the Agitators had for some time been asking 'unity for what?' On 17 July Ireton brought forward the Heads of Proposals, a new constitution which he had drafted in association with Cromwell and Lambert. This proposed biennial Parliaments, a franchise redistributed in accordance with contribution to taxation, a modified episcopal state church with toleration outside it, and various specific provisions, including confirmation of the abolition of the Court of Wards (abolished by order of the House of Commons in February 1646), the ending of forest laws and monopolies, reform of the law and of tithes. But the King and the House of Lords were to be retained, and although the franchise was to be redistributed, nothing was said about its extension. The Agitators were already, in Clarendon's words, speaking 'insolently and confidently against the King and Parliament, and ... professed as great malice against all the lords as against the King'.[10]

Once London was occupied, and Parliament at the Army's mercy, the generals resumed negotiations with the King on the basis of the Heads of Proposals. But Charles was interested only in gaining time, until he could persuade a Scottish army to invade England and rescue him. Meanwhile the Levellers had put forward their rival constitution, the Agreement of the People, and this won considerable support in the Army and especially from the Agitators. At Putney, at the end of November, this constitution was discussed in the Army Council. (On 18 July the Heads of Proposals had been referred to a committee of this Council, which included Agitators, but in the flurry of the occupation of London nothing seems to have come of it.) At Putney, for the first time, the two rival ideas of

the future constitution of England faced each other. Com-
missary-General Ireton, soon to become Cromwell's son-
in-law, called for a modification of the existing constitution by a geographical extension of the franchise to the
men of property, those who have 'a permanent fixed
interest in this kingdom ... the persons in whom all land
lies, and those in corporations in whom all trading lies'.
Colonel Rainborough and the Levellers on the other hand
called for a wide extension of the franchise downwards to
all save paupers and wage labourers.

Cromwell and Ireton also had to defend their negotiations with the King, which Rainborough had opposed in
the Commons. Their 'credit and reputation had been
much blasted', the Agitator Sexby told them to their
faces. Cromwell doubted the feasibility of the Leveller
proposals. 'The expressions in it are very plausible, ... if
we could leap out of one condition into another.' But 'how
do we know if, whilst we are disputing these things, another company of men shall gather together, and they
shall put out a paper as plausible perhaps as this?' What
Cromwell wanted was not a perfect theoretical scheme
but 'that that, as before the Lord, I am persuaded in my
heart tends to uniting us in one to that that God will manifest to us to be the thing that he would have us prose-
cute'. 'It is not enough for us to propose good things,
but it behoves honest men and Christians' only to make
proposals that they think will work. Professions of confidence were not enough: 'we are very apt all of us to
call that faith that perhaps may be but carnal imagination
and carnal reasonings.' He was not 'wedded and glued
to forms of government'. Forms of constitution were 'but
a moral thing ..., dross and dung in comparison of
Christ'. At all costs he wanted to avoid 'such a real and
actual division as admits of no reconciliation'. He advocated a committee, a prayer-meeting: and was accused
by the other side of playing for time 'till we have our

throats cut'. 'Let us be doing,' Cromwell replied; 'but let
us be united in our doing.'

Whilst Ireton concentrated on defending the propertied
franchise, Cromwell tried to find compromises between
the two positions. 'Perhaps there are a very considerable
part of copyholders by inheritance that ought to have a
voice?' Although King and House of Lords should not
be abolished, their power might be considerably restricted.
God may have marked them out for destruction, but 'let
those that are of that mind wait upon God for such a way
when the thing may be done without sin, and without
scandal too'. On 4 November the Army Council voted –
against Cromwell and Ireton – in favour of extending the
franchise to all except servants, and on the next day a
resolution was carried 'that the Army might be called to
a rendezvous and things settled'.[11] There were plans for a
great demonstration of solidarity by Spitalfields weavers,
who were to march in their thousands to the rendezvous.
Cromwell was up in arms at once. He spoke fiercely at a
General Council of the Army against 'the danger of their
principles who had sought to divide the Army', declaring
that the suffrage proposals of the Agreement of the
People 'did tend very much to anarchy'. Despite opposition, he got the Army Council to ask Fairfax to send the
Agitators back to their regiments until after the rendezvous.

Meanwhile a sensational event occurred. The rendezvous was fixed for 15 November. On 11 November the
King escaped from his captivity at Hampton Court. His
destination was still unknown to the Army when it as-
sembled. Charles had in fact fled to the Isle of Wight,
which was commanded by Cromwell's cousin, Robert
Hammond. The whole episode played so completely into
Cromwell's hands that many believed that he contrived
the King's escape. This cannot be proved: but there is
evidence, apart from its convenience for Oliver, that

makes one wonder. Oliver Cromwell visited the Isle of Wight between 4 and 12 September: no reason has ever been given for this visit. It occurred just after Hammond had resigned command of his regiment, and had been appointed Governor of the island (31 August, confirmed by Parliament on 6 September). This was at Hammond's own request, the reason given being that 'he found the Army resolved to break all promises to the King and he would have nothing to do with such perfidies'. On 10 or 11 November Cromwell wrote to his cousin Edward Whalley, who happened to be commanding the King's guards at Hampton Court, to warn him of rumours of a plot to assassinate the King. Whalley immediately showed the letter to the King (why?), whose plans for escape had already been concerted with John Ashburnham and Sir John Berkeley. These royalists had been the two people through whom Oliver and Ireton had conducted both open and clandestine negotiations with Charles, and Clarendon describes Ashburnham as wholly dependent on Cromwell and Ireton.[12] Berkeley had been specially selected by the two officers to mediate between them and the King. It was Ashburnham who – after meeting Hammond on his way to take up his governorship of the Isle of Wight – recommended that Charles go there. In 1656 Berkeley was dismissed by Charles II from the service of James Duke of York, and came under suspicion of being in communication with Cromwell – for which there is some circumstantial evidence.

A further complication, on which it is difficult to obtain satisfactory evidence, is offered by contemporary hints that many of the other ranks in the Army were King's men at heart, or at least had been worked on by royalist agents. 'Who knows not,' said Wildman, 'that the forces in pay will be at the King's beck whenever he be warm in his throne? Did not many at Ware cry out for the King and Sir Thomas [Fairfax]?'[13] It is likely that many even of those who cheered for the Agitators and the Levellers failed to understand the political subtleties of their ideas. Arrears and indemnity, yes; the Agreement of the People, perhaps less clearly understood. Such an explanation would help to account for the ease with which the Leveller hold on the Army was broken. Many of the Levellers themselves in defeat negotiated with the royalists, regarding them as a lesser evil than Oliver Cromwell.

If the whole escape and its timing were uninfluenced, Cromwell had indeed good reason for believing that he enjoyed the special protection of God. Instead of a general rendezvous of the Army, Fairfax ordered three separate assemblies. When the first took place at Cork-bush Field, near Ware, the troops knew that Charles had escaped but not where he had gone. Another civil war might well be imminent: all Cromwell's arguments for preserving the unity of the Army were suddenly reinforced. The troops were faced by a skilfully-drafted remonstrance from Fairfax, in which he rebuked the Agitators for dividing the Army at this critical moment, promised to press for regular pay, pensions and indemnity for the Army, for an early dissolution of Parliament and franchise reform so that the Commons should be '(as near as may be) an equal representative of the people that are to elect' (a totally ambiguous phrase, well calculated to deceive the unwary). If military discipline was not restored, Fairfax would resign his commission.

It was irresistible in the circumstances. There was trouble from two regiments which were there without orders, following the Army Council's vote for a general rendezvous rather than the General's orders for three separate ones. But after a scuffle they submitted. One of the ringleaders, Private Richard Arnold, was shot, and eleven imprisoned. The others accepted Fairfax's Remonstrance. At the other two rendezvous there was no incident. Hammond at once sent his chaplain from the Isle of Wight to urge his fellow-officers 'to make use of their success upon the Agitators', and sent Berkeley back to resume negotiations.

But the generals' victory was less complete than it appeared, and from its incompleteness we can guess something of the strength of feeling on the other side. Representations were made to Cromwell and Ireton from 'two third parts of the Army', to warn them that 'though they were certainly to perish in the attempt, they would leave nothing unessayed to bring the Army to their sense; and if all failed, they would make a division in the Army and join with any that would assist in the destruction of their opposers'. Cromwell was alleged to have decided, not for the first time, 'that, if we cannot bring the Army to our sense, we must go to theirs, a schism being evidently destructive'. In mid-December the King rejected Parliament's terms for a settlement, and signed an agreement by which the Scots agreed to intervene with an army on his behalf. At a meeting of the General Council, Cromwell admitted that 'the glories of the world had so dazzled his eyes that he could not discern clearly the great works the Lord was doing'. Richard Arnold could not be brought back to life, but his imprisoned comrades were liberated, and the Army was united again in fact as well as in form. On 3 January the House of Commons voted against any further negotiations with the King, Cromwell speaking strongly in favour of the motion and reinforcing his arguments by laying his hand upon his sword. The gesture was underlined twelve days later when the Army again entered Whitehall to persuade the House of Lords to concur with this Vote of No Addresses. A new Committee of Safety was set up, with Cromwell on it, and given considerable independence of Parliament. The General Council of the Army voted itself out of existence on 8 January. When the second civil war broke out, the Council of Officers pledged themselves, after

victory, to call Charles I to account for the bloodshed he
had caused.

III

In the summer of 1648 there were revolts in South Wales,
Kent and Essex, followed by an invasion from Scotland.
The rising in South Wales was led by former Parlia-
mentarian officers, renegades against whom Cromwell was
particularly bitter.[14] After defeat, one of their leaders was
shot; so were those who commanded the defence of Col-
chester, where Fairfax won after a long and bitter siege.
When Cromwell reported his defeat of the invading
Scottish army at Preston in August, he recommended to
Speaker Lenthall that 'they that are inflexible and will
not leave troubling the land may speedily be destroyed'.
It looks as though he may already have decided that there
was no other way to deal with Charles, and pressure from
the Army must have done much to bring this conviction
home to him.

The Presbyterians, the majority in the House of Commons, had never wished for too decisive a victory for
either side. They still hoped the King would save them
from the 'heretical democracy' – freedom of discussion
and organization for the lower classes – which the Army
advocated. In May 1648 they had passed a savage act
against heresy and blasphemy. They resumed the weary
negotiations with the King while Cromwell pursued the
defeated royalists into Scotland at the beginning of
October, and then sat down to besiege Pontefract. He
stayed there for six weeks, unaccountably, while sensational decisions were being taken in London. On 16 November a Remonstrance from the Council of Officers,
drafted by Ireton, called for the death sentence on
Charles and 'his chief instruments' in both wars. On 6

December the Army occupied London again, and Colonel
Thomas Pride purged the House of Commons, thoroughly
this time. The coup seems to have been Ireton's, not
Cromwell's. The latter at once returned to London, declaring 'that he had not been acquainted with the design;
yet since it was done he was glad of it'. (On 2 December
he had similarly approved the officers' Remonstrance 'for
the speedy executing of impartial justice upon all offenders
whatsoever'.)

'We in this northern army were in a waiting posture,
desiring to see what the Lord would lead us to,' Oliver
had told Hammond a few days previously. What had he
been waiting for? Miss Wedgwood suggests that he had
hoped to avoid a forcible purge by persuading the Commons to purge themselves.[15] From the North he had had
a curious and often-quoted correspondence with Hammond, in which Oliver seemed to be trying to reassure
himself just as much as his cousin. 'How easy it is to find
arguments for what we would have, and how easy to take
offence at things called Levellers, and run into an extre-
mity on the other hand, meddling with an accursed
thing' (6 November 1648). 'Our fleshly reasonings en-
snare us.' 'Let us look into providences, surely they mean
somewhat. They hang so together, have been so constant,
so clear and unclouded.' We must not act 'before and without faith', but to be passive now may be more dangerous
than to be active. Is not 'the whole fruit of the war like
to be frustrated' by continuing to negotiate with the
King? 'Dost thou not think this fear of the Levellers (of
whom there is no fear), that they would destroy nobility,
had caused some to rake up corruption?' (25 November).
So Cromwell silenced his own doubts in conversation
with Robin Hammond.[16]

The men who were taking control of events now,
though not Levellers, were indeed of a significantly lower
social class. On 21 November Hammond (who really had

had scruples about Army policy) was recalled from the
Isle of Wight and replaced by Colonel Ewer, a former
serving man. Colonel Thomas Harrison, who removed
the King to Windsor after Pride's Purge, was the son of a
grazier or butcher. Pride himself, who purged the gentry
from the House of Commons – without any orders from
Fairfax, it was said – had been a drayman or brewer's
employee; Colonel Okey a tallow-chandler, Hewson a
shoemaker, Goffe a salter, Barkstead a goldsmith or
thimble-maker, Berry clerk to an iron works, Kelsey a
button-maker; Colonel Philip Jones had been born to £8
or £10 a year. We need not take all this contemporary
gossip too literally: but the general point remains valid,
that the men who came to power in December 1648, and
who were responsible for the execution of Charles I,
were men well below the rank of the traditional rulers of
England. A committee of the Army which met on 15
December 'to consider of the best ways and grounds for
the speedy bringing of the King to justice', as well as
other great delinquents, contained no one above the rank
of lieutenant-colonel. 'What were the lords of England but
William the Conqueror's colonels? Or the barons but his
majors? Or the knights but his captains?' men had asked
even earlier in the civil war.[17] Such men had social opinions which might well alarm scions of old families like
the Hammonds and the Cromwells.

Hammond was arrested on 28 November, the day on
which Oliver was asked to return to London immediately.
His journey took him eight days, and when he arrived the
purge was over. Meanwhile Ireton was conferring with
the Levellers. They were at work on a new version of the
Agreement of the People. When Cromwell got back to
London, he still tried to save Charles's life. Ireton seems
to have decided earlier. Burnet, a well-informed near-
contemporary, tells us that he 'was the person that drove
it on: for Cromwell was all the while in some suspense

about it'.[18] It was not until the end of December that Cromwell publicly accepted that 'the providence of God hath cast this upon us' in a speech to the House of Commons. Yet once trial and execution had been decided on, Cromwell threw himself into it with the vigour he always showed when his mind was made up, when God had spoken. 'I tell you we will cut off his head with the crown on it,' he replied to Algernon Sidney's arguments against the validity of the tribunal being set up. He shouted down one of the judges who raised a protest during the trial. He was alleged to have held Henry Ingoldsby's hand and forced him to sign the death warrant. Outside the House of Commons he called 'those that are gone in shall set their hands, I will have their hands now'.[19]

Pride's Purge of Parliament was succeeded by a similar purge in London. Parliament voted that no royalists or persons who since December 1647 had supported a personal treaty with the King could elect or be elected to Common Council. The result was that two-thirds of that body lost their seats and were replaced by radicals.[20] There were similar changes in many other towns, though not enough have yet been investigated.

The execution of the King marked a point of no return. Henceforth compromise between Army leaders and defeated royalists was impossible, at least for a long time to come; and Pride's Purge had equally alienated the conservative Parliamentarians. The brusque use of military force had outraged the Levellers and many radical supporters of the revolution. They eyed the new régime with the gravest suspicion as it put into effect some of their own policies but in a way that they found totally unacceptable. They were soon to rise in revolt against it. The English republic rested on a very narrow social basis.

V

THE LORD GENERAL:
1649-53

How shall we behave ourselves after such mercies? What is
the Lord adoing? What prophecies are now fulfilling? Who
is a God like ours? To know his will, to do his will, are both
of him.

CROMWELL to the Rev. John Cotton,
Boston, New England, 2 October 1651

Every good Commonwealthsman is diligent, some would
advance trade to the utmost, and others would advance
liberty to the utmost; indeed all other things men seek to
improve them to the utmost; but oh the little care is found
among men to advance the kingdom of the Lord Jesus Christ
to the utmost!

STEPHEN MARSHALL, *A Sermon preached to the
Honourable House of Commons*, 26 January 1648

I

The uneasy dualism of power which had existed since the Army's first intervention in politics in June 1647 had now ended. There could no longer be any doubt where real power lay. Cromwell was the first chairman of the Council of State which the House of Commons set up on 17 February 1649, although peers sat side by side with him. It was certainly with his approval that the execution of the King was followed by those of the Duke of Hamilton, the Earl of Holland, Lord Capel and Colonel Poyer, the leaders of the 1648 royalists. In a speech to the General Council of Officers on 23 March Cromwell referred to these executions as 'a great fruit' of the second civil war which God had given them. He was, as usual, arguing that 'there is more cause of danger from disunion among ourselves than by anything from our enemies'. He listed these enemies in ascending order of disagreeableness: 'I had rather be overrun with a Cavalierish interest than a Scotch interest; I had rather be overrun with a Scotch interest than an Irish interest; and I think of all this is the most dangerous.' 'Now that should awaken all Englishmen, who are perhaps willing enough he [Charles Stuart] should have come in upon an accommodation, but not [that] he must come from Ireland or Scotland.'

Charles I had been executed in no spirit of republican doctrinairism. There were republicans among the supporters of the Rump – Henry Marten and Edmund Ludlow, for instance – but Cromwell seems fairly consistently to have favoured a settlement 'with somewhat of mon-

archical power in it', as he put it in December 1652.
Levellers and other republicans opposed the new Commonwealth. Monarchy was not formally abolished in
England until 17 March, and the House of Lords two days
later. The upper House, Cromwell told the Scots fifteen
months later, was 'at that time very forward to give up
the people's rights, and obstruct what might save them,
and always apt enough to join with kingly interest against
the people's liberties'. In 1653 he was reported as telling
London aldermen 'that the King's head was not taken off
because he was King, nor the Lords laid aside because
Lords ... but because they did not perform their trust'.
It was a pragmatic not an ideological objection. One
suspects that financial considerations may have helped to
prompt even the abolition of monarchy and House of
Lords, since acts at once followed for selling the personal
estates of the royal family and of royalists who refused
to compound – all to pay for the Army about to be sent
to Ireland, to whose command Cromwell was nominated
on 15 March 1649.

Meanwhile Oliver had been setting about his usual task
of trying to restore relations with the Presbyterians whom
he had so recently defeated, both before and after the
execution. This would have been at the expense of the
Levellers, against whom his speech to the Council of
Officers had largely been directed. The Levellers felt that
they had been outwitted by the officers in that the purge
of the House of Commons, the execution of the King and
abolition of the Lords had not been accompanied by a
realization of the aims of the Agreement of the People.
That document had played its part and was now forgotten. There was no sign that the House of Commons
would dissolve itself, no extension or even redistribution
of the franchise, no law reform or abolition of tithes, nor
any of the other social reforms they had argued for. Instead there was naked military dictatorship; and they

feared Oliver's further ambitions. 'You shall scarce speak
to Cromwell about anything,' said a Leveller pamphlet of
21 March 1649, 'but he will lay his hand on his breast,
elevate his eyes and call God to record; he will weep,
howl and repent even while he doth smite you under
the fifth rib.' 'Oh Cromwell! Whither art thou aspiring?'[1]

The Leveller leaders were arrested, dragged before the
Council of State, where Lilburne, his ear to the keyhole,
heard Cromwell thump the table and cry out 'I tell you,
sir, you have no other way to deal with these men but to
break them or they will break you; yea and bring all the
guilt of the blood and treasure shed and spent in this
kingdom upon your heads and shoulders, and frustrate
and make void all that work that . . . you have done. . . .
To be broken and routed by such a despicable, contemptible generation of men' was unthinkable. It was only
three months since Oliver had assured Robin Hammond
that there was no fear of the Levellers. But then he had
been arguing a case, and indeed may have meant that the
Levellers were too 'despicable and contemptible' to be
feared. At all events he was now determined to break
them. One reason for this may have been that the Levellers were extending their political activities from London
and the Army to the country at large.[2]

When the decision had been taken to send an army to
Ireland,[3] the occasion was seized to weed out the
Leveller-influenced regiments. There was a mutiny in
London, and Robert Lockyer, who had fought all through
the civil war, was shot as ringleader. Despite this, in
May there were mutinies in four more regiments, which
turned into a full-scale Leveller revolt. Parliament declared mutiny in the Army to be treason. The revolt was
suppressed after a lightning night attack by Cromwell
on the rebels at Burford, not without suggestions of
treachery on his part. Three leaders were shot after the
surrender, and a fourth, William Thompson, was caught

and shot three days later. The Leveller mutiny was over.
Fairfax and Cromwell returned to Oxford, where they
were given honorary degrees by that formerly royalist
university, and to London where they were feasted by the
City. On the latter occasion the grace recalled the biblical
curse on him who removes his neighbour's landmark.[4]
Property had been saved.

II

The mutinies, in 1649 as in 1647, were caused by refusals
to be drafted to Ireland. But this time there was no chance
of support from the generals. The latter were now the
government; and the government had decided that Ireland must be subdued once for all. For this there were
many reasons. The Irish had been in revolt since November 1641. Suppression of the revolt there had been
delayed only because neither King nor Parliament could
trust the other to command the force to be sent. But now
the question of power in England had been finally settled.
Meanwhile for seven and a half years Ireland had been
an open back door to foreign invasion. Advantage had
not been taken of this since the great powers on the
continent had been locked in the Thirty Years' War. But
the Treaties of Westphalia in 1648 had ended the German
war, though England's most dangerous potential adversaries, France and Spain, still fought on. There were many
German troops now unemployed which might well be
used for an invasion of Ireland. Hopes were held especially of the Duke of Lorraine, as early as 1645 and as late
as 1651.[5] It is possible that the speed with which Charles I
was rushed to the scaffold was in part motivated by fear
of foreign intervention; it is certain that regicide intensified the hostility with which the Parliamentary cause was
viewed by continental monarchs. If Charles Stuart was to

be restored to the English throne, his likeliest route seemed to be via Ireland. His supporters in England had been defeated in two civil wars; the pro-royalist Hamiltonian party in Scotland was in eclipse following its disastrously ineffective invasion of England in 1648. Charles could now win support from Scotland only by an unpalatable surrender to the party of the Presbyterian Kirk. But in Ireland there were still armies in the field which were at least wholeheartedly opposed to the regicide Parliament. And Prince Rupert was hovering off the coast with a squadron of eight ships.

The Irish situation was confused. One army, commanded by George Monck, professed allegiance to Parliament: it had a precarious foothold in and around Dublin. The Marquis of Ormonde commanded an army of protestant English settlers, though not all of his nominal supporters were enthusiastic royalists. A powerful Parliamentarian showing in Ireland could easily rally support. The Catholics were divided into two factions – the Old English, most of whom were moderate royalists, and the Ulster tribesmen, owing allegiance to Owen O'Neill and hostile to all Englishmen. There was also a group of Ulster Scots, who like their countrymen at home were torn between their hatred of popery and their hatred of regicide and religious toleration.

The problem was to find a formula to unite as many as possible of these diverse groups. Ormonde hoped to join English and Scottish settlers with the Irish against the regicide republic. O'Neill, cooperating with the papal nuncio Rinuccini, hoped to unite all Catholic Irish in a nominal allegiance to Charles, thus snatching the lead from the English settlers and in effect uniting Irishmen against the English colonizers. Parliament could use fear and hatred of the Catholic majority at least to neutralize most of the English and Scottish settlers. There was a curious moment in May 1649 when Monck at the head of the Parliamentary forces signed an armistice which involved actual military cooperation with O'Neill against Ormonde's attempt to unite English and Scottish settlers behind Charles. This coincided with the Leveller policy for Ireland, which was to unite the common people of the two countries. ('The cause of the Irish natives in seeking their just freedoms' – the words are attributed to Walwyn – 'was the very same with our cause here in endeavouring our own rescue and freedom from the power of oppressors.'[6]) If the Levellers had won control of the English Army the history of Anglo-Irish relations might have been very different and much happier. As late as 25 March – three days before the arrest of Lilburne, Walwyn and Overton – the Council of Officers voted that the army in Ireland should not be used either to 'eradicate the natives or to divest them of their estates'.

But Monck's armistice had no ideological significance. This tough professional soldier was concerned only to gain time and to preserve his army until the English expeditionary force came to his relief. By the time news of the armistice reached England, the Levellers had been shattered at Burford. For two months the English public was told nothing of the armistice agreement. When it was finally revealed in August, Monck was publicly rebuked by the House of Commons. He loyally covered up the fact that Cromwell and the Council of State had known all along – a loyalty which Cromwell did not forget later. As late as October 1649 Cromwell in a letter to Parliament was stressing the cooperation between O'Neill and Ormonde 'so that now, I trust, some angry friends will think it high time to take off their jealousy from those to whom they ought to exercise more charity'.

By now the English expeditionary force was ready to sail to Ireland, with Cromwell in command. The brutality of the Cromwellian conquest of Ireland is not one of the pleasanter aspects of our hero's career, and I have no desire to whitewash his conduct. But we must get the campaign and its aftermath into historical perspective, and try to see it through the eyes of Cromwell and his contemporaries as well as those of posterity. In the first place, though Cromwell must bear responsibility for the military conduct of the conquest, the policy behind it was not his alone. It was that of the English government as a whole. Nor would this aspect of the Rump's policy be unpopular in itself with other factions of the English ruling class. That the native Catholic Irish should be subordinated to England was common ground between both parties in the Long Parliament in 1641–2: the dispute was only over command of the army which was to subdue them. The hatred and contempt which propertied Englishmen felt for the Irish is something which we may deplore but should not conceal. Even the poet Spenser, who knew Ireland well, the philosopher Bacon and the poet Milton, who believed passionately in liberty and human dignity, all shared the view that the Irish were culturally so inferior that their subordination was natural and necessary. Religious hostility reinforced cultural contempt. And the strategic considerations which I have mentioned, reinforced by the anxieties to which the second civil war had given rise, added overtones of fear to the contempt and hatred. A great number of civilized Englishmen of the propertied class in the seventeenth century spoke of Irishmen in tones not far removed from those which Nazis used about Slavs, or white South Africans use about the original inhabitants of their country. In each case the contempt rationalized a desire to exploit. In these matters Cromwell was no better and no worse than the average Englishman of his time and class. Only a few intellectuals of the radical left in England seem to have been exempt from this appalling attitude, and their ideological influence was slight, since it ran counter to the extreme protestant assumptions which most of the radicals shared. Cromwell's troops in Ireland, though they must have contained many soldiers who in England had supported the Levellers, showed no disposition to fraternize with the native Irish.

What Cromwell does seem to have decided, as military commander who was also a leading member of the English government, was that Ireland must be suppressed as swiftly, decisively and cheaply as possible. For this there were many reasons. First, the international situation, the possibility of foreign intervention via Ireland to restore monarchy, demanded that the back door be swiftly slammed and bolted. Charles Stuart, now calling himself Charles II, arrived at Jersey *en route* for Ireland a few days after the massacre of Drogheda. Secondly, the internal situation in England, where the government was conscious of hostility from right and left, called for quick successes without the imposition of heavy burdens on the taxpayer. The Irish campaign (and the navy) were financed by the sale of dean and chapter lands and of royal fee-farm rents. Vast sums had been raised in England in the early 1640s on the security of Irish lands, for wholesale confiscations had been envisaged from the start. Repayment at the expense of Irish landed proprietors would do much to consolidate the support of the moneyed men for the republican régime. Ireland was in every sense the first English colony.

Thirdly, we must not allow hindsight to blind us to the precariousness of Oliver's personal position. We know that he returned from his Irish victories with vastly enhanced prestige. But this was not inevitable. Ireland had been the grave of many military reputations from Elizabeth's Earl of Essex onwards – and the latter's position in English politics looked far securer before he sailed for Ireland than did Cromwell's in 1649. It is indeed highly probable that many of those MPs who pressed the Irish command upon an unwilling Oliver did so in the hope of cutting him down to size. If he had got bogged down in a long-drawn-out campaign in Ireland, control of the government in England might well have passed to men unfriendly to him and all that he stood for. These considerations may not excuse Oliver's conduct of his Irish campaign; but at least they help to explain his ruthless determination to break Irish resistance swiftly, finally – and at the cheapest possible rate.

Certainly he ran no risks with his Irish campaign. Nowhere is his concern for the detail of military preparation better evidenced than in the six months between his nomination as Commander-in-Chief and his actual departure for Ireland. Before accepting the proffered command he assured a General Council of Officers that if his name was to be used to attract recruits, he must 'be well satisfied concerning a just and fitting provision for them before they went'. He finally accepted the command, the day after the arrest of Lilburne, Walwyn and Overton, only on condition that it be 'sufficiently provided'. He was a member of the committee which persuaded the City to lend £120,000 on the security, *inter alia*, of the sale of royal fee-farm rents. The banquet which the City gave to Fairfax and Cromwell was not only a symbol of thanksgiving for the suppression of the Levellers, it was also a strong demonstration of support for the commander of the Irish expedition which the Levellers had opposed.

Cromwell was wise to insist on adequate financial backing. Out of sight tended to mean out of mind. On 25 June a newspaper reported a letter from Sir Charles Coote to Cromwell, complaining that his six regiments in Ireland had received eight months' pay in eight years. Within the next four days the Commons voted £400,000 from the excise to provide for the army, and authorized a further loan of £150,000. Cromwell lingered at Bristol for a month from mid-July until mid-August when the £100,000 cash promised him actually arrived: he had assured his troops they would not embark until it was to hand. On 2 August, ten days before Oliver sailed, Michael Jones, Monck's successor in command of Parliament's army in Ireland, had won a crushing victory over Ormonde's forces at Rathmines. The armistice with O'Neill had done its job and could now be repudiated with impunity.

Cromwell's first action on reaching Ireland was to forbid any plunder or pillage – an order which could not have been enforced with an unpaid army, and which introduced something quite new into Irish warfare. Two men were hanged for plundering, to enforce the point. This at once produced its effect on Ormonde's protestant troops, many of whom deserted to the Parliamentary army. Ormonde wrote to Charles Stuart that he feared Cromwell's money more than his face; and well he might. Before leaving England Cromwell had secured the co-operation of Lord Broghill, the former royalist son of Richard Boyle, first Earl of Cork, the most famous of the great plundering colonizers of Ireland. ('If there had been one like Boyle in every province,' said Oliver, 'it would have been impossible for the Irish to have raised a rebellion.') Broghill's intrigues were to bring many of the Irish protestant settlers over to accepting the rule of Parliament: he was to be a significant figure in Oliver's future career.[7]

On 11 September occurred the sack and massacre of Drogheda. Virtually the whole garrison, and all priests that were captured, were slaughtered. Montaigne had written, nearly 70 years earlier, of 'the custom we hold in wars, to punish, and that with death, those who wilfully opinionate themselves to defend a place which, by the rules of war, cannot be kept'.[8] Cromwell had summoned the town, and warned its defenders of the consequences of prolonging a hopeless resistance. Nevertheless, the savagery of the massacre was different from anything that had happened in the English civil wars (except to Irish camp followers): it recalled the horrors of the German Thirty Years' War. Cromwell, in his report to the President of the Council of State, hoped that 'this bitterness will save much effusion of blood'. A modern historian has compared it to the dropping of the A bomb on Hiroshima and Nagasaki, which brought the Japanese surrender in 1945.[9] In his more considered report to the Speaker of the House of Commons Cromwell again showed his anxiety lest Parliament should fail to keep him financially supplied: 'although it may seem very chargeable to the state of England to maintain so great a force, yet surely to stretch a little for the present, in following God's providence, in the hope the charge will not be long, I trust it will not be thought by any (that have not irreconcilable or malicious principles) unfit for me to move for a constant supply, which, in human probability as to outward means, is most likely to hasten and perfect this work. And indeed, if God please to finish it here as He hath done in England, the war is like to pay itself.' A week after Drogheda the Council of State wrote to Cromwell instructing him to let all forfeited estates in Ireland at the highest possible rent, and use the proceeds to pay for his army. The war would not finance itself unless it was finished quickly. So the massacre at Drogheda was followed by another at Wexford, which had long been a thorn in the side of English traders as a privateering centre. Again the town refused to surrender, and after an eight days' siege it was sacked. Anything from 1500 to 2000 troops, priests and civilians were butchered. Since the inhabitants were dead or fled, Cromwell reported, the town was available for English colonists to settle. 'It is a fine spot for some godly congregation,' wrote the Rev. Hugh Peter 'where house and land wait for inhabitants and occupiers.'[10] The news reached England just in time to counterbalance the adverse effect for the government of Lilburne's acquittal by a London jury on 26 October.

By this time losses due to military action, to sickness and to the need for leaving garrisons, had reduced Oliver's men from 15,000 to 5,000. He had reached the danger point from which so many English armies in Ireland had failed to recover. 'It is not to be imagined,' Ormonde wrote, 'how great the terror is that those successes and the power of the rebels have struck into this people. They are so stupified that it is with great difficulty that I can persuade them to act anything like men towards their own preservation.' It could be argued that only the terror which Cromwell's name aroused in the Catholic Irish saved him from the fate of so many of his predecessors – this together with the attractive power of his successes for the protestant settlers, whom Broghill brought in in large numbers. But we should also not forget the medical supplies and food which Cromwell had provided, far better than any previous English commander in Ireland.

He continued to hurry, campaigning far later into the winter than normal. ('We could not satisfy our consciences to keep the field as we do', he wrote on 26 October, 'were it not that we hope to save blood by it . . . in prosecuting the enemy whiles the fear of God is upon them.') When on 14 November he wrote to Parliament for money, clothes, shoes and stockings for his troops, he insisted that 'the extending your help in this way, at this time, is the most profitable means speedily' to make Ireland 'no burden to England, but a profitable part of its Commonwealth'. 'And if I did not think it your best thrift, I would not trouble you at all with it.' The conquest and colonization was a business operation. Money, boots and stockings were sent at once. 'A considerable part of your army,' Cromwell reported on 25 November, 'is fitter for an hospital than the field.' But he did not go into winter quarters for another three weeks, still pointing out that the Irish 'have so much of Ireland still in contribution as ministers to them a livelihood for the war, all the natives, almost to twenty, being friends to them but enemies to you'. Money must continue to be supplied, the sea must be patrolled to prevent supplies and ammunition coming in from the continent. It was guerrilla war, of a type with which we have become familiar in the twentieth century, with the bulk of the population sympathizing with the guerrillas against the invaders. Savagery seems an inevitable accompaniment of such wars.

Cromwell's policy was successful. The Young Pretender (as contemporary pamphlets called him) was still in Jersey waiting: it was not until February 1650 that he abandoned hope of Ireland and returned to the continent. Ormonde still had more troops than Cromwell, but he had neither money nor adequate supplies. Nor could his fortifications stand up against the powerful and mobile English artillery. Consequently he lost influence with the native Irish, and the influence of the Ulstermen and the priesthood grew. More and more protestant settlers transferred their allegiance to the Parliament. Cromwell improved on the occasion by issuing a Declaration which sharply distinguished between the Irish Catholics, all of whom he held responsible for the rebellion of 1641, and the English settlers. 'Ireland was once united to England. Englishmen had good inheritances which many of them purchased with their money. . . . They had good leases from Irishmen for long time to come; great stocks thereupon; houses and plantations erected at their cost and charge. . . . Ireland was in perfect peace and, . . . through the example of the English industry, through commerce and traffic, that which was in the natives' hands was better to them than if all Ireland had been in their possession.' 'Do you think that the state of England will be at [£]5 or 6 millions charge[11] merely to procure purchasers to be invested in that for which they did disburse little above a quarter of a million? – Although there be a justice in that also,

which ought and I trust will be reasonably performed to
them.' But there was a better reason. 'We come (by the
assistance of God) to hold forth and maintain the lustre
and glory of English liberty in a nation where we have
an undoubted right to do it; wherein the people of Ireland
. . . may equally participate in all benefits, to use liberty
and fortune equally with Englishmen, if they keep out of
arms.' The implications of that passage for Cromwell's
definition of 'English liberty' are worth pondering. Seven
months later Oliver was telling the Scots that his invasion
of their country was 'a just and necessary defence of ourselves, for preservation of those rights and liberties which
divine Providence hath, through the expense of so much
blood and treasure, given us; and those amongst you have
engaged they will, if they can, wrest from us'. At least
those liberties were not to be exercised in Scotland.

After a bare six weeks in quarters, Cromwell recom-
menced his campaign at the end of January 1650, writing again to the Speaker for money. ('I desire the charge
of England as to this war may be abated as much as may
be.') Local levies barely pay the cost of garrisons. 'If the
marching army be not constantly paid, . . . it will not be
for the thrift of England, as far as England is concerned
in the speedy reduction of Ireland.' 'If moneys be not
supplied,' he reiterated on 2 April, just after the capture
of Kilkenny had dealt a further blow to the Irish, 'we
shall not be able to carry on your work. . . . But if it be
supplied, and that speedily, I hope, through the good
hand of the Lord, it will not be long before England will
be at an end of this charge. . . . Those towns that are to
be reduced, . . . if we should proceed by the rules of other
states, would cost you more money than this army hath
had since we came over. I hope, through the blessing of
God, they will come cheaper to you,' thanks to the work
of Broghill and others. But this too would cost some
money, even if a good investment. In fact the protestant

settlers were now hurrying to submit, and by 18 May Cromwell could return to England.

Something must be said about Cromwell's attitude towards Irish Catholicism. The tolerance which is so striking a feature of his religious thought of course applied only to protestants, to those with the root of the matter in them, to God's children. Yet in England he was prepared in fact to tolerate Catholics as well as Episcopalians: Roman Catholic historians agree that their co-religionists were better off during the Protectorate than they had ever been under James or Charles ɪ. But in Ireland it was different. 'For that which you mention concerning liberty of conscience,' he told the Governor of Ross, 'I meddle not with any man's conscience. But if by liberty of conscience you mean a liberty to exercise the mass, I judge it best to use plain dealing, and to let you know, where the Parliament of England have power, that will not be allowed of.'[12] In his Declaration of December 1649 he told the Irish Catholic priesthood that the mass had been illegal in Ireland for 80 years before the rebellion of 1641, and that he was determined to reinforce this law, 'and to reduce things to their former state on this behalf.' Technically he was right. But there had never been such a law-enforcing power in Ireland as his army. Again we must refer, by way of explanation though not justification, to the *political* associations of Irish Catholicism, to the lead which the priesthood and the papacy itself had undoubtedly taken in the Irish revolt, to the fact that whereas the 1640s had (rather to the surprise of Puritans and Parliamentarians) revealed the political *weakness* of popery in England, and its lack of effective foreign contacts,[13] the same decade had revealed the utter failure of eighty years of proscription to uproot Catholicism in Ireland or to sever its links with Rome. It was a *political* religion in a sense in which Catholicism in England had ceased to be political. This would be Cromwell's justification for

hanging priests and shooting officers, whereas – apart from
the dreadful sacks of Drogheda and Wexford – other ranks
and civilians were usually given quarter.

To Cromwell's racial contempt for the Irish, and his
commercial-calculating attitude towards the colonization
of Ireland, we must add a conscientious enthusiasm for
conferring the benefits of English civilization on the
natives, whether they liked it or not. There is a curious
private letter of 31 December 1649 in which Oliver tried
to persuade John Sadler to accept the office of Chief
Justice of Munster. 'We have a great opportunity to set
up, until the Parliament shall otherwise determine, a way
of doing justice amongst these poor people, which, for the
uprightness and cheapness of it, may exceedingly gain
upon them, who have been accustomed to as much in-
justice, tyranny and oppression from their landlords, the
great men, and those that should have done them right as,
I believe, any people in that which we call Christendom.'
This was not the only argument Cromwell used: he also
offered Sadler £1000 a year ('more than hath usually been
allowed. . . . I desire you not to discourse of the allowance
but to some choice friends.') Sadler was not convinced
either by the idealistic or by the economic argument. The
post was conferred on John Cook, who had managed the
case against Charles I. He gave great pleasure to Cromwell
because, 'by proceeding in a summary and expeditious
way', he 'determined more cases in a week than Westminster Hall in a year'. 'Ireland', Cromwell assured
Ludlow, 'was as a clean paper in that particular, and
capable of being governed by such laws as should be
found most agreeable to justice, which may be so impartially administered as to be a good precedent even to
England itself; where when they once perceive property
preserved at an easy and cheap rate in Ireland they will
never permit themselves to be so cheated and abused as
now they are.'[14] It is a fascinating glimpse if not of

Cromwell's utopia, at least of what he thought was that of Ludlow and his republican friends. One of them, John Jones, hoped that 'all men of estates' would 'be banished, and the Irish ploughman and the labourer [be] admitted to the same immunities with the English'.[15] This would at least have been a positive policy for Ireland, however paternalistic: better than what actually happened.

III

In England Cromwell was in some demand. The government was under fire from left and right, its social basis dangerously narrow. When Bulstrode Whitelocke's son James enlisted for a regiment in Cromwell's Irish army, Oliver observed that 'he was the only gentleman of England that came as a volunteer to serve under him'.[16] The Leveller leaders had had to be released after Lilburne's acquittal. Lilburne was then elected to the London Common Council, but was forbidden by Parliament to take his seat. The government had had few successes during the past year, and consequently made the most of Cromwell's Irish victories. His despatches were ordered to be printed and read in all churches – with reason, since Cromwell described his Irish victories as 'seals of God's approbation of your great change of government, which indeed was no more yours than these victories and successes are ours'. But in fact the prestige was his, not Parliament's or God's. As it became increasingly clear that Ireland was secure and that the main threat now lay on the side of Scotland, the government anxiously called for Cromwell's return, so that they could have the benefit of his prestige and the protection of his military skill. Early in January the Council of State told him to prepare to return to England as soon as possible. But Cromwell proved as dilatory now as he had been just before Pride's

Purge. It was not until 2 April that he even referred to
the order, not until the beginning of June that he was
back in London. Whether this delay was due simply to a
desire to finish off the Irish campaign (which he did not),
or whether he was expecting new political developments
in England, we do not know.

Cromwell was needed because Fairfax refused to take
command of the intended invasion of Scotland, where
Charles Stuart had been proclaimed King not only of
Scotland but also of England and Ireland. Fairfax was
prepared to fight a defensive war against a Scottish invasion, but disliked England being the aggressor against
those with whom 'we are joined in the National League
and Covenant'. Cromwell did his best to persuade his
general to change his mind – undoubtedly genuinely, for
Fairfax's public defection could not be good for morale
at this critical juncture. When he failed, Cromwell was
at once appointed Commander-in-Chief. It was at about
this time that Marvell wrote his *Horatian Ode upon
Cromwell's Return from Ireland,* in which he saw Oliver
as the personification of the English Revolution, a historical force rather than an individual.

During his month's stay in London Cromwell's preoccupations were as much political as military. He managed
to charm the republican Ludlow by declaring his desire
for law reform, by defending the execution of Richard
Arnold at Ware as necessary to preserve the unity of the
Army (it is interesting that Ludlow should have harked
back to this); and persuaded him to accept the office of
General of the Horse in Ireland. There he would be use-
fully employed, and removed from the possibility of political activity in England. Interestingly, in view of Oliver's
historical discussion with Ludlow, the late Agitator Sexby
was authorized to raise a regiment for service in Ireland,
though this was later transferred to Scotland. Another
formidable ex-Agitator, Joyce, was promoted to Lieuten-

ant-colonel, no doubt for similar reasons, and sent to command the remote garrison of Portland. When he marched north, Cromwell's last supper was with John Lilburne. They embraced at parting, and (according to Lilburne's account) Cromwell promised to 'put forth all his power and interest that he had in the world, to make England enjoy the real fruit of all the Army's promises and declarations', a happily vague phrase which Lilburne hoped would mean 'successive Parliaments equally chosen by the people'. Cromwell thus secured his rear against the radicals, for whom the Scots must always seem a greater evil even than the Independent Grandees; but Lilburne at least might have recalled a similar reconciliation in 1648: the disillusionment now was to be as great.

As in Ireland, Cromwell looked meticulously after his supply. The fleet was used to ship provisions via Newcastle and Dunbar. Despatches flew back to the Council of State, demanding clothing, medical stores, backs, breasts and pots, spades, pistols, saddles, pikes and muskets. When the Scots were routed at Dunbar on 3 September, this was the only major engagement in which Cromwell had not enjoyed numerical superiority. But in every other respect – discipline, morale, equipment – his force was far superior. Cromwell's letter reporting to the Speaker followed up the radical political gestures he had made before leaving England. 'Curb the proud and the insolent, such as would disturb the tranquillity of England though under what specious pretences soever [to whom does this refer?]; relieve the oppressed, hear the groans of poor prisoners in England; be pleased to reform the abuses of all professions, and if there be any one that makes many poor to make a few rich, that suits not a Commonwealth.' So Cromwell paid his debt to Ludlow and Lilburne: the phrases were not marked by their precision. George Fox afterwards alleged that 'O.C. at Dunbar fight had promised to the Lord that if he gave

him the victory over his enemies, he would take away
tithes etc.', a reform for which his Irish officers had peti-
tioned Parliament just before leaving England over a year
earlier.[17]

Dunbar was a decisive victory, but it did not end the
campaign. It may even have strengthened Charles's hand
by weakening the authority of the Kirk, on whose insistence royalists had hitherto been excluded from the
Scottish army. Cromwell switched from military to propaganda weapons against 'our brethren of Scotland'. 'Are
we to be dealt with as enemies because we come not to
your way?', he had asked in a Declaration justifying the
original English advance into Scotland. 'I beseech you in
the bowels of Christ, think it possible you may be mistaken', he had adjured the Kirk a month before Dunbar.
'We look at ministers as helpers of, not lords over, the
faith of God's people', he told the Governor of Edinburgh
Castle on 12 September. Turning to the Kirk's criticism of
Independent lay preaching, Oliver thundered: 'Are you
troubled that Christ is preached? Is preaching so inclusive
in your function? ... Your pretended fear lest error
should step in is like the man that would keep all the
wine out of the country lest men should be drunk.[18] It
will be found an unjust and unwise jealousy to deny a
man the liberty he hath by nature upon a supposition he
may abuse it. When he doth abuse it, judge.' The fine
Miltonic phrases in favour of natural liberty form an
interesting contrast to Cromwell's sharper words to Irish
Catholics; but there is a common factor in his resolute
defence of the religious rights of laymen. 'So Antichristian
and dividing a term as clergy and laity', he had told the
Irish clergy, was unknown to the primitive church. 'It
was your pride that begat this expression, and it is for
filthy lucre's sake that you keep it up, that by making the
people believe they are not so holy as yourselves, they
might for their penny purchase some sanctity from you;

and that you might bridle, saddle and ride them at your pleasure.' That passage echoes the early reformers, Luther and Tyndale.

In 1651 Parliament had professed to believe that the nobility and gentry of Scotland had been 'the chief actors in these invasions and wars against England', and that their tenants had been drawn in unwillingly. So they promised such easy rents 'as may enable them . . . to live with a more comfortable subsistence than formerly, and like a free people'.[19] Cromwell's theological disputations, though he no doubt enjoyed them for their own sake, were the counterpart of this political campaign to detach the middling sort. Oliver's propaganda was aimed especially at the radical wing of Presbyterians, the Covenanters of Glasgow and the South-West, who mistrusted Charles ii and his 'malignant' supporters. Cromwell succeeded in persuading many of them to adopt a position of neutrality, in some cases even of cooperation. The Governor of Edinburgh Castle, whether or not he was influenced by Cromwell's attack on clericalism, was linked with the radicals and allowed himself to be persuaded by them to surrender Edinburgh Castle long before his situation was desperate. As in Ireland, Cromwell won greater victories by diplomacy even than by the sword.

But it was slow work. Throughout the winter, spring and summer of 1650–1, Cromwell could not bring the Scottish army to a decisive engagement; and meanwhile he complained bitterly of the quality of his reinforcements, especially of the officers.[20] 'This is the grief,' he told Harrison in May, 'that this being the cause of God and of this people, so many saints should be in their security and ease, and not come out to the work of the Lord in this great day of the Lord.' But a chaplain in his army – William Good – explained it differently. War weariness, a feeling that 'the officers and Parliament men had made great estates up to themselves, that there was little justice

in their Parliament men but much bribing; that they did
all for self-preservation at the best; that God's people had
but, as it were, taken quarter under and from them'.
These points were often made. As early as 1649 the radical
preacher Joseph Salmon said that the Army was really
interested only in its own preservation, no longer in principles.[21] Royalist and Presbyterians had for long been
drawing attention to the immense properties acquired by
Parliamentarian and Army leaders: soon men like Milton,
William Dell and Vavasor Powell on the other side equally
emphasized their corrupting effects. This spirit of disil-
lusion among the radicals made possible the wide-reaching
Presbyterian-royalist plot in England, for which Christopher Love, a Presbyterian minister, was tried and condemned at the end of June. But the régime was still strong
enough to cope with opposition from the right. The expo-
sure and collapse of this plot in England at last set
Cromwell's hands free in Scotland.

As July passed into August he lured the Scottish Army
away from its fastness at Stirling to an invasion of England
which was now hopeless. Cromwell followed at leisure,
and Parliamentary forces converged on the invaders
from all over England. Even Fairfax lost his doubts now
that England had been invaded; he organized the Yorkshire militia. Charles's advance on London was checked,
and he was shepherded south-west to Worcester. On the
day he entered that city Love and a fellow conspirator
were executed, to discourage Presbyterians from further
activity.

The 'crowning mercy' of Worcester was fought on 3
September, exactly a year after Dunbar. The Scots had
obtained few recruits on their march through the West
of England, and were outnumbered by two to one. Though
they put up a stouter resistance than might have been
expected, the result was never in doubt. Cromwell in his
despatch after the battle concentrated on making political

Edward Montagu, Second Earl of Manchester; artist unknown.

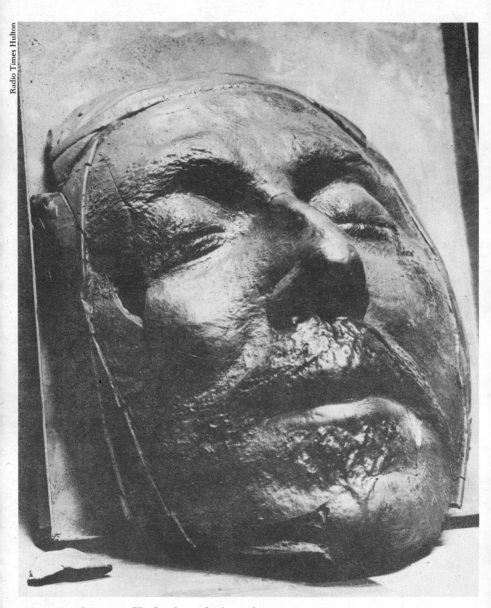

Wax cast of Cromwell's death mask; from the specimen
in the British Museum.

Colonel John Lilburne, from
a print prefixed to his trial, 1649;
engraved by R. Cooper.

John Owen, theologian;
engraved by R. White.

Major General Henry
Ireton; drawn and
engraved by
Harding and Gardiner.

Hugh Peters,
Puritan divine
and parliamentarian,
executed for treason
at Charing Cross.

Cromwell's wife, Elizabeth;
artist unknown.

Richard Cromwell, third son of Oliver;
artist unknown.

Robert Devereux, Earl of Essex.

Cromwell dissolves the "Long Parliament," 1653.

Oliver Cromwell, by Lely, 1653.

Cromwell's mother,
by Haskins.

Cromwell's house.

points: 'the country riseth upon [the defeated Scots] everywhere.' The militia behaved admirably, and God had shown his approval of 'the nation and the change of the government, by making the people so willing to the defence thereof'. The militia was traditionally the force of the gentry, and therefore jealous of the power of the Army; but it had lately been remodelled. Nevertheless, just in case, the militia men were packed off to their homes forthwith.

The Worcester campaign had demonstrated at least one thing – the wisdom of Parliament's policy of 'slighting' castles, which had been deliberately entered upon at the end of the first civil war, and reinforced after the second.[22] Worcester itself had been singled out for special measures.

Two days before Worcester, Monck had sacked Dundee amid scenes of massacre and plunder rivalling Drogheda and Wexford, though with less excuse. Scotland was leaderless and open to English conquest and annexation. 'Negotiations' for union between the two countries began in February 1652, though they were not completed by legislation until 1654. The aim of English policy in Scotland was, by offering free trade with England, to conciliate tenants and the commercial classes. 'It is the interest of the Commonwealth of England to break the interest of the great men in Scotland,' wrote Colonel John Jones two months after Worcester, 'and to settle the interests of the common people upon a different foot from the interests of their lords and masters. . . . The great men will never be faithful to you so long as you propound freedom to the people and relief against their tyranny.'[23] Serfdom and feudal tenures were abolished, and private jurisdiction of landlords, in the hope of forcing them to follow the model of the English gentry by investing in the improvement of the estates. Union of the two countries had been advocated by John Knox nearly a century earlier: such supporters as the English army now found in

Scotland came from the towns, which, Monck wrote, 'are generally the most faithful to us of any people in this nation'. 'The middle sort of this people grow up into such a substance as makes their lives comfortable if not better than they were before,' Cromwell told Parliament in 1658.

IV

Scotland and Ireland were included within the provisions of the Navigation Act of 9 October 1651, which established an imperial monopoly of trade and shipping. This was aimed against the Dutch merchants, who in the preceding thirty years had built up a near-monopoly of the English carrying trade, and who equally prohibited English merchants from trading to their colonies. Before the beginning of the civil war, the House of Commons in its 1642 Book of Rates had outlined a policy of protection: the Long Parliament, men recalled in 1654, had been 'a trading Parliament'.[24] (When commissioners for the government of the plantations in America and the West Indies were appointed by Parliament in November 1643 Oliver Cromwell was one of them: he was reappointed in 1646.)

The conclusion of civil war made possible an elaboration of this policy. In August 1650 a Council for Trade was set up to consider 'how the trades and manufactures of this nation may most fitly and equally be distributed to every part thereof', and 'how the commodities of this land may be vented to the best advantage thereof into foreign countries'.[25] The secretary of this Council was Benjamin Worsley, friend of Samuel Hartlib the great educational reformer and promoter of industrial and agricultural improvements. It contained merchants from many areas outside London as well as from the capital. Worsley himself had close contacts with Maurice Thompson, author of the Navigation Act.[26] 'The government of the Commonwealth and that of its trade' are 'exercised by the same individuals', wrote the Venetian Ambassador in June 1651:[27] he seems to have been right. The Navigation Act involved 'a reorganization of English trade policy from one based on monopoly companies to one based on national monopoly'.[28] It was the first attempt in English history at treating the colonies as part of a single economic and political system. In 1657 Parliament confirmed and extended the Act.

The idea that an English republic would forward a more powerful commercial policy had long been in the minds of at least French observers. In August 1644 the Venetian Secretary in England reported home that 'France is exceedingly concerned to support a moderate monarchy in this kingdom as against a republic, which ... would be more formidable, especially for its naval strength'.[29] Two years later Cardinal Mazarin observed that 'in a republic, taxation being voluntary and coming by consent and by agreement of everyone for a policy unanimously agreed, they will pay without murmurings or regrets whatever is necessary to make that policy succeed'.[30] His resident in England reported in 1651 that the rulers of England toiled for the public as if for their private interest, living 'without ostentation, without pomp, without emulation of one another'.[31]

In pursuance of this policy the Rump offered union to the Dutch republic, on terms – the Dutch Ambassador complained – not dissimilar to those which had just been imposed on Scotland. The English object, Mr Farnell argues, was simply to transfer the entrepôt trade from Amsterdam to London. When the Dutch refused to allow their colonies to be peacefully incorporated in the British empire, the Dutch War was another way of attempting to achieve the same end.[32] Evidence for Cromwell's attitude towards the Dutch War is ambiguous. There are suggestions that he was unenthusiastic about it, though the Dutch regarded him as one of their bitterest enemies. It may well be that Cromwell's long-term strategic aims would have been satisfied with a military base on the continent, and that beyond that he had no desire to crush or humiliate another protestant power. Negotiations with France for the surrender to England of Dunkirk – besieged by a Spanish army – seem to have been initiated by Cromwell at the very end of 1651, as his personal venture. In April of the next year five thousand English soldiers were ready to sail for Dunkirk; but Mazarin refused to yield to England's terms, and instead Blake scattered the French fleet, and Dunkirk surrendered to the Spaniards the following day. Cromwell's design on Dunkirk came to fruition only in 1657. But whatever Cromwell's attitude may have been, a significant commercial interest certainly wanted to crush their Dutch rivals.

Cromwell concluded peace with the Netherlands once power was in his own hands. But he did not hurry, nor did he offer particularly lenient terms. Henceforth there were, Thurloe told the restoration government, 'no greater considerations in England than how to obviate the growing greatness of the Dutch'.[33]

This grandiose imperial policy – conquest of Ireland and Scotland, the Dutch War – was financed by the sale of crown lands, of dean and chapter lands, and the lands of recalcitrant royalists. Even so taxation had to be increased. There were proposals for financial reform, to bring all the *ad hoc* financial bodies which had sprung up in the 1640s under Exchequer control, rather as the financial bodies which had sprung up in similar circumstances in the 1530s were brought under Exchequer control in 1554.

The policy of confiscations alienated conservatives without giving much satisfaction to the radicals, since little was done to help smaller men to acquire land. Radical demands for law reform and the abolition of tithes seemed as far from realization as ever – though both had been demanded in the Heads of Proposals, in petitions from the officers just about to sail for Ireland in July 1649, and tithes at least had been debated at Putney. Cromwell had told Ludlow (when he was trying to win him over before departing for Scotland) that 'it was his intention to contribute the utmost of his endeavours to make a thorough reformation of the clergy and law'. But, he continued, 'the sons of Zeruiah are yet too strong for us, and we cannot mention the reformation of the law but they presently cry out we design to destroy property; whereas the law as it is now constituted serves only to maintain the lawyers and to encourage the rich to oppress the poor'. Cromwell seems to have echoed the last phrase in his despatch after Dunbar.[34]

The reforming movement still had staunch supporters among the officers. It was ominous that when in August 1652 they began again to intervene in politics they asked for abolition of tithes and law reform, as well as for dissolution of Parliament. Cromwell did not sign this Declaration of the Army, but many of his protégés did, and he can hardly have been unaware of their action. His position in the eighteen months after Worcester was rather like that in the year 1646. He was the most important figure in the government – in November 1651 and again in November 1652 he topped the poll in re-elections for the Council of State. Yet he did not control policy; he was aware of the impatience of Army radicals; and he spent a great deal of time in behind-the-scene conversations, trying to find a programme on which as much unity could be secured as possible. In December 1651 he held a conference at which he expressed himself in favour of 'a settlement with somewhat of monarchical power in it'. At the end of September 1651 the gossip in Hamburg was

'what great man we shall have either as King or Protector?'[35] Over a year later Cromwell asked Whitelocke
bluntly, 'What if a man should take upon him to be
King?'

All the time pressure for Parliament to dissolve itself
increased, although it was not easy to see how it could
be replaced. Elections on the old franchise were unlikely
to produce a Parliament which would willingly accept
Army rule; yet how else could the causes which the
officers favoured, and indeed their own personal security,
be guaranteed?[36] In November 1651 Cromwell seems to
have asked an astrologer whether he would himself be
re-elected in a new Parliament.[37]

'How to make good our station, to improve the mercies
and successes which God hath given us, and not to be
fooled out of them again, nor to be broken in pieces by
our particular jarrings and animosities one against another, but to unite our counsels' – so Cromwell put to
Whitelocke a year later what was indeed becoming the
problem. Whitelocke pretended to think that Cromwell
meant that the danger came from 'the emulation of the
officers' and mutinies of the private soldiers. Cromwell
explained that the corruption and delays and unaccount-
ability of MPs were even more to blame. 'Some course
must be thought on to curb and restrain them, or we shall
be ruined by them.' Whitelocke rejected Cromwell's hint
that he might be made king by saying this would reduce
the question to 'whether Cromwell or Stuart shall be our
king'. He proposed instead a treaty with Charles Stuart.[38]

Cromwell found himself increasingly frustrated by his
failure to produce agreement. The country was suffering
from war weariness, a desire to return to normal methods
of government and normal levels of taxation. As 1653
succeeded 1652 the officers, conscious both of their un-
popularity and of the absence of reforms, became more
and more impatient and threatening. After the battle of

Worcester an anti-clerical like Milton had regarded 'hireling wolves, whose gospel is their maw' as the main enemy whom he hoped Cromwell would now tackle. Yet Parliament did nothing to disestablish the church – which would have been the effect of abolishing tithes. Cromwell, Ludlow tells us, played up to Army radicalism by saying that the Rump intended to support 'the corrupt interests of the clergy and the lawyers'. So far from reforming the English church, Parliament roused resentment by refusing to renew the Commission for the Propagation of the Gospel in Wales – the Army's favourite instrument for evangelizing that politically unreliable country.

The issue came ultimately to turn on arrangements for the transitional period, after the Rump had agreed to a dissolution. Cromwell and the generals advocated the disappearance of Parliament and the handing of power to a provisional government, in which they themselves would naturally preponderate, to supervise and control elections. How otherwise, Cromwell pertinently asked, could one know 'whether the next Parliament were not like to consist of all Presbyterians'. 'Thus, as we apprehended, would have been thrown away the liberties of the nation into the hands of those who had never fought for it.' This was after the event. The official version which the generals published to justify the dissolution ran:

> After much debate it was judged necessary and agreed upon, that the supreme authority should be by the Parliament devolved upon known persons, men fearing God and of approved integrity, and the government of the Commonwealth committed unto them for a time, as the most hopeful way to encourage and countenance all God's people, reform the law and administer justice impartially; hoping thereby the people might forget monarchy, and understanding their true interest in the election of successive Parliaments may have the government settled upon a true basis, without

hazard to this glorious cause, or necessitating to keep up armies for the defence of the same.[39]

That sounds a pretty long-term programme for an interim government! At all events, a majority in the Commons preferred to continue in existence themselves to supervise elections. At a meeting of officers and MPs on 19 April 1653 deadlock was reached, but some sort of assurance was given that no final decisions would be taken without further discussions. This gentleman's agreement was apparently repudiated by back-bench MPs next day, and they started to rush through the bill for dissolution without meeting the officers' demand for an interim authority under their control. The assumption is that Parliament intended to control the election of its successors.

Cromwell felt that his hand had been forced. He intervened just in time to stop the new bill becoming law: he forcibly dissolved the House. 'You are no Parliament, I say you are no Parliament; I will put an end to your sitting. Call them in, call them in.' Harrison went out and returned with musketeers who brought the Speaker down from his chair and ejected the MPs. Oliver 'commanded the mace to be taken away, saying "What shall we do with this bauble? Here, take it away".'[40] So ended the Long Parliament, which had sat for twelve and a half years. 'When they were dissolved,' Oliver said afterwards, 'there was not so much as the barking of a dog, or any general or visible repining at it.'

V

There seems little doubt that by the 1650s the modest country gentleman had been more than a little elated by his successes, and that his self-confidence had hardened. His doctrine of providences slipped over easily into a theory of justification by success.[41] He had some excuses.

As early as 1645 Sir Thomas Fairfax, in asking for Cromwell's reappointment to military command despite the Self-Denying Ordinance, had stressed 'the constant presence and blessing of God that have accompanied him'. For their own propaganda reasons the Independents in the 1640s and the government of the Rump in the 1650s had boosted his reputation to bolster their interests. 'These are seals of God's approbation of your great change in government,' Cromwell wrote to the Speaker from Ireland in November 1649. 'These victories and successes' are God's rather than ours; yet 'both are the righteous judgments and mighty works of God'. 'A divine presence hath gone along with us in the late great transactions in this nation,' he wrote to a friend a month later. 'I do not condemn your reasonings: I doubt them', he told another friend who objected to the argument from success. 'I have not sought these things,' he wrote to Richard Major after his appointment to the Scottish command. 'Truly I have been called unto them by the Lord and therefore am not without some assurance that he will enable his poor worm and weak servant to do his will and to fulfil my generation.' The 'and therefore' is becoming ominous. Oliver's brother-in-law John Desborough agreed that 'your victories have been given you of [God] himself; it is himself that hath raised you up amongst men, and hath called you to high employments'. 'High places,' Desborough continued on a warning note, 'are slippery, except God establisheth our goings.'[42]

Cromwell pressed the argument from God's favour vigorously against the Scots, who 'in answer to the witness of God upon our solemn appeal' answered – what else could they say? – that they had 'not so learned Christ to hang the equity of [their] cause upon events'. 'But did you not solemnly appeal and pray?' Cromwell retorted. 'Did not we do so too? And ought not you and we to think, with fear and trembling, of the hand of the great

God in this mighty and strange appearance of his [at Dunbar]; but can slightly call it an event! . . . Shall we after all these our prayers, fastings, tears, expectations and solemn appeals, call these bare events? The Lord pity you!' 'With fear and trembling,' yes; but with a growing recognition that Oliver Cromwell had been chosen as God's instrument. The providences seemed to conspire to establish this fact. 'The greater the trust, the greater the account,' he wrote to Hammond in the frustrating months between Dunbar and Worcester. Ireland and Scotland combined to build up this sense of divine favour, which was certainly behind him when he dissolved the Rump in April 1653, rebuking its members for their sinfulness.

The dissolution however had been brought about by an uneasy coalition of right and left, and in itself solved nothing. All turned on what succeeded the Long Parliament. There was considerable disagreement about the next step. Since no electorate could be trusted to vote the generals into power, the next assembly ('diverse persons fearing God and of approved fidelity and honesty') was nominated 'by myself with the advice of my Council of Officers'. The words are those of the summons, signed by Oliver Cromwell as Commander-in-Chief, to the members of what was later to be known as the Barebones Parliament. We do not know how the 140 names were selected. Some were recommended by gathered churches: others by individuals like Major-General Harrison. Socially they were of a lower class than those normally elected to Parliament. Clarendon said they were mostly 'inferior persons, of no quality or name, artificers of the meanest trades'. Even though he adds that there were 'some few of the quality and degree of gentlemen, and who had estates',[43] this exaggerates grossly. Sixty of the members (nearly half) either had been or were to be members of elected Parliaments, and most of them were of respectable standing. There were, one contemporary said, 'not so many lords of manors' as in a normal House of Commons, and it has been suggested that the leadership of the assembly 'was in the hands of Londoners to a greater extent, probably, than in any other Parliament either before or since'.[44] Their enthusiasm for trade was contrasted with the attitude of the gentry in the next Parliament of 1654.[45] They refused to bring the Dutch War to an end, but insisted on fighting until the Netherlands were crushed.

Cromwell, strongly influenced by the Harrisonian wing in the Army, regarded the meeting of this assembly as the high point of the Revolution, the moment at which all its contradictions would be resolved. He greeted the members in an ecstatic speech, and resigned his power into their hands. 'Truly you are called by God to rule with him and for him', he assured them repeatedly. 'I confess I never looked to see such a day as this – it may be nor you neither – when Jesus Christ should be so owned as he is at this day and in this work. Jesus Christ is owned this day by your call.' Their task, he told them, was to undertake the government until 'God may fit the people for such a thing' – rescued as they had so recently been 'out of their thraldom and bondage under the royal power'. 'This may be the door to usher in the things that God has promised, which have been prophesied of, which he has set the hearts of his people to wait for and expect. ... You are at the edge of the promises and prophecies.'

This speech is very revealing of one aspect of Cromwell's complex personality – the millennarian aspect, his optimistic and irrational belief that God would solve the problems which the Rump had found so intractable. That he really intended to hand over power there can be no doubt. The Dutch Commissioners were instructed no longer to address their communications to 'His Excellency and the Council of State' but simply to 'the Council of State'. The members of the assembly, apparently on their own initiative, voted themselves the name of Parliament,

though the original plan seems to have been rather that
they should act as a constituent assembly.

But alas. The millennium did not come. The Barebones
Parliament proved to be divided in the same way as those
who called it, into radicals and conservatives. Nevertheless its historical reputation as an assembly of religious
fanatics is quite unjustified. The members approached
their tasks in a thoroughly businesslike way. They appointed a committee to consider reform of the whole legal
system, and a vote was taken to abolish the dilatory
Court of Chancery. An act was passed for the relief of
creditors and poor prisoners. Other committees were instructed to make recommendations for the relief of the
poor and the victims of enclosure; and for the advance-
ment of learning. The cumbrous financial system was to
be unified and rationalized; the excise, especially burden-
some to the poor, was to be abolished. Tenants were to be
protected against the oppressions of royalist landlords,
but landlords were to be empowered to break entails.
Following the abolition of church courts by the Long
Parliament, new arrangements were made for probate of
wills and for the registration of births, marriages and
deaths. Marriage was made a civil ceremony. The Assembly tried to find a better system for the maintenance
of the clergy than tithes, and wanted to iron out inequali-
ties in clerical incomes. They proposed to deprive laymen
of the right to present ministers to benefices, though with
full compensation. The reformers proposed to codify the
law, as had recently been done successfully in Massachusetts. That is the meaning of the oft-quoted phrase
about reducing the great volumes of the law 'into the big-
ness of a pocket book, as it is proportionable in New
England and elsewhere'. The reforms which are said to
have shocked the lawyers included proposals that pick-
pockets and horse thieves should not be executed for the
first offence; that burning should cease to be the death

penalty for women; that accused persons refusing to plead should no longer be pressed to death; that genuine bankrupts should be released, while the goods of fraudulent debtors should be seized and sold. Most of the reforms which they adopted were the work of the very respectable committee which had been appointed by the Rump.

The measures which the radicals envisaged were aimed at reorganizing the country's administration after a revolution in which many old institutions had been overthrown or profoundly modified. One of Cromwell's correspondents had written to him in November 1650: 'Hitherto in the change of government nothing material as yet hath been done but a taking off the head of monarchy and placing upon the body or trunk of it the name and title of a Commonwealth.' He called for radical administrative reform if a true republic was to be established, for 'equality and independence of persons and places'. Otherwise we 'cannot assure ourselves from a return to monarchy'.[46] He was right. So far the revolutionary governments had carried on with the old state machinery, plus improvised additions. But reform did not come in 1650, and it was defeated in 1653. When it did come, in and after 1654, it did not amount to a radical reconstruction. Professor Aylmer's researches suggest that what took place in 1654 was a general administrative reform in the interests of conservative efficiency. Fees, perquisites and bribes had already been reduced under the Commonwealth; rationalizations took place, and the government of the 1650s was more businesslike and less corrupt than those which came before and after it. But because of the failure of Barebones nothing was done which would prevent the head of monarchy being restored to the trunk: on the contrary, 1654 seems 'to have been a step towards 1660 and the victory of oligarchy'.[47]

The conservatives in 1653 were upset by the radicals' reforming programme. They felt, or claimed to feel, that property was in danger. The Presbyterians, a royalist correspondent stated, were alienated by Barebones's attack on tithes, which could lead to an attack on all property, 'especially since elected Parliaments, the bulwark of property, is taken away'.[48] The French Ambassador reported in November moves for a *rapprochement* between Presbyterians and Independents against their radical enemies and to reassert the old forms of government.

Cromwell came to think of the Barebones Parliament as 'a story of my own weakness and folly'. Though he spoke in favour of law reform in his initial speech to the assembly, he was not prepared for the abolition of Chancery or of ecclesiastical patronage and tithes. Since Barebones proposed at the same time that higher Army officers should serve for a whole year without pay, most of the latter were easily persuaded that the dangerous assembly must be got rid of. On 12 December the conservatives got up early, and after speeches denouncing the Parliament for 'endeavouring to take away their properties by taking away the law, to overthrow the ministry by taking away tithes and settling nothing in their rooms', they voted an end to their meeting. Then they marched off to the Lord General, to whom they surrendered the authority they had received from him five months before.

As usual we do not know whether Cromwell planned the coup: he denied it. But he was certainly prepared to accept and act upon it. Within three days a new constitution, the Instrument of Government, had been accepted: it had been under discussion by the officers for a month or so. On the next day, 16 December, Oliver Cromwell was proclaimed Lord Protector. In a public ceremony he took an oath to rule 'upon such a basis and foundation as by the blessing of God might be lasting, secure property, and answer those great ends of religion and liberty so long contended for'. In his speech after taking the oath Oliver reiterated his determination so to govern that 'the gospel might flourish in its full splendour and purity, and the people enjoy their just rights and property'. 'Ministry and property were like to be destroyed', Oliver reminded his officers in February 1657. 'Who could have said anything was their own if they had gone on?'

VI

It is impossible to exaggerate the psychological importance of the failure of the Barebones Parliament for Oliver Cromwell. The historian looking back may see the breach with the Levellers as the turning point of the Revolution, the point of no return. But for Oliver 1653 was undoubtedly the high point of the Revolution; after the failure, as he saw it, of Barebones to unite God's people, his high hopes had gone. Perhaps, he reflected after the event, he had sinned in being too anxious 'to be quit of the power God had most providentially put into my hand', and had relinquished it too eagerly and too optimistically to the Barebones Parliament. He did not make the mistake of relinquishing power to his later Parliaments. He insisted to his first elected Parliament 'I called not myself to this place' of Protector. Henceforth Oliver's optimism has left him. He was a tired, disillusioned old man, still confident that he enjoyed a special relationship with God, but with few positive ideas left, on the defensive. He no longer hoped to realize the rule of God's people in England: he saw himself as a constable whose task was to prevent Englishmen from flying at one another's throats. He was forced back upon the support of an Army purged of radicals, an Army which in the last resort had to be paid by taxes collected from the propertied class, the natural rulers of the countryside.

The Revolution was over. Oliver Cromwell was the saviour of propertied society. In 1649 the Levellers had been annihilated. One group of radicals – Vane, Haslerig, Marten, Ludlow, Sidney – had been driven from power in April 1653; Ireton had died in Ireland. Now Harrison, Rich and the Army radicals, together with Moyer and the City radicals, were also driven out. The dissolution of Barebones saved the trading monopoly of the Newcastle oligarchy.[49] John Lambert, who drafted the Instrument of Government, and the conservative wing of the generals, mostly of gentry origin (Desborough, Sydenham, Lisle, Colonel Edward Montagu, of the family of Cromwell's old rival) formed Cromwell's Council, together with three baronets (Sir Gilbert Pickering, Sir Charles Wolseley and Sir Anthony Ashley Cooper – the last two prominent in the self-dissolution of the Barebones Parliament). Cromwell's own connections were well represented (Desborough, the Protector's brother-in-law, Major, Richard Cromwell's father-in-law, Lawrence, Oliver's landlord at St Ives, Montagu, now a dependant). Three of the Councillors – Lisle, Ashley Cooper and Montagu – were to become peers after the restoration.

Other advisers of the new régime included Lord Broghill, ex-royalist, for Ireland; Monck, the professional soldier, for Scotland. Nathaniel Fiennes (son of Lord Saye and Sele) and the Earl of Mulgrave were soon added, who still further strengthened links with the aristocracy. The key figure came to be John Thurloe, protégé of Oliver St John, who had been associated with Cromwell since at least June 1647, and seems to have been in charge of his personal affairs since October 1650, if not before. He had been Secretary to the Rump's Council of State and to the Council under Barebones; the latter put him in charge of the intelligence service.

The new government proceeded to annul some of its predecessor's acts, notably that which looked after the interests of creditors against impoverished debtors. Reform of Chancery was entrusted to the safe hands of three lawyers. Even the Long Parliament's act forfeiting two-thirds of the estates of Roman Catholic delinquents was repealed. Cromwell's plans for unity were no longer restricted to the party whose leader he had been: he saw his task now as being to unite the nation. Hyde wrote from Paris, with grudging admiration, that 'Cromwell proceeds with strange dexterity towards the reconciling all sorts of persons, and chooses those out of all parties whose abilities are most eminent'. The City of London returned to government by conservatives, though Maurice Thompson managed to switch his loyalty in time. The City showed its gratitude by feasting the Lord Protector on 8 February 1654. But not a single cheer greeted Oliver as he rode in state through the streets of London.

To the radicals Oliver was now the finally lost leader. Lilburne, Wildman, Sexby and other Levellers turned to negotiation with the royalists rather than accept the new régime. George Fox and the Quakers never forgave Cromwell for failing to carry out his alleged promise before the battle of Dunbar to abolish tithes.[50] The Fifth Monarchist Vavasor Powell greeted the Protectorate by asking his congregation whether the Lord would have 'Oliver Cromwell or Jesus Christ to reign over us?' A few months earlier the two had not seemed to be rivals.

VI

THE LORD PROTECTOR:
1653-55

In this manner, and with so little pains, this extraordinary man, . . . without the assistance and against the desire of all noble persons or men of quality, or of three men who in the beginning of the troubles were possessed of £300 land by the year, mounted himself into the throne of three kingdoms, without the name of king but with a greater power and authority than had ever been exercised or claimed by any king.

CLARENDON, *History of the Rebellion*, V, pp. 287–8

Ask we the nations of this matter, and they will testify, and indeed the dispensations of the Lord have been as if he had said, England, thou art my first-born, my delight amongst the nations, under the whole heavens the Lord hath not dealt so with any of the people round about us.

Declaration of the Lord Protector, 23 May 1654

If the Lord take pleasure in England, and if he will do us good, he is able to bear us up. Let the difficulties be whatsoever they will, we shall in his strength be able to encounter with them . . . For I look at the people of these nations as the blessing of the Lord . . . And the people being the blessing of God they will not be so angry but they will prefer their safety to their passions, and their real security to forms, when necessity calls for supplies. Had they not been well acquainted with this principle, they had never seen this day of gospel-liberty.

CROMWELL, Speech at dissolution of first
Parliament, 22 January 1655

I

On 23 December 1653 Secretary Thurloe wrote to Bulstrode Whitelocke, England's representative in Sweden, 'This change ... hath a very general acceptance, especially among the lawyers, the ministers and the merchants, who conceived themselves most in danger from the temper of the last Parliament'. Henceforward England would be governed no more by 'arbitrary committees', but by the laws of the land.[1] The Protectorate meant the victory of conservatism in church and state. A member of the old family of the Howards, who had been reactionaries even in the days of monarchy, was made colonel of the regiment of Nathaniel Rich, dismissed for his radical views. The whole army was under constant process of transformation from the ideologically committed force of the 1640s to the formidable professional arm of the later 1650s. Edward Montagu – son of the Earl of Manchester, Cromwell's old rival – was appointed Admiral, with the specific task of purging radicals from the fleet.[2] He was soon on bad terms with the stalwart old republican Robert Blake, who was better at winning battles than at trimming his sails to court breezes.

In August 1655 a colonel, an alderman and another commissioner were appointed to regulate printing. From the following month no news item might legally be published without Thurloe's permission. Gone were the exuberant days of free discussion: opposition pamphlets could appear only illegally. The author of *Areopagitica* soon slipped out of the public service. Only two newspapers survived, *Mercurius Politicus* and *The Publick Intelli-gencer,* each edited by Marchamont Nedham under Thurloe's supervision. In November 1653 Nedham had assured Cromwell that if he looked after fundamentals, 'the most substantial men of every rank and profession . . . will be interested in the very point of self-preservation to adhere unto your Excellency'. The former royalist Nedham's political theory was entirely pragmatic: he thought that 'the way of government in free nations is not to be accommodated unto schemes of freedom which lie in melancholy contemplation, but must be suited to that form which lies fairest for practical convenience'[3]. Many men consoled themselves with such reflections. The eminent lawyer Matthew Hale thought 'it was no sin to take a commission from the usurper . . . it being abso-lutely necessary to have justice and property kept up at all times'.[4]

To his first Parliament Cromwell proclaimed his sup-port for the existing social order: 'a nobleman, a gentle-man, a yeoman: that is a good interest of the nation and a great one. The magistracy of the nation, was it not al-most trampled underfoot, under despite and contempt by men of Levelling principles? . . . Did not the Levelling principle tend to reducing all to an equality? . . . What was the design but to make the tenant as liberal a fortune as the landlord? . . . It was a pleasing voice to all poor men, and truly not unwelcome to all bad men.' His audi-ence, composed of magistrates, landlords and other rich men, must have been reassured that the days of radicalism were over. 'We would keep up the nobility and gentry,' Oliver repeated to his second Parliament. The new tend-ency showed itself in a variety of ways. In March 1654 the excise was extended to many hitherto untaxed objects of popular consumption. In London the oligarchy came back to power. Between 1640 and 1654 there had been no Lord Mayor's shows: they were resumed in 1655. John

Evelyn first saw women painting themselves in May 1654; by August of that year it even seemed safe to address a bishop by his title, 'the times being now more open'.[5] Growing conservatism in the colonial sphere as in all others may be illustrated by Oliver's restoration to Lord Baltimore in 1657 of his proprietorial rights in Maryland. The 'natural rulers' began to raise their heads again in many quarters. Edmund Waller hailed his cousin as

> One whose extraction from an ancient
> Gives hope again that well-born men may shine.[6]

The well-born if royalist Waller was made a Commissioner for Trade by the Protector, one of whose daughters married the grandson of the Earl of Warwick, and another Lord Fauconbridge, son of a royalist, soon to be a Privy Councillor to the restored Charles II.

In March 1655 the ex-royalist Lord Broghill, who had cooperated with Cromwell in subduing Ireland, and a year earlier had proposed that Oliver should take the title of King, became President of the Council for Scotland. His advent inaugurated a more conservative policy there. The Scottish Council was instructed 'to encourage commerce, advance manufactures and fisheries' and 'consider how to improve them'. As in Ireland, royalist fighting men were either transported to the West Indies or encouraged to take service overseas.[7] Many Scottish royalists rallied to the Protectorate, including Sir William Lockhart, who married Cromwell's niece and became his ambassador to France. In September 1656 the Scottish Presbyterian Baillie wrote that 'all who are wise think that our evils would grow yet more if Cromwell were removed'.[8] Oliver was, for many Scots, the least of all *possible* evils. The attempt to win over the Remonstrant or radical party in the Kirk was abandoned in 1657: Broghill instead tried to consolidate the Resolutioners into a pro-Protectorate majority. After the restoration of Charles II the leaders of the Remonstrants were hanged: the leader of the Resolutioners became an Archbishop.

In Ireland the replacement of Fleetwood by Oliver's second son Henry, and the modification of the transplantation policy, were equally the result of the move to the right in England. But in Ireland this move had to be made more carefully in view of the preponderance of radicals among the officers of the army of occupation, and the English government's absolute dependence on it to hold the Catholic majority of the population in subjection. The army there was gradually reduced from 34,000 to 20,000 – still a vast burden to the country. Instructions to Henry Cromwell's Council in March 1656 suggested taking Irish children away from their parents at the age of ten in order to bring them up in industry and protestantism; but the administration seems to have been incapable of managing so complicated a scheme.

We should see Cromwell's Irish policy as part of his general imperial policy. The native Irish were treated much as the original settlers of New England treated the Indians. Cromwell wrote to New England to try to persuade 'godly people and ministers' to move to Ireland. His own influence as Lord Protector was in the direction of moderating the policy of wholesale transplantation, so that only landowners were shifted: the mass of the population was required as labourers and payers of rent. Ireland had been included within the scope of the Navigation Act of 1651, and the same customs and excise were paid as in England. But of course it was the English settlers who benefited, as in New England: native Irish and papists were excluded from corporate towns. Ireland must not be over-taxed, Cromwell said, lest 'the English must needs run away for pure beggary and the Irish possess the country again'. After 1660, Charles II's government reversed the policy of allowing English settlers in Ireland

equal treatment with inhabitants of England, while doing
nothing to better the lot of the native Irish.

In England the Protector made every effort to come
to terms with the 'natural rulers' in two Parliaments.
Royalist conspiracy continued, but it became more desperate as it grew increasingly clear that so long as Cromwell had the Army's support he was invulnerable. This
desperation is shown by royalist willingness to enter into
plots with some of the less reputable Levellers – John
Wildman, Edward Sexby, Miles Sindercombe. We do
not know how far these men represented the body of
Levellers, nor indeed whether anything like a body of
Levellers still existed. Nor do we know how seriously the
negotiations were intended by either side. 'Give us money,
and we will give you a port,' the Levellers said in effect:
'give us a port and we will give you money,' was the
reply. There was little coordination of efforts, and less of
aims. Nevertheless, the coincidence in time of royalist
and Leveller plots alarmed the government. Wildman was
arrested while dictating 'A Declaration of the free and
well-affected people . . . in arms against the tyrant Oliver
Cromwell', only a month before Penruddock's royalist
rising of 1655. And some Levellers were certainly demora-
lized by the defeat of 1649. Richard Overton acted as spy
for Thurloe. Sexby ended by advocating Oliver's assas-
sination in the wittiest pamphlet of the fifties, *Killing No
Murder*, impudently dedicated in 1657 to the Lord Protector – 'the true father of your country; for while you
live we can call nothing ours, and it is from your death
that we hope for our inheritances'.[9]

All this had at least the advantage for Oliver that in
his speeches to Parliament he could, in Baxter's words,
'conjure up at pleasure some terrible apparition, of Agitators, Levellers, or such like, who as they affrighted the
King from Hampton Court shall affright the people to fly
to him for refuge'.[10] Oliver denounced his enemies on the

left as irresponsibles who were objectively playing the
game of the royalists. ('They must end at the interest of
the Cavalier at the long run,' he told his second Parliament in September 1656.) He tried to rally the propertied
by exaggerating the social-revolutionary objectives of the
Levellers. It is 'some satisfaction, if a Commonwealth must
perish, that it perish by men, and not by the hands of
persons differing little from beasts; that if it needs must
suffer, it should suffer rather from rich men than from
poor men'.

Yet the Protector could not maintain his régime for ever
on such horror stories. In the last resort he was sitting
on bayonets and nothing else. The Instrument of Government had written into the constitution, as a first charge
on the revenue, an army of 30,000 men: this was beyond
the power of elected Parliaments to change. The Council
was packed with the generals and their friends and relations, and this too Parliament was powerless to change.
' 'Tis against the will of the nation: there will be nine in
ten against you,' the Presbyterian divine Edmund Calamy
had told Cromwell when asked for advice about dissolving the Rump. 'But what if I should disarm the nine,'
Oliver replied, 'and put a sword in the tenth man's hand?
Would not that do the business?' It did the business
well enough for a short time, and might have done it for
longer if the Army had continued to be a united force
believing in its cause. But the breach with the Levellers,
the failure of Barebones, and the repeated purgings,
had ended all that. The Army was now a very efficient
professional force, no longer the people of England or the
people of God in arms. The 'natural rulers' were determined to get rid of it as soon as they possibly could.

II

Oliver hoped to reunite the landed class in support of his foreign policy. In the early years of the republic, exalted visions of international revolution were still prevalent. Gossip said that Cromwell once remarked to Lambert 'Were I as young as you, I should not doubt, ere I died, to knock at the gates of Rome.'[11] 'If he were ten years younger,' another report said, 'there was not a king in Europe he would not make to tremble.'

> As Caesar he ere long to Gaul,
> To Italy an Hannibal,
> And to all states not free
> Shall climacteric be.

So Marvell had seen Cromwell's role after his return from Ireland in 1650. Oliver toyed for some time with the idea of intervening in south-western France in support of the Bordeaux rebels: the ex-Leveller Sexby was there on behalf of the Council of State from 1651 to 1653. In 1654 George Fox was urging Oliver to 'rock the nations as a cradle'; 'the King of France should have bowed his neck under thee, the Pope should have withered as in winter'.[12] As late as 1657 Fox was still using words which are very different from his later pacifism, upbraiding the Army for its failure to carry the revolution to Spain and Rome. I have collected elsewhere[13] some of the evidence for the hopes of an international revolution led by England, held by men so diverse as Alexander Leslie, commander of the Scottish army, John Milton, Hugh Peter, Admiral Blake.

But by the end of 1653 such thoughts no longer corresponded to reality. English foreign policy was now conceived in hard practical terms of national and commercial interest. Two lines of policy emerged. One, popular in the

City and the Rump, was that which aimed at annihilating
Dutch commercial rivalry, by agreement if possible, by
war if not. This would open up to English merchants the
trade of India and the Far East, seriously restricted since
the massacre of Amboyna in 1623. This policy inspired the
Navigation Act and the first Dutch War: an eloquent
defence of it may be read in Slingsby Bethel's *The
World's Mistake in Oliver Cromwell* (1668) and *The
Interest of Princes and States* (1680). This course of action
completely abandons religion as a consideration in deter-
mining foreign policy. The second course, more popular
with the Presbyterian country gentry, was aimed at forcing
a way in to the Spanish monopoly area of the West Indies
and America. It was a continuation of the Providence
Island Company's policy, and if successful would have
given England bases in the sugar and tobacco islands of
the Caribbean and a strong position in the trade in African
slaves to America, including Spanish America.[14] War
against Spain had the additional advantage that it could
still be described in religious terms as an anti-Catholic
crusade.

The fierce anti-Dutch policy had been the product of a
City pressure group, and was strongly supported by the
radicals in the Barebones Parliament. Cromwell was not
associated with the extreme anti-Dutch party. But Thurloe
tells us that he supported the war on *salus populi* lines.
The Commonwealth should do anything to preserve its
trade.[15] In 1654 Cromwell equipped and despatched an
expedition to cooperate with New Englanders in the capture of the Dutch settlements on the mainland of North
America. This plan was frustrated by the signing of peace,
but the force then carried out Cromwell's alternative instructions by capturing Nova Scotia. This might have
been a second beginning of English colonization of
Canada, where Charles I had surrendered an earlier settlement in 1629. But Charles II gave Nova Scotia back to

the French in 1668. Samuel Pepys believed that Oliver had far too accurate an appreciation of its economic advantages – coal and copper especially – to have agreed to such a surrender.[16] Although in 1656 Cromwell was accused by the Baptist Captain Chillenden of selling English trade to the Dutch,[17] the peace terms of 1654 were not unfavourable to England, and indeed the secret agreement excluding the House of Orange from office in the Netherlands dashed one of the main hopes of the royalists, and forced many of them into reluctant acquiescence in the existence of the Protectorate. Their two countries, Cromwell had told the Dutch Ambassadors in July 1653, if they agreed together, 'could overrule all others and control the markets and dictate the conditions'. Cromwell seems to have been interested, especially in 1653, in attracting Dutch capital to England, where liquid assets were alarmingly short. But he was equally determined, a shrewd German observer tells us in October 1654, to oust the Dutch from the leadership of the protestant interest.[18]

After concluding peace with the Netherlands, Cromwell moved towards a pro-French and anti-Spanish alignment, such as had always been popular with the Presbyterians. The pro-Spanish policy was that of clothing interests dependent upon imports of Spanish wool and on trade with Old Spain. But war with France was also disadvantageous to the clothing industry, as Oliver pointed out to his first Parliament, 'by reason of the advantages taken by other states to improve their own and spoil our manufacture of cloth and hinder the vent thereof'. The Treaty of 1655 with France was primarily a commercial treaty. An anti-Spanish policy however had the advantage of appealing to traditional patriotic and protestant sentiments, of throwing Charles Stuart into the arms of the national enemy. The conquest of Dunkirk offered a bridgehead on the continent, that of Hispaniola

or Jamaica the possibility both of commercial advantages
in the New World and of solving the régime's financial
problems by the capture of Spanish treasure. It is easy to
dismiss the last consideration as wishful thinking, just
because we know that the grand coup of capturing the
Spanish Indies fleet never came off. But the Dutch had
done it 30 years earlier, and English use of sea power in
the 1650s was even more powerful and systematic. In
September 1656 Captain Richard Stayner destroyed ships
containing £2 million of treasure, and captured booty
worth £600–700,000, which was brought across England
from Portsmouth to London in 38 wagonloads, so as to
gain the maximum publicity. Seven months later Blake
destroyed the Spanish treasure fleet at Santa Cruz.
Merchants trading to Old Spain disliked the war, but
there can be no doubt of its popularity in its early days.
Parliament in 1656 voted *nem. con.* in favour of it.[19] It
was only after Oliver's death that the war became unpopular, when its high cost in taxation had brought no
immediate compensating returns, and when anti-Dutch
feeling rose again because Dutch merchants were too
obviously profiting by England's involvement.

The Western Design was Oliver's main contribution to
the development of English imperial policy, and it is
important to see it in perspective. Firth described it as
'the most fruitful part of his external policy', which 'produced the most abiding results'.[20] It had nothing in common with the raids of the Elizabethan sea-dogs, with
which it is sometimes misleadingly compared: Oliver's
was a determined attempt to occupy and settle perma-
nently a stable base in the West Indies. 'The design in
general is to gain an interest in that part of the West
Indies in the possession of the Spaniard', its first commander was told. Englishmen would settle there 'from
other parts'. Cromwell tried hard to persuade New Englanders or Irish protestant settlers to transfer to Jamaica.

Another aim was 'the mastery of all those seas', in order to maintain the Navigation Act and humble the Netherlands. Dutch ships were seized at Barbados and on the high seas. The ultimate objective was to break open the Spanish monopoly of South American trade, including the silver trade: and in the short run the government undoubtedly hoped to profit by seizing Spanish silver fleets. But the important part of the scheme was government-sponsored settlement. Just as the union of England and Scotland had been followed by an offer on similar terms of union to the Netherlands, so the conquest and settlement of Ireland was to be followed by conquest and settlement of the West Indies. The two were in fact connected by the transportation of Irish, Scots and others to the West Indies; an attempt was also made to get New Englanders to move to Jamaica.

The Western Design had a long pre-history, which I have traced elsewhere,[21] Sir Walter Ralegh advocated it, though in practice his privately-financed expeditions could never resist being diverted by the hope of plunder. The merchants who sponsored the Pilgrim Fathers and the settlement of Massachusetts may have had long-term anti-Spanish designs; but no government support was forthcoming for their colonizing efforts. One of the five Commissioners in charge of Cromwell's expedition was Edward Winslow, the Pilgrim Father. The Providence Island Company came as near as private enterprise could get to putting the policy into effect, by planting a colony right in the Spanish Main. But this Puritan enterprise also degenerated into a pirate station when government support was lacking and the island was 'by the hard and undue dealing of such as then swayed the affairs of this realm exposed to the rapine of the public enemy'.[22] The connecting links between this company and the Parliamentary opposition of the 1640s have often been noted,[23] as has the importance of ex-members of the Company in

Cromwell's entourage in the 1650s. His Manifesto against
Spain of October 1656 referred specifically to the Providence Island venture. What has not so often been
stressed is that Maurice Thompson, right-hand man of
Cromwell's Western Design, had also been a contractor
for the Providence Island colonists, and financed the
follow-up voyage of Captain Jackson in 1642.[24]

A major effort of state power was needed if a base in
the West Indies was to be secured and maintained. In the
1630s Sir Thomas Roe had called – in vain – for an Anglo-
Dutch alliance to invade the Spanish Indies.[25] Cardinal
Richelieu had cast greedy eyes on the islands, but had
concluded 'Il y a peu à espérer de ce côté-là, si par une
puissante guerre on ne se rend maître des lieux que le
roi d'Espagne occupe maintenant'.[26] Cromwell mounted
this 'mighty war' – without a Dutch alliance. It is a historic turning-point. For the next 150 years the West
Indies were crucial to English imperial and foreign
policy. Jamaica was the centre of the slave trade,
first supplying slaves for other West Indian islands,
then for the southern colonies on the mainland of
America. The eighteenth-century prosperity of Bristol and
Liverpool is unthinkable without Jamaica and the slave
trade. There is continuity here too, for the colonists of
Providence Island had employed slave labour in large
quantities.[27]

Through the person of Maurice Thompson, the Western
Design was linked to the policies of the East India Com-
pany. Thompson had been the architect of the Navigation
Act. In 1649 he advocated a scheme for colonizing Assada,
an island off Madagascar. Its first Governor was Colonel
Robert Hunt, former Governor of Providence Island.
Cromwell was said to have announced his intention of
endeavouring 'the settlement of a national interest in
India'. In correspondence with the government in 1654
both the rival factions in the East India Company

assumed more state support and protection might be expected in future.[28] It is hardly a coincidence that the Company lent the government £50,000 in 1655, and that its charter was confirmed in October 1656. In February 1657, on the motion of Thurloe's brother-in-law, Martin Noell, the Council advised the Protector to strengthen the Company's monopoly, and in October a new charter was issued which marked the final defeat of the free-trading element which had seemed so strong in the early 1650s.

Why, in view of its great importance, was the Western Design so badly prepared that it failed of its first objective, Hispaniola? It is the only one of Cromwell's military endeavours which can be criticized on this score. The naval and military commanders, it has been suggested, may have been chosen in order to get them out of England; they quarrelled and both came home at the earliest opportunity, taking no further part in protectorate political life. Admiral William Penn contributed to the restoration of Charles II – after which, it is fair to remember, he proved a good naval officer. Whether or not the commanders were men whom the government wanted out of the way, there is no doubt that many other ranks were selected for reasons of that kind. Regimental commanders were given the chance of nominating men for the expedition, and naturally took the opportunity of getting rid of undesirables. The immediate responsibility was Desborough's, rather than Oliver's; but this merely shifts the problem. Why did Cromwell delegate so great a responsibility without keeping a proper watch himself on what was happening? It may be that he was too confident that the Lord would provide: he brushed aside Lambert's very practical objections with this phrase in the only report we have of discussions on the subject in the Council. Certainly Oliver saw the check at Hispaniola as a rebuke from the Lord. On the other hand we should recall that it was far and away the most ambitious combined operation yet staged by an English government, and we should perhaps emphasize its considerable success even more than its partial failure.

Oliver's imperial and foreign policies were part of a single grand design. The dissolution of the Rump and of the Barebones Parliament caused a shift in the aims of policy, but no change in its commercial orientation. The Navigation Act was maintained, and indeed strengthened by Parliament in 1657; the Dutch were contained; French privateers – a real menace to English trade in the early 1650s – were checked. Blake's exploits in the Mediterranean in 1654–5 were an essential part of the design, for they curbed French ambitions in Italy and aspirations for a hegemony of the Mediterranean. The Portuguese Treaty of 1654, ratified only thanks to Blake's fleet, gave English merchants entry into the whole vast Portuguese empire in west and east, and offered European markets to compensate for the loss of those of Old Spain. 'It is a peace,' Cromwell told his first Parliament, 'that your merchants make me believe is of good concernment to their trade, their assurance being greater, and so their profit in trade thither, than to other places.' When he added that English traders to Portugal would enjoy liberty of conscience – something none of his monarchical predecessors had ever been strong enough to extract – he was loudly applauded.

Under Charles I, Cromwell was alleged to have said, 'England had ruined the protestant party in France'; and now 'England must restore it'. But this soon turned into a plan for obtaining the cession of Bordeaux to England.[29] Thurloe later explained that Oliver wanted to draw the French Huguenots 'to a dependence upon him, and thereby keep an interest in France in all events, and also to do that which was most acceptable to his people as to all other protestants in the world, whose cause and interest he professedly asserted on all occasions and laid the foundation of becoming the head and protector of them'.[30] Cardinal Mazarin certainly took the threat seriously and regarded the secret clause in the Treaty of 1655 by which each party renounced assistance or shelter for the internal enemies of the other as 'the fundamental point of the whole treaty'. We are apt to think of this clause only in connection with the English royalists whom Oliver was anxious to have expelled from France. By 1655 England was no longer international-revolutionary. Whatever may have been true of the republic, the protectorate was a conservative national government – a trend which Mazarin supported.[31]

Cromwell hoped that 'all, but especially true Englishmen, will lay aside their private animosities among themselves', and not 'let slip out of their hands the most noble opportunities of promoting the glory of God and enlarging the bounds of Christ's kingdom; which, we do not doubt, will appear to be the chief end of our late expedition to the West Indies against the Spaniards, to all who are free of those prejudices which hinder people from clearly discerning the truth'. Spain, he told his Second Parliament, was 'described in Scripture to be papal and Antichristian'. 'The papists in England, they have been accounted, ever since I was born, Spaniolized.' And now Antichristian Spain 'hath espoused Charles Stuart.' In stressing the religious aspects of a war against Spain Oliver was undoubtedly personally sincere. But it was also good propaganda, drawing on the whole Foxe tradition of the battle of God's Englishmen against Antichrist. English propaganda also utilized the writings of Las Casas on behalf of the Indians, a translation of which by Milton's nephew John Philips was published in 1656 as *The Tears of the Indians: Being an Historical and true Account of the Cruel Massacres and Slaughters of above Twenty Millions of innocent People*. This translation, dedicated to the Protector, called on him to avenge the Indians, 'an eye for an eye, a tooth for a tooth'. The demand had been anticipated in Milton's *Defensio Secunda pro Populo Anglicano* (1654) and was duly repeated in the Manifesto of October 1656 in which Oliver justified the war against Spain.

It is hardly likely that Oliver's religious views were decisive in the formation of foreign policy – a matter in which the Council shared. When the decision lay between fighting either France or Spain, the religious argument could have been used either way. Spain was the arch-Catholic power whilst France in the Thirty Years' War had fought on the 'protestant' side. On the other hand, if Oliver had opted the other way, he could have posed as the liberator of the French Huguenot population. He did in fact enquire closely into their views, sending various emissaries to France for this purpose, and one factor at least in his choosing a French alliance was the distinct unwillingness of the Huguenots to be liberated.

Cromwell's desire to take the lead of the protestant interest from the Dutch was also a matter of power politics at least as much as of ideology: we may compare Russo-Chinese rivalries at present. One of those European protestants whom Oliver aspired to lead wrote to his government in October 1654 that 'neither financial nor military aid should be expected from this country, unless you would consider adopting the status of an English protectorate'. This was from a shrewd observer, who regarded Cromwell as 'the greatest hero of the century'.[32] He was writing to Bremen, whose annexation to England Cromwell proposed a year or two later. It would be, he thought, among other things, a bridle on the protestant Dutch.

'Bring us back a protestant alliance' are reported to have been the Protector's last public words to Bulstrode Whitelocke before he left for Sweden at the end of 1653; but his private discussions with Whitelocke on the subject deal exclusively with political and economic matters. Oliver wanted to be sure of keeping the Baltic open to English traders. Once England had secured entry to Swedish ports on equal terms with the Dutch, he proved anxious to avoid the military alliance which Charles x of Sweden pressed on him. Despite a great deal of talk about an offensive and defensive alliance, the only agreement signed with Sweden was a commercial treaty, in July 1656. But two years later Oliver was reported as saying that if Charles x conquered the Danes, England would demand Elsinore in compensation; ' "which if once I have," said Oliver, "the English shall have the whole trade of the Baltic Sea. I will make the Dutch find another passage, except they will pay such customs as I shall impose" '.³³ 'If they [the Habsburgs] can shut us out of the Baltic Sea,' he had asked Parliament earlier in the same year, 'and make themselves masters of that, where is your trade? Where are your materials to preserve your shipping?' As for the protestant interest, it was useful to be able to employ a man like John Dury, with an international reputation as a worker for protestant unity, as diplomatic representative to Sweden, Germany, Switzerland and the Netherlands.³⁴ And there is no doubt that Oliver shared the general English indignation at the massacre of the Vaudois, as well as making diplomatic capital out of it. But it gave him just the lever he wanted at the time for putting pressure on France. Another example of the victory of commercial over religious considerations in foreign policy was the Protector's refusal to help the Venetians against the Turks because too much English capital in the Mediterranean was vulnerable to Turkish attack.³⁵

Finally, what needs most of all to be stressed, because historians have come to take it for granted, is the fantastic scope of Cromwell's foreign policy. It is taken for granted because it set the pattern for the future. But we must see it as contemporaries saw it. In the 1620s and 1630s England had been powerless to take any action while the fate of Europe was being decided in the Thirty Years' War. Neither James nor Charles gave any effective help to the former's son-in-law when he was driven out of his hereditary domains of the Palatinate. The Massacre of Amboyna and the destruction of the English settlement on Providence Island alike went unavenged until the 1650s. English merchants were driven out of the East and West Indies. England could not prevent Dutch and Spanish fleets fighting in her waters. North African pirates carried seamen off to slavery even in the English Channel. As the Venetian Ambassador put it in June 1638: 'The interest and share of the Spaniards in the government here obscure reason'. Two years later he concluded: 'England . . . has become a nation useless to all the rest of the world, and consequently of no consideration.'[36]

The transformation a mere fifteen years later is astonishing. The governments of the 1650s were the first in English history to have a world strategy. After Blake had subdued the pirates of Algiers, Cromwell envisaged maintaining control of the Mediterranean by the occupation of Gibraltar or Minorca. Bremen would give the entry to Germany. Dunkirk would be a bridle on Dutch and French alike. The Western Design, as we have seen, was linked with the plans of the East India Company: the seizure of Cartagena was contemplated. Preparations were made for expelling the Dutch from New Amsterdam, the French from Canada. Not all of these grandiose schemes were realized, and others were frustrated by Oliver's successors. It was only after the restoration that Slingsby Bethel was able to argue plausibly that the alliance with France against Spain had made possible the subsequent preponderance of Louis xiv.[37] But it was Charles's disbandment of Oliver's army, neglect of the navy and sale of Dunkirk that made the sudden rise of French power possible. It might be argued that Cromwell's foreign policy stretched the resources of the country too far, that it was political necessity and not choice that made Charles II economize, that a generation of consolidation was needed before Oliver's global imperial designs could be resumed. It might also be argued that the Levellers were right in thinking such a policy not in the best interests of the English people. But, for good or ill, England's world position was transformed out of all recognition. England, in Professor Abbott's words, 'began to turn definitely from its position as an island chiefly agricultural to a world power chiefly industrial and commercial'. 'First to his Englishmen,' Milton had said;[38] whether God or some other high authority was responsible, England was undoubtedly first on the road to the modern world.

In 1633 it was observed that 'England . . . has no minister of her own at any court of Europe' except Constantinople, and the envoy there was sent and paid for by merchants.[39] But now all Europe counted, as far afield as Russia, Poland, Brandenburg. In 1655 the Prince of Transylvania sent an envoy to beg Cromwell's help; in 1656 the Duke of Courland did the same. There were rumours that the Protector intended to attack Archangel, and that he had established relations with the rebel Cossack leader, Bogdan Khmelnitsky.[40] Cromwell's reputation as 'an intimate colleague, if not the contriver, of the King of Sweden's expedition for Poland . . . makes all Italy very meek and humble', an English diplomat wrote thence in October 1656. Oliver's intervention was sought to end war between Venice and the Turks, so that the latter might be free to attack Poland. Thurloe discussed with the Venetian Ambassador the desirability of sending an English representative to the Morea. The Jews sought re-admission into England under Oliver's protection. The Sultan of Morocco sent him presents, and treaties were signed with Algiers, Tetuan and Tunis, establishing English naval bases there. The King of Florida sent his brother to 'settle trade and friendship with England', and to suggest a joint enterprise against the Spanish empire. 'A national interest in India' came within the Protector's purview.[41]

In his essay *Of the True Greatness of Kingdoms and Estates,* Francis Bacon had prophetically written: 'The wealth of both Indies seems in great part but an accessory to the command of the seas.' English strategy after the Revolution was based on a conscious use of sea power on a world scale that was new in execution if not in conception. In 1649–50 Ireland was kept free from foreign intervention, and Blake blockaded Prince Rupert's fleet in Kinsale. In March 1650 Blake followed Rupert to Portugal and shut him up in the Tagus for six months, finally capturing or destroying most of his ships. In September 1652 Blake's victory over a French fleet ensured the Spanish capture of Dunkirk. In 1654–5 – performing the unique feat of keeping at sea throughout the winter – the English admiral frustrated French designs on Naples, and brought Portugal to accept a virtual English protectorate. The forcing of treaties on Tetuan and Tunis introduced a new type of gunboat diplomacy, of which the next three centuries were to see a great deal. In 1656–7 Spain was effectively blockaded. The English navy cleaned up privateering, from Algiers to Dunkirk, in a way that no other power could: Blake in the Mediterranean, Penn in the Caribbean, Goodson in the Baltic, were phenomena hitherto unknown, presaging Britain's future. English merchants were now protected in the Mediterranean and Baltic in a way that would have been quite impossible for early Stuart governments, as is attested by innumerable diplomatic documents issued on their behalf (see Abbott's *Writings and Speeches of Oliver Cromwell* and Milton's *State Papers*).

III

But the foreign policy did not pay for itself, any more than the decimation tax imposed on royalists by the Major-Generals paid for them. Yet finance was the crucial problem. If the troops could not be regularly and fully paid – as they had been at the beginning of the Protectorate – the régime itself would be insecure. The Rump's proposal to restore Exchequer supremacy was brought to fruition in 1654. But the decimation tax was outside the course of the Exchequer, and so were the assessments – a sort of Chamber finance at the Protector's direct disposal. The financial problem was the principal reason for calling Parliaments, as Oliver made clear in his speech to his first Parliament. The land fund and fines, from which deficits were met down to 1653, were now exhausted. To ram the point home, a London merchant, George Cony, in November 1654 challenged the whole legal basis of the Instrument of Government by refusing to pay customs. He was an old friend of Oliver's, and reminded him that 'the tyranny of princes could never be grievous but by the tameness and stupidity of the people'.[42] At his trial the pleas echoed those of the Hampden Case. Cony's lawyers were sent to the Tower, and Chief Justice Rolle resigned rather than try the case. The fact that Cony submitted *after* the dissolution of Parliament witnessed only to the government's military power. Cony's protest was followed in August 1655 by a similar refusal to pay taxes from the bearer of the ominous name of Peter Wentworth, who declared that 'by the laws of England no money ought to be levied upon people without their consent in Parliament'. He too submitted under protest. Parliament's concern was always to lower taxes. 'It was in every man's sense to go as low as possibly could consist

with our safety,' it was said of the first Parliament. 'If we
did not ease them [our constituents] in their purses, we
should never think to oblige them ever to us.'[43] Thus
Parliament voted £1,100,000 for the army and navy, at
a time when they were costing £2 million; and even this
sum was conditional on the government accepting Parliament's revision of the Instrument; just as the Petition and
Advice accorded the Protector a regular revenue only
with the clause 'no part thereof to be by a land tax'.

Ludlow believed that after the dissolution of the Barebones Parliament Oliver became the Protector of the
corrupt part of the lawyers and clergy, those opposed to
radical reform.[44] But Cromwell never abandoned at least
a verbal interest in law reform. Before Parliament met in
1654 his Council had passed a number of reforming ordinances – for the relief of creditors and poor prisoners,
codifying the law on the maintenance of highways, uniting
England and Scotland and subsidizing Scottish universities, for the reorganization of the English Exchequer.
Bills were in preparation for reform of the law, Oliver
told his first Parliament – as, men no doubt recalled, they
had been under the Rump! Chancery had been reformed.
Parliament suspended this latter reform, but it was reinforced after the dissolution, and confirmed by the second
Parliament of the Protectorate. In his opening speech in
September 1656 Oliver still declared that 'there is one
general grievance in the nation: it is the law'. 'To hang
a man for six and eightpence and I know not what – to
hang for a trifle and acquit murder.' The Speaker dwelt
forcefully on the need for law reform when presenting
the Humble Petition and Advice to Oliver on 31 March
1657: he must have supposed that this would be acceptable. Three weeks later the Protector was still complaining
of the law's delays and high costs. This Parliament also
discussed government bills for establishing county regis-
ters and local courts (another of the Rump's plans), and

confirmed the abolition of feudal tenures and the Court of Wards.

Jeremy Bentham in 1817 thought that Cromwell's interest in law reform 'ranks that wonderful man higher than anything else I ever read of him'.[45] But it is noteworthy that the reforms which did occur were again in the interests of conservative efficiency rather than of any radical change. Bentham was praising Oliver's hopes, no doubt genuine enough, rather than his achievements, which were limited by the men with whom he had chosen to work.

VII

KING?

1656-58

You Cavaliers . . . must needs laugh in your sleeves at our
dissensions, and the struggle there is amongst us, who shall
have the government, and promise your King, not without
reason, great advantages from our disagreement.

> JOHN BRADSHAW, to Peter Barwick, winter 1657–8, in
> Peter Barwick, *The Life of Dr John Barwick* (trans-
> lated by H. Bedford, abridged and edited by C. F.
> Barwick, 1903), p. 82

Sir Henry Vane: If you be minded to resort to the old
government, you are not many steps from the old family.
They will be too hard for you if that government be restored.

> Ed. J. T. Rutt, *Diary of Thomas Burton* (1828), III,
> p. 180: in the House of Commons, 9 February 1659

My Lord, I have stood by you as an idle spectator upon this
deck of state ever since your Lordship laid hold on the helm
of English affairs, and have seen you for your own safety and
interest unhappily constrained to cast overboard the most
considerable rights and privileges of the people, the valuable
commodities you found the ship of state after a dangerous
voyage well fraught with. Had you been necessitated by
any other storm and tempest than that raised by your own
fears and jealousies to manage this unruly vessel, you had
surely been pitied rather than blamed and cursed.

> D.F. (=John Goodwin), *A Letter of Address to the
> Protector* (1657)

I

After the failure of his first Parliament and some unsuccessful royalist and republican conspiracies in the
early months of 1655, Oliver accepted his generals'
scheme for direct military rule. The country was divided
into eleven districts, and over each a Major-General was
set, to command the local militia as well as his own
regular troops. In addition to their defensive military
function, one of their main tasks – one which Oliver
Cromwell singled out for special praise even whilst repu-
diating them – had been to drive local government, to
see that JPs and deputy-lieutenants did their job. Laud
and the Rump's committees had been feeble whips compared to the scorpions of the Major-Generals. Many of the
'natural rulers' had already withdrawn or been expelled
from local government, and a proclamation at the time of
setting up the Major-Generals also excluded all ex-
royalists from the commission of the peace or any share
in local government. The Major-Generals took over many
of the functions of Lords Lieutenants, formerly agents of
the Privy Council in the counties. But their social role was
very different. Lords Lieutenants had been the leading
aristocrats of the county. Some Major-Generals were low-
born upstarts, many came from outside the county: all had
troops of horse behind them to make their commands
effective. This was the more galling at a time when many
of the traditional county families were beginning to benefit economically from the restoration of law, order and
social subordination. The rule of the Major-Generals

seemed to them to jeopardize all of these. There was not much temptation to return to local government under such circumstances.[1]

The Major-Generals interfered, on security grounds, with simple country pleasures like horse-racing, bear-baiting, and cock-fighting – not 'to abridge gentlemen of that sport [horse-racing] but to prevent the great confluence of irreconcilable enemies', as Whalley put it.[2] The Major-Generals were instructed not only to set the poor on work – the JPs' job anyway – but to consider by what means 'idle and loose people' with 'no visible way of livelihood, nor calling or employment, . . . may be compelled to work'. They were to see that JPs enforced the legislation of the Long Parliament (and indeed of the Parliaments of the 1620s) against drunkenness, blasphemy and sabbath-breaking – offences which the justices were ready enough to punish in the lower orders, but in them only. The Major-Generals were to make all men responsible for the good behaviour of their servants. They were to take the initiative against any 'notorious breach of the peace'. They were to interfere in the licensing of alehouses – a matter on which the House of Commons had defeated even the great Duke of Buckingham. They also interfered, often quite effectively, against corrupt oligarchies in towns. They had little confidence in juries of gentlemen and well-to-do freeholders, and Cromwell himself shared the prejudice.[3] Above all they took control of the militia, the army of the gentry, away from the 'natural rulers'. Quite apart from the latter's objections to having their running of local government supervised, controlled and driven, the whole operation was very costly. At least justices of the peace and deputy-lieutenants were unpaid. In the summer of 1655 10–12,000 men had been disbanded; but the 'standing militia of horse' raised by the Major-Generals cost £80,000 a year: decimation of royalists by no means covered this sum.

It was made clear at the beginning of the second Parliament of the Protectorate that financial grants would be linked with the abolition of the Major-Generals, just as the Humble Petition and Advice presented to Oliver in March 1657 insisted that no part of the revenue to pay for the Army was to be raised by a land tax. The Major-Generals left behind them in the memory of the ruling class a fixed hatred of standing armies that is one of the most important legacies of the revolutionary decades.

One consideration which should not be ignored is the anxiety which contemporaries – including Cromwell himself – showed about the danger of 'cantonizing the nation'. National unity was something which had been laboriously won in the sixteenth century. Thomas Adams in James I's reign rejoiced that England was not 'cut into cantons by a headless, headstrong aristocracy'. In 1640 Edward Hyde used the phrase 'cantonize out a part of [the] Kingdom' when condemning the Council in the North.[4] During the interregnum, the Councils in the North and in Wales had been abolished, the local power of the feudal aristocracy curtailed, the authority of Whitehall and the pull of the London market extended over the whole country. It seems obvious to us that the Revolution established much greater unity of England – and indeed of the British Isles, if we recall the conquest of Ireland and Scotland – and for the first time of the British Empire (the Navigation Act).[5] But contemporaries worried about centrifugal tendencies. They were no doubt influenced by the Netherlands, where the republic's unity derived mainly from the dominance of Holland, and the other provinces clung on to their independence, often with paralysing effects on policy. They were also disturbed in the 1650s by events in Switzerland, where protestant and Catholic cantons were at war, a war – as Cromwell repeatedly insisted – which had been brought on by external papist intervention. They had every reason to

remember France. Du Bartas-Sylvester, Ralegh and Fulke
Greville all spoke of France as 'endangered ... to be
cantonized' during the sixteenth-century civil wars. In
the 1620s the French Huguenots had been accused of
wanting to cantonize the kingdom after the Dutch
fashion.[6] In the early 1650s England had nearly intervened
in the Fronde – an intervention which might have created
a breakaway republic in the south-west. Men would also
notice the revolts from Spanish sovereignty of Portugal,
Catalonia and Naples, Cossack risings against Russia and
Poland. Remembering the disunity of Italy and Germany,
it might seem that none of the national states built up
with such difficulty in sixteenth-century Europe were
going to survive.

The Levellers proposed a great deal of decentralization,
local courts at York, greater county autonomy. William
Walwyn said that the Swiss cantons were the nearest to
his ideal. In 1647 Cromwell had argued against Leveller
constitutional projects, 'Would it not make England like
Switzerland, one canton of the Swiss against another, and
one county against another? And what would that produce but an absolute desolation to the nation?' Next year
Bishop King suggested that the Army was carrying out
Leveller plans:

> For new Committees, and your armed supplies,
> Canton the land in petty tyrannies.

The argument was to be used even more forcibly
against the rule of the Major-Generals. It was, said Trevor
in Parliament, 'a new militia, raised with a tendency to
divide this commonwealth into provinces, a power too
great to be bound within any law; in plain terms, to
cantonize the nation'.[7] Ludlow and Clarendon echoed the
phrase: Cromwell 'divided England into cantons, over
each of which he placed a bashaw with the title of Major-
General'; 'like so many bashaws with their bands of janis-

saries'.[8] The royalists also used the phrase 'cantonizing', meaning to divide the country into associations of counties grouped together for military purposes.[9] 'Cantonizing' indeed became a cant phrase of the time.[10] It presented a threat to county society as well as to national unity. Military government made the executive too strong, and yet created the possibility of regional fission. What the natural rulers wanted was a federation of counties securely ruled by themselves, with no power, central or regional, strong enough to counterbalance their territorial influence.

II

But the Petition and Advice went much further than mere reaction against the rule of the Major-Generals would seem to justify, and offered the crown to Oliver Cromwell. Kingship had been proposed in one form or another many times before 1657. Two months after the execution of Charles I the Levellers hinted that the Army Grandees' 'creatures' had decided 'that the power must be reduced to one'.[11] Cromwell himself among others mooted the idea in 1651–2. He dismissed a proposal to restore Charles Stuart by saying 'He is so damnably debauched, he would undo us all'; 'Give him a shoulder of mutton and a whore, that's all he cares for.'[12] He asked in November 1652: 'What if a man should take upon himself to be king?' The idea that Oliver might be crowned was put forward by Lambert in December 1653, by Broghill in December 1654. It was proposed in Parliament later in the same month by the regicide Augustine Garland, supported by Sir Anthony Ashley Cooper and Henry Cromwell. The suggestion cropped up again in May and July 1655, and Colonel Jephson seems to have been touting the idea around independently at the same time as the Humble Petition and Advice.

Several questions were involved: a repudiation of the Instrument of Government, on which alone the title of Protector was based; a return to the forms of the old constitution, rejecting revolutionary illegality; a reassertion of the hereditary principle; an unambiguous declaration of the succession, thus removing the uncertainties of a situation in which stability depended on Oliver's life. There might be objections on as many grounds. Republicans naturally disliked monarchy, and democrats the hereditary principle; kingship seemed to many a denial of the Good Old Cause for which they had fought. The end of revolutionary illegality, and the establishment of a hereditary succession, would put paid to personal ambitions which a general (John Lambert, for example) might have to succeed Oliver. The conflict between the hereditary and the elective principle went very deep, and related to the whole programme of the career open to the talents of which Oliver had been in a sense the spokesman. The Barebones Parliament was alleged to have declared nobility contrary to the law of nature.[13] In his first Parliament the Protector was given the right to create *life* peerages, and he himself spoke against the hereditary principle at the dissolution. But the position of King was known to and bound by the laws, notably those passed in 1640-1 and accepted (however reluctantly) by Charles I. Moreover, under a statute of Henry VII rebellion against a *de facto* king was defined as treason. An ex-royalist poet wrote in 1656:

> He's traitor helps a traitor to a throne,
> Yet who resists him on it may be one.[14]

The royalist rebel Penruddock, who was executed in 1655, had said that if Oliver had been a crowned king, he would have known that his revolt was treasonable.

By 1656 the problem of the succession had become acute. Oliver's second Parliament was as concerned about it as any of Elizabeth's Parliaments had been, and Cromwell was perhaps no more willing than the Virgin Queen to nominate a successor. The hereditary principle, just because of its arbitrariness, had some advantages. Government by Major-Generals had profoundly upset the 'natural rulers', whose own position depended on their hereditary rights. In January 1657 it was noted as 'the distinguishing character' of those who opposed the Militia Bill (which would have prolonged the Major-Generals' rule) 'that they were for the hereditary rank'. Significantly, Oliver's son-in-law Claypole as well as Broghill was among them. The man who first brought up the question of kingship in this Parliament was the Presbyterian John Ashe, 'the greatest clothier in England', but an upstart whose wealth had never made him acceptable to the royalist Wiltshire gentry. Ashe was supported by George Downing and followed by Sir Christopher Packe, Merchant Adventurer and ex-Lord Mayor of London. Packe was anxious for 'the settlement of the nation and of liberty and property'.[15]

Cromwell too was always 'hugely taken with the word settlement'. Another consideration which may have weighed with him in rejecting military rule – as he clearly had not thought of doing when he was persuaded to summon a Parliament – is that in November 1656 final agreement had been reached between Thurloe and the royalist traitor Sir Richard Willis, discussions between whom had started just about the time when the decision to call a Parliament was arrived at. Henceforth the Protector's government had full information about all royalist risings, and could crush them in advance. The job that the Major-Generals had been created to do no longer existed.[16]

In the last analysis it was the lower-class upstart officers, headed by Pride and some of Oliver's oldest comrades-in-arms, who organized the Army to force Cromwell to refuse the crown. Pride was reported as saying that if Oliver accepted kingship he would shoot him in the head

at the first opportunity he had.[17] Pride's petition against
kingship was signed by a majority of the officers in
London: it invited 'two out of each regiment in the Army
to own and subscribe it'. This echo of the representative
principle of 1647 at once aroused Oliver's vigilance, and
led to the traditional remedy, paying up arrears. It may
have precipitated the fall of Lambert, once Fleetwood
and Desborough had been placated by acceptance of the
Petition and Advice without the crown. It may well have
been to appease them and their like that the ingenious
device was worked out by which a substantial number of
generals and colonels – including Fleetwood, Desborough,
Philip Jones, Pride, Hewson, Goffe, Barkstead, Berry and
Tomlinson, but not Lambert – were given seats in the
Other House, where they could have an effective veto
on the Commons' legislation. The original draft of the
Petition and Advice subjected the Protector's nomination
of the upper chamber to the approval of the Commons:
abandonment of this in the Additional Petition and
Advice must have been one of the bargains reached behind the smoke-screen of Cromwell's many speeches.

Certainly the final dissolution of Parliament on 4 February, after hopeless quarrels in the Commons over recognition of the Other House, was related to agitation among
the rank and file of the Army. It was followed by the
cashiering of the officers of Oliver's own old regiment, 'that
had served him fourteen years, ever since he was captain
of a troop of horse', said one of them plaintively. They
were replaced by mere professionals. 'He had left them
and not they him', Colonel Biscoe told Oliver in the
presence of a number of other officers; 'He had dismissed
six as honest officers as any were in his army.'[18] The senti-
ment must have been widespread among the old revolutionaries. Cromwell received many letters urging him to
reject the crown. One from William Bradford said: 'I am
of that number, my Lord, that still loves you, and greatly

desires to do so, I having gone along with you from
Edgehill to Dunbar'. It was Cromwell's enemies, he
thought, who had voted for kingship.[19] On this the appropriate comment is James II's: support for the restoration
in 1660 came especially from such 'as had been of that
party which advised Cromwell to take the crown upon
him'.[20]

Repeated efforts had been made to rid the Army of its
radical elements by packing them off to Ireland, Scotland,
the navy, Jamaica. 'He weeded, in a few months' time,
above a hundred and fifty godly officers out of the Army',
Lucy Hutchinson wrote, 'with whom many of the religious soldiers went off, and in their room abundance of
the King's dissolute soldiers were entertained'. The old
ruling families began to return to local government. Acceptance of the Petition and Advice amounted in fact to
a change of government. Under the Instrument of
Government the Council had been nominated for Cromwell, and he had little power to alter it: under the
Petition and Advice he chose his own. He kept some of
the old members, but used the occasion for a thorough
reshuffle. If he had accepted the crown he would in one
sense have enjoyed *less* real power, at all events *vis-à-vis*
Parliament. 'A name that the law knows not, and that is
boundless', he agreed, 'is that under which a man exer-
ciseth more arbitrariness'. The monarchy's wings had been
well clipped by the legislation of 1640–1. The Petition and
Advice liberated Oliver from the Council, largely composed of generals, which the Instrument had imposed on
him. The Council, for instance, was said to have overruled
him in 1655 when they thought he was being too tolerant
to Episcopalians.[21] The Major-Generals had recommended
the summoning of Parliament (not due until 1657), and
had introduced the Militia Bill against Oliver's wishes –
or so he told them. They had made him their drudge, he

told a meeting of 100 officers: they made a very kick-shaw of him in London, Henry Cromwell echoed.

Another significant fact is that Pride's petition was drafted by John Owen, hitherto Cromwell's right-hand man in ecclesiastical affairs, and in the government of Oxford University. Owen, in a telling simile, compared the disagreements among the godly in the 1650s to the fate of colonists in a new country, who were infected by their environment.[22] Oliver may have been reluctant to break with those divines who were closest to his own outlook, though Owen 'forfeited much of his favour at court' from now onwards. The journalist Marchamont Nedham's crack to the Protector had been pertinent: town talk was that Philip Nye (who also opposed king-ship) should be Archbishop of Canterbury, and Owen Archbishop of York. That bit deep. 'No bishop, no king': monarchy, and agreement with Parliament in defiance of the Army, would have entailed a much more conservative religious policy. In November 1657 Cromwell's daughter Mary married Lord Fauconberg according to the forms of the common prayer book. It was Fauconberg to whom the regiment of the fallen Lambert had been given.

III

One of the reasons for the Petition and Advice was the case of James Nayler. Nayler, whose standing with the Quakers in 1656 was equal to that of George Fox, had symbolically ridden into Bristol on an ass, with women strewing palms in his way and giving him honours which onlookers thought blasphemous. This trivial event was seized upon by the enemies of religious toleration to make a major demonstration in Parliament against the consequences of the lax religious policy of the Protector and the Major-Generals. It must be seen against the back-

ground of a rapid spread of Quakerism which – whatever
it later became – seemed to men of property little better
than a revival of the Leveller movement. After a debate
which reveals the savagery of frightened men, Nayler was
sentenced to be flogged, pilloried, branded, his tongue to
be bored, and then to be imprisoned indefinitely. This
was a milder punishment than many MPs wanted. The
enemies of religious toleration seemed to have won a
resounding victory. But, like the Scots at Dunbar, they
laid themselves open to devastating counter-attack from
the flank. The Protector's simple question, on what
authority they had acted against Nayler, though it did
the latter no good, brought the constitutional problem to
a crisis from which the Petition and Advice resulted: for
there was no answer to the question under the Instrument
of Government. Oliver even used the 'need of a check or
balancing power' to argue in favour of the Petition to
his officers: 'for the case of James Nayler might happen
to be your own case'.

Liberty of conscience, Cromwell had told his first
Parliament, was one of the fundamentals of the Instrument which might not be challenged. But any elected
House of Commons was always anxious to persecute. It
was in part to meet the alarm of the propertied class at
unrestricted and uncontrolled lay preaching that Triers
and Ejectors were instituted – as Oliver went out of his
way to reassure the City Fathers in the first weeks of the
sitting of the 1654 Parliament. In 1584–5 Parliament had
proposed to make a commission of laymen the arbiters of
the fortunes of the clergy.[23] Cromwell's Ejectors were all
laymen. The Triers included 11 laymen together with 14
Congregationalist, 10 Presbyterian and 3 Baptist ministers. They were to review all ecclesiastical appointments
made since the dissolution of the Rump – in the period
of radical ascendancy. MPs were interested in property
as well as in theology. Francis Osborn put it neatly

when he wrote in about 1654: 'He was a Presbyterian
and an impropriator, and so will be true to the priests'
interest, whatever he is to O.P.'[24] One reason for the
gentry's objection to the Triers was revealed in a debate
in the Commons in March 1659. Serjeant Maynard said
that 'Triers at Whitehall ... have done more than the
Pope or the bishops ever did to take away men's ad-
vowsons'.[25]

The Parliament of 1654 had called in question the relatively liberal terms of the Instrument, as well as taking
direct action against the Unitarian Bidle. Their proposed
confession of faith marked a return to the Presbyterianism
of the 1640s – 'in substance the same which were agreed
by the Assembly of Divines and presented to the King
at the Isle of Wight', wrote Thurloe without a trace of
disapproval.[26] They voted that Parliament should share
in enumerating 'damnable heresies', and wished to deprive the Protector of his veto in this respect. This must
have caused great indignation in the Army, for although
at the beginning of the Parliament Cromwell had spoken
against too wide an extension of toleration and for an
endowed ministry, in his speech dissolving Parliament he
referred significantly to God having 'spoken very loud on
the behalf of his people, by judging their enemies in the
late war and restoring them a liberty to worship with the
freedom of their consciences ... I know a cause which
yet we have not lost, but do hope we shall take a little
pleasure rather to lose our lives than lose.' He returned
to the point twice, praising the Instrument of Government because it allowed the Protector to hinder 'Parliaments from ... imposing what religions they will on the
consciences of men'. 'What greater hypocrisy', he expostu-
lated with those who whored after Presbyterianism, 'than
for those who were oppressed by the Bishops to become
the greatest oppressors themselves so soon as this yoke
was removed?'

Yet Oliver became increasingly irritated with the various radical groups – Fifth Monarchists, Baptists and Quakers – who refused to accept his broad state church. His *via media* in religion, as in politics, became increasingly narrow. He told John Rogers that tithes were not Antichristian, to which Rogers replied: 'You were once of another mind, and told me you'd have them pulled down.' It would be very treacherous, Oliver told his second Parliament, to 'take away tithes, till I see the legislative power to settle them another way'. The whole history of the 1650s can be told in terms of tithes. Milton and many other supporters of the Commonwealth had been disappointed by the Rump's failure to get rid of them. The Barebones Parliament proposed their abolition, with compensation. The Instrument said they would be replaced by a more satisfactory system 'as soon as may be'; but meanwhile they should be paid. The Baptist Henry Jessey recorded Oliver as saying he could be called juggler if tithes were not abolished by September 1654.[27] The proposed Parliamentary constitution of 1655 merely declared that tithes should go on being paid, 'until some better provision be made *by the Parliament*', the words italicized being a sufficient guarantee of inaction. The Humble Petition and Advice not only assumed the payment of tithes, to impropriators as well as to ministers, but seriously restricted the circle of ministers eligible to receive them. 'The Presbyterian party in England', wrote Baillie in the winter of 1657–8, 'is exceeding great and strong, and, after the Army, is the Protector's chief strength against the sectaries, who generally are out of conceit of him'.[28] Oliver seemed to have made his choice. It was only a small step forward to the Parliamentary persecution of sectaries after 1660.

'And who made them judges of grace, my Lord?' John Rogers asked about the Triers. It was a question Cromwell would have found troublesome four or five years earlier even if he did not in 1655. Thurloe at any rate clearly preferred Presbyterians to Fifth Monarchists: 'The Presbyterian speaks as well of the Kingdom of Christ as these men, and many of them as holy, and I am sure much more knowing even in spiritual things'. But spiritual things were not perhaps the efficient Secretary's strongest subject. After the catastrophe of Barebones, Cromwell was dissatisfied with all religious parties. 'When shall we have men of a universal spirit?' he asked in December 1654. 'Every one desires to have liberty, but none will give it.' 'Nothing will satisfy them unless they can put their finger upon their brethren's consciences, to pinch them there,' he told Parliament in the following month. So he came to see himself 'as a constable to part them and keep them in peace' when 'men falling out in the street would run their heads one against another.'

By September 1655 he snapped at a defender of John Bidle that he would not 'show favour to a man that denies his Saviour and disturbs the government'. One suspects that the latter offence was almost the greater of the two. In February 1655 a proclamation withdrew the hitherto existing right for members of the congregation to speak 'after the priest had done'; this was confirmed by Parliament in June 1657.[29] And meanwhile the Council was doing a great deal to augment the stipends of ministers. It would be uncharitable to suppose that the special concern shown for the welfare of ministers in market towns at the end of May 1656 had anything to do with the impending Parliamentary elections, since town livings were notoriously badly endowed.

The Cromwellian state church was very similar to what John Owen had recommended to the Rump in 1652 – an establishment surrounded by self-supporting nonconformist churches tolerated by the state. 'This government,' Cromwell told his first Parliament, 'hath endeavoured to put a stop to that heady way ... of every man making himself a minister and a preacher', and had entrusted the approbation of ministers to Presbyterians and Congregationalists. Milton heartily disapproved. Baxter approved of the Triers, despite their tolerance of Independents and Baptists. 'One of the chief works [Oliver] did was the purging of the ministry'; godliness had in Baxter's view been greatly advanced during the 1650s. Baxter and his like concentrated on pressing Parliament to draw the lines of orthodoxy tighter, so that only conservatives should enjoy the state-guaranteed maintenance of tithes. Vane warned against them in 1656: 'Since the fall of the bishops and persecuting presbyteries, the same spirit is apt to arise in the next sort of clergy that can get the ear of the magistrate.'[30] In presenting the Petition and Advice to Oliver the Speaker said 'the permission of the exercise of more religions than one ... I hope shall never be in these nations.'[31] The Petition represented a victory for the religious conservatives, though the church still lacked the sort of discipline they wanted to see and which Baxter had tried to build up in his widely-imitated Worcestershire Association of ministers – a sort of voluntary Presbyterianism from below. But voluntary discipline of this sort is a contradiction in terms. Baxter was one of those who would have been prepared to accept the House of Cromwell as *de facto* monarchs. When it failed, his demand for discipline made him ready to pay the price not only of a Stuart monarchy but even of episcopacy.[32]

In 1652 Hugh Peter had enthusiastically urged New Englanders to return to their mother country, as he himself had done in 1641. By 1654 he thought they should stay where they were, because of England's 'great uncertainty and changes'. But by March 1658 the uncertainty was over, at least for him. 'Truly upon all accounts,' he wrote, 'I think New England best, if clothing and bread may be had'.[33] He failed to take his own

advice, and was hanged, drawn and quartered three years
later.

Baxter, the Quaker John Camm and the Rumper
Slingsby Bethel all suggested that Oliver deliberately
maintained divisions among the religious sects in order
to play one off against another. His attempts to keep on
terms with the religious radicals, his many patient conversations with George Fox (who advised him to reject
the crown) and other Quakers, with John Rogers and
other Fifth Monarchists, fit this interpretation. It also
explains Cromwell's *de facto* tolerance of papists: he inherited from his Stuart predecessors the policy of trying
to win over those among the Catholics who were prepared to give guarantees of loyalty: it was only under
pressure from Parliament that this policy weakened. We
can indeed see Charles II as the heir to Oliver's policy in
his attempt to build up a party on which he could rely
against the persecuting majority in the House of Commons, a party uniting protestant and Catholic dissenters –
though Charles's personal sympathies were with the latter
as Oliver's were with the former.

IV

Oliver's health was failing from the beginning of 1658.
He was 'at his wit's end', contemporary observers tell us,
'not well in body or mind', 'mad', 'still sick and keeps his
bed'. 'The poor man seems to speak and act much like
one that have lost his lock of strength and wisdom that
he once had', runs a phrase that anticipates *Samson
Agonistes,* adding 'surely he hath not wanted Dalilahs to
deprive him of it'.[34] The analogy can be extended. Milton's
Samson is not only the poet himself: he is also a symbol
for the Army, whose *Declaration* of 14 June 1647, made
by 'no mere mercenary army', he echoes:

I was no private, but a person raised
With strength sufficient and command from heaven
To free my country. If their servile minds
Me their deliverer sent would not receive,
But to their masters gave me up for nought
Th' unworthier they; whence to this day they serve . . .

Samson's 'known offence' which 'disabled' him had been a betrayal similar to that against which the poet had warned in 1655: 'Unless you will subjugate the propensity to avarice, to ambition . . . you will find that you have cherished a more stubborn and intractable despot at home than ever you encountered in the field. . . . You will become royalists as well as they, and liable to be subdued by the same enemies or by others in your turn.'

The final blow to Oliver's health came from the painful illness (cancer) of his favourite daughter, Elizabeth. She died on 6 August 1658; pneumonia carried off the Protector less than a month later, on his lucky day, the day of Dunbar and Worcester, 3 September. The storm which preceded Oliver's death was the greatest known in the memory of most Englishmen, and was seen by contemporaries as symbolic.

> Tossed in a furious hurricane
> Did Oliver give up his reign.

wrote Samuel Butler.[35] Oliver remained ambiguous to the last in his attitude to the hereditary principle. Did he nominate his eldest son as his successor, as Thurloe said he did? Or did the Council get together and decide that the succession of Richard would be the least divisive of all possible solutions, as Ludlow and Burnet suggest? The evidence is 'very dark and imperfect'.[36]

The other Elizabeth Cromwell, Oliver's wife, survived till 1672. She remains a shadowy figure. 'Thou art dearer to me than any creature,' Cromwell wrote to her after Dunbar, adding rather dampingly: 'Let that suffice.' The only letter from her that survives is mildly nagging: 'And truly my dear if you would think of what I put you in mind of some, it might be to as much purpose as others, writing sometimes a letter to the President and some time to the Speaker. . . .'

It was Oliver's cofferer John Maidstone who wrote the simplest epitaph after his master's death, in a letter to John Winthrop: 'A larger soul, I think, hath seldom dwelt in a house of clay than his was.' Let that suffice.

V

The Lord Protector's effigy lay in state for many weeks after his death, 'multitudes daily crowding to see this glorious but mournful sight'. We are reminded of the crowds that thronged to gaze on Lenin's embalmed corpse in the Red Square. But two years after Oliver's death his corpse was dug up and hanged at Tyburn.

One of those who went to look at Oliver lying in state was the Quaker, Edward Burroughs. He was horrified that the man who had led the New Model Army, the great enemy of idolatry, should now himself be set up as an idol for people to gape at. 'I knew the man, when he was living, and had the knowledge of his spirit'; and Burroughs was sure Oliver would have disapproved of the show:

But upon another consideration, I said 'This is come to pass after this manner, though he was once zealous against popery, yet he did too much forget that good cause, and too much sought the greatness and honour of the world, and loved the praise of men, and took flattering titles and vain respects of deceitful men, and many great abominations were upheld through him, as tithes and old mass-houses and ordaining of ministers by men's will, and the false worships and sprinkling of infants and such-like popish stuff; . . . and he suffered the servants of the Lord to be persecuted and imprisoned

for denying and crying against such things as were popish;
... that all men might see the first cause is lost'.... And I
began to recall ... what a gallant instrument for the Lord
he once was: and how many glorious and noble victories
God once gave him.... And then said I, 'Alas, alas! Is it
ended all in this? All his former good service for God and
the nations? ... And is this the end and final farewell of once
noble Oliver? What, only the sight of an image carried
and set up?'[37]

Curiously, the adoring steward and the censorious
Quaker agree on Oliver's nobility of spirit. Thomas Carlyle
would have thought they were right.[38]

VI

When we try to grasp Oliver Cromwell's elusive personality, it seems that he had some of the qualities associated
with a manic depressive. Both his own doctor at Huntingdon and the specialist Sir Theodore Mayerne remarked
on his great inclination towards melancholy. A nineteenth-
century doctor diagnosed hypochondriasis, the result of
living in low, marshy country.[39] Cromwell was always
liable to be ill in a crisis, as in the spring of 1647, or on
receipt of bad news, as in 1655 when he heard of the
failure to capture Hispaniola. On the other hand there
is much evidence for his manic phases. 'He was of a
sanguine complexion,' wrote Richard Baxter, whose tem-
perament was very different; 'naturally of such a vivacity,
hilarity and alacrity as another man is when he hath
drunken a cup too much.'[40] (A similar remark was made
about Major-General Harrison.) 'I am very often judged
for one that goes too fast that way' ('in our affections
and desires'), Cromwell admitted to the Army Council.
'It is the property of men that are as I am, to be full of

apprehensions that dangers are not so real as imaginary; to be always making haste, and more sometimes than good speed.'

This accords with his elation on the battlefield. At Dunbar 'he did laugh so excessively as if he had been drunk, and his eyes sparkled with spirits. . . . The same fit of laughter seized him just before the battle of Naseby.' It accords too with the decisive action which sometimes followed weeks of indecision, as in the dissolution of the Rump and of his last two Parliaments. Solemn discussions about the future constitution in January 1648 ended by Oliver throwing a cushion at Ludlow's head and being chased out of the room by him. At the signing of the King's death warrant Oliver and Henry Marten were inking one another's faces like schoolboys. This capacity for horseplay, his 'familiar rustic carriage with his soldiers in sporting' (Baxter), naturally endeared him to his troops. 'Oliver loved an innocent jest,' said one of his officers.

Cromwell was no intellectual: the cast of his mind was practical, pragmatic, never doctrinaire. At Putney he left the discussion of theory to Ireton, intervening himself only with practical proposals for compromise – which did not appeal to the ideologues on either side. He had not much use for introspection. 'The voice of fear is, "If I had done this, if I had avoided that, how well it had been with me".' These were vain reasonings. Baxter noted another characteristic of Cromwell's – his preference for listening to others rather than arguing with them. In 1656 he and his Council heard even the intransigent republican John Bradshaw 'with patience, I must acknowledge'.[41] Sir William Waller put it unflatteringly but not inaccurately when he wrote that 'whilst he was cautious of his own words (not putting forth too many, lest they should betray his thoughts) he made others talk until he had, as it were, sifted them, and known their most intimate designs.' We see the technique in action in the many interviews which Abbott prints. This could lead to later disillusionment. John Rogers said in February 1655 'Every man almost that talks with you is apt to think you of his opinion, my Lord, whatever he be.' The point was valid: but so was Oliver's swift retort, 'Nay, *you* do not.' Rogers's remark helps to explain why so many of Cromwell's associates later became so bitter against him. The Scot Blair thought him 'an egregious dissembler and a great liar'.[42] The Levellers, Colonel Hutchinson and Ludlow came to the same conclusion. Lilburne, who began by believing Cromwell was 'sound at the heart and not rotten-cored', 'the most absolute single-hearted great man in England, untainted and unbiassed with ends of your own', thought very differently a few years later. Cromwell's passion for preserving unity, especially of the Army, but also of the supporters of the Cause in general, made him almost instinctively move towards those he had just outmanoeuvred and defeated, so as not to drive them to desperation: but the tactic was liable to misinterpretation.

On one point there is general agreement: he lacked the vulgar externals of ambition. Those who like to reduce politics to personal and family rivalries can make much of the quarrel between the Cromwell and Montagu houses. At the beginning of the century the Cromwells were the greater family. But by the 1620s the prudent lawyer Henry Montagu had become first Earl of Manchester; and had bought Hinchinbrooke from the improvident Cromwells. In the affair of Huntingdon corporation Manchester humiliated Oliver, and as we have seen they crossed swords again over Cromwell's refusal to pay his knighthood fine and his defence of the Fenmen.[43] But the sword proved mightier than the gown: by 1645 Oliver had triumphed over his commanding officer, the second Earl of Manchester, and reasserted his family's supremacy in the county. In the 1650s Edward Montagu was a client and faithful agent of the Protector's, though he managed

to trim his sails in 1660 and win out in the end – to become
Earl of Sandwich and Viscount *Hinchinbrooke*.

Oliver made money out of his political career, of course.
He had his army pay (£1095 a year as Lieutenant-General,
plus substantial allowances), and for a time that of Lord-
Lieutenant of Ireland (£8000 a year, £3650 when in
England). In January 1646 he was voted £2500 a year in
lands, of which a year later he forwent £1000 a year for
5 years. (He was already potentially a landowner in Ireland by virtue of his subscription to the re-conquest
in 1641.) After the battle of Worcester Parliament voted
Cromwell lands worth £4000 *per annum*. So Oliver was
already a considerable landowner before December 1654,
when Parliament settled £70,000 a year on the Protector for the expenses of his household and family.

Sir Philip Warwick recalled the 'mean figure' which
Cromwell cut at the beginning of the Long Parliament.
In August 1652 the Venetian Ambassador commented on
'his unpretending manner of life, remote from all display
and pomp, so different from the former fashion of this
kingdom.' Men noticed the 'plain black clothes, with grey
worsted stockings' which Oliver wore when he dissolved
the Rump. Even when he was Lord Protector a Quaker –
a severe critic – commented on his rough coat, 'not worth
three shillings a yard', and his court was so far from
ostentation that royalist propagandists preferred to con-
centrate on Mrs Cromwell's meanness. This changed a
good deal during the second Protectorate: in June 1658
Lady Conway said – rather surprisingly – that Cromwell
'has introduced the Spanish habit and port'.[44] But presumably this was, or was believed to be, politically necessary.
Cromwell's remark to the French Ambassador in 1647,
that a man never rises so high as when he does not know
where he is going,[45] seems as true of him as such remarks
ever can be. He had few illusions, at any rate after the
traumatic experiences of 1647–9 and 1653. This is sug-

gested by his remark at Northampton to John Lambert in June 1650 about a cheering crowd: 'These very persons would shout as much if you and I were going to be hanged.' Lambert recalled the remark 10 years later, when he entered Northampton on his way to the imprisonment which ended only with his death.

Historians are beginning to appreciate how much the interregnum in general and Cromwell in particular did for British education and British cultural life. But the legend of the philistine Puritan, hostile to art and culture, dies hard in popular imagination. Dr Nuttall has, I hope, established the fact that most cathedrals whose desecration is conventionally ascribed to Oliver Cromwell were in fact desecrated by sixteenth-century bishops or (more rarely) by the troops of either side in the civil war in the course of military operations or out of control of their officers. The only reliable evidence we have on the subject invariably shows Cromwell trying to protect the monuments of antiquity.[40] In May 1649 Cromwell, fresh from shooting down the Levellers at Burford, told the University of Oxford that 'no commonwealth could flourish without learning'. In December he assured John Tillotson, the future Archbishop who married Oliver's niece, that he was 'ready to embrace all opportunities of showing favour to the universities'. Nor were these mere words. As Chancellor he did a great deal for Oxford: his generosity is still commemorated by the Bodleian Library. Owen, his favourite chaplain, was Dean of Christ Church and Vice-Chancellor; one of the prebends of Christ Church was Oliver's brother-in-law, Peter French. John Wilkins, who married French's widow, became Warden of Wadham and centre of the group which later formed the Royal Society; Jonathan Goddard, physician to Cromwell's armies in Ireland and Scotland, became Warden of Merton. Even Clarendon admitted that Oxford

under the Protectorate 'Yielded a harvest of extraordinary
good and sound knowledge in all parts of learning'.[47]

In Glasgow Cromwell made good a thirty-year-old promise of £200 towards new buildings which Charles I
had not honoured. The Council in Scotland in March
1655 was instructed to reform the universities, and they
received further financial assistance, mostly from church
lands, as in 1650 Parliament had endowed Trinity College,
Dublin, with lands formerly belonging to the Archbishop
of Dublin and the Dean and Chapter of St Patrick's. A
Scottish College of Physicians was set up. From 1650
Cromwell interested himself in a project for a new university at Durham, primarily in order to help with the
propagation of the gospel in those dark places; it actually
came into existence under the Protectorate. History, and
especially Sir Walter Ralegh's *History of the World*,
Oliver recommended to his eldest son, together with
mathematics and cosmography: 'These fit for public services, for which a man is born.' We do not know whether
Oliver kept up his early interest in mathematics,[48] but he
was a friend of the mathematician Edmund Wingate,
patronized John Pell, and regarded 'mathematical demonstration' as the most certain form of truth.

Cromwell was very far from being the Puritan killjoy
of vulgar convention. 'To keep wine out of the country
lest men should be drunk' seemed to him an utterly absurd suggestion. His Council used to meet on Sundays,
and the 1654 Parliament had its opening session on a
Sunday. Indignant MPs retaliated by passing a sabba-
tarian bill. Oliver was fond of music and horses. Dr
Scholes has taught us to see his court as an important
patron of music:[49] so it was of painting, sculpture and
literature. The miniaturist Samuel Cooper held office
under the Protector.[50] Sir William Davenant's *The Siege
of Rhodes* was performed in 1656, the first English
opera, and was followed in 1658 by the same dramatist's

The Cruelty of the Spaniards in Peru and *The History of Sir Francis Drake,* whose propaganda uses to the Protectorate are obvious. It was under Oliver's rule that actresses first appeared on the London stage. Brian Walton's *Polyglot Bible,* a major cooperative work, mentions with gratitude Oliver's support for the project; after the Restoration this was disavowed and it was said to have been inserted merely at the insistence of 'the great dragon.' Among men of letters who enjoyed Cromwell's patronage and sang his praises we may name Milton, Marvell, George Wither, Edmund Waller, John Dryden, Samuel Hartlib and Thomas Sprat, later the historian of the Royal Society and a bishop. Thanks to the intervention of Milton, the Protector restored confiscated Irish property to Spenser's grandson.

VIII

THE PEOPLE OF ENGLAND
AND THE PEOPLE OF GOD

When we shall come to give an account to them [the electorate] we shall be able to say, Oh! we have quarrelled for and we contested for the liberty of England.

CROMWELL, Speech to first Parliament, 12 September 1654

The condition of the people [is] such as the major part a great deal are persons disaffected and engaged against us.

CROMWELL, Conference with Committee of Parliament on reducing the armed forces, 23 November 1654

The consequences of the immediate extension of the elective franchise to every male adult would be to place power in the hands of men who have been rendered brutal and stupid and ferocious by ages of slavery.

P. B. SHELLEY, *A Proposal for putting reform to the vote throughout the kingdom,* 1817

I

Few politicians can have been so innocent of political theory as Oliver Cromwell. 'I can tell you, sirs,' he said to two MPs in 1641, 'what I would not have, though I cannot what I would'.[1] He truthfully claimed not to be wedded and glued to forms of government. They were 'but a moral thing', 'dross and dung in comparison of Christ'.[2] In the Putney Debates Ireton and the Levellers discussed fundamental principles: was the vote a natural right of freeborn Englishmen, or was it a right attached to certain forms of property? Cromwell intervened with practical suggestions for compromise, not to say horse-trading: perhaps some copyholders might be given the vote? He is said to have cited Buchanan on the responsibility of kings, but he was no republican: his enemies described him as 'king-ridden'. Early in 1648 Cromwell and his friends annoyed the republican Ludlow by refusing to commit themselves to a preference for monarchy, aristocracy or democracy: 'Any of them might be good in themselves, or for us, according as providence should direct us.' The farthest Oliver would go was to say that a republic might be desirable but was not feasible – and one suspects that he only said this to please Ludlow. As late as 12 January 1649 Cromwell opposed a motion to abolish the House of Lords, with the highly characteristic argument that it would be madness at a time when unity was so essential. Political practice was always more important for him than constitutional theory. He subsequently justified the abolition of King and Lords not on any ground of political principle but 'because they did not perform their trust'. If Oliver, as Major Huntington alleged, said that 'every single man is judge of justice and right, as to the good and ill of a kingdom',[3] it was an *ad hoc* argument rather than a settled conviction: I suspect he only said that godly men might sometimes have to take such decisions on their own responsibility.

Oliver was associated with no specific '-ism' in politics, just as he was not known as a member of any religious sect: no dissenting body today claims him as one of their early members. This was not inconvenient politically. The sterility of mere opportunist empiricism, or action for action's sake, was mitigated by Oliver's belief that he conformed his actions to God's will.[4] But of course he had his social and political prejudices. He always thought 'a settlement of somewhat with monarchical power in it' likely to be best for England. He disliked perpetual Parliaments and arbitrary committees, because of their tendency to interfere with the rights of private property. Here we see that fear of a strong executive which haunted the English gentry from Laud to James II, and which was roused especially by Cromwell's Major-Generals. To his first Parliament he defined the four fundamentals of the Instrument of Government as (i) government by a single person and Parliament; (ii) no Parliament to make itself perpetual; (iii) liberty of conscience; (iv) control of the militia by Protector and Parliament.

Oliver had no use for democracy. 'Where is there any bound or limit set,' he asked at Putney, 'if . . . men that have no interest but the interest of breathing' shall have voices in elections? But again he might be prepared to compromise: it was only when he saw that 'they which had no interest in estate at all should choose a representation (and they, being the most, were likely to choose those of their own condition), that this drive at a levelling and parity etc. he could not but disclaim and discountenance'.[5] He seemed at Putney to accept Ireton's Hobbist view that men should keep their covenants made, unless (a characteristic escape clause) God's providence clearly spoke otherwise. The revolutionary leader could be very coy about using violent means. 'That you have by force I look upon as nothing,' he said,[6] except on those not infrequent occasions when Oliver decided that God wished it to be used: such were, we must suppose, the civil war, the Army's interference in politics in 1647, the execution of Charles I, the dissolution of the Rump, the rule of the Major-Generals.

In so far as Oliver thought about the social structure, it was in wholly traditional terms. 'A nobleman, a gentleman, a yeoman: that is a good interest of the nation, and a great one,' he told his first Parliament; 'we would keep up nobility and gentry', he assured his second. In these speeches he equated poor men with bad men, and said that if a commonwealth must suffer, it was better that it should suffer from the rich than from the poor. His enemies realized much more clearly than he did (in the 1640s, at least) how far his insistence on promotion by merit in his army, and on the career open to the talents generally, subverted this traditional social order. Even in the 1650s it was Oliver's practice, Thurloe later told Charles II, 'to seek out men for places, not places for men'.

The Self-Denying Ordinance and the New Model Army were in fact portentous events in the modernization of English political life. In medieval society there had been two types of revolt. A great lord might abjure his fealty, and levy war against the king as his equal: this type of revolt had ceased to be a serious threat by the sixteenth century. What survived was peasant revolt, which threw up its own leaders, often claiming to be sent by God, and tried to persuade gentlemen to come along with

them, ostensibly under compulsion. The advantage of this
was that the Cades, the Askes, ran the risks and paid the
penalties: the greater men could betray the revolt at the
appropriate time and realign themselves with authority.[7]
The Self-Denying Ordinance rejected the traditional
ruling-class leaders with their feudal following, and yet
Parliament took full responsibility for the revolution:
leaders who had come to the fore in action were accepted,
however reluctantly, as commanders of the New Model
Army. The Earl of Essex's indignation at 'the audacity
of the common people' marks the beginning of a new
epoch. It was Cromwell who initiated it. Notwithstanding
the wealth which some individuals amassed, the government of the Commonwealth and Protectorate was less
corrupt than that of the monarchy.[8] The payment of
salaries and a diminished reliance on fees, perquisites and
bribes, the Council's reluctance to impose oaths on subjects,[9] are all evidence of something more modern. But
the civil service was still rudimentary: Cromwell's
Council dealt with far too much trivial detail for efficiency.

Underlying all the disputes between Oliver Cromwell,
the Levellers and his Parliaments, was one fundamental
problem: the problem of the electorate. After 1647 the
Revolution had gone much further than the average MP,
or the average gentleman or merchant whom he represented, could approve. Religious toleration, for instance,
was something which no Parliament elected on the traditional franchise would ever accept. The Levellers, who
agreed with Cromwell in wanting toleration to be preserved at all costs, favoured a wide extension of the
franchise to all except servants and paupers. Cromwell
and his like found this unacceptable on social grounds,
and they also had reasonable doubts of its feasibility. The
mass of the population was totally unsophisticated politically, very much under the influence of landlords and

parsons: to give such men the vote (with no secret ballot, since most of them were illiterate) would be to strengthen rather than to weaken the power of the conservatives. Shelley's argument quoted as epigraph to this chapter was equally valid in the mid-seventeenth century. 'In most parts,' said Richard Baxter, 'the major vote of the vulgar ... is ruled by money and therefore by their landlords.'[10] 'Everywhere the greater party are for the King', admitted a pamphlet of 17 October 1648. 'If the common vote of the giddy multitude must rule the whole, how quickly would their own interest, peace and safety be dashed and broken!'[11] What if the mob 'had demanded that Charles should be restored to the kingdom?' Milton asked in 1654.[12]

This was a real problem, a problem which recurred in later revolutions. Rousseau thought that men might have to be forced to be free; the Jacobin dictatorship, and the Bolshevik dictatorship of the proletariat, justified themselves as covering the period in which the sovereign people were being educated up to their new responsibilities. The Levellers, having failed to capture control of the Army, never faced the necessity of holding the rest of the population down. Their reluctance to use force is sympathetic, but it helps to account for their practical failure.

Many others tried to grapple with the problem. Hugh Peter in 1646 wanted to use the Army 'to teach peasants to understand liberty'.[13] In November 1650 Thomas Scot, a member of the Council of State, wrote to Cromwell that 'England is not as France, a meadow to be mowed [by taxation] as often as the governors please; our interest is to do our work with as little grievance to our new people, *scarce yet proselitized*, as is possible'.[14] In November 1651 that shrewd and thoughtful observer Colonel John Jones was asking 'what qualifications will persuade a people sensible of their present burdens, and not of the reasons

and necessity of them, to choose those persons that laid
the burdens (or their adherents) to be the next representative? What interest in England is like to carry the
general vote?' If electoral qualifications were imposed,
who would decide whether they had been observed? 'If
force interpose, will they not cry out that their freedom
is invaded? If the hearts of the people be generally for
the present government and governors, what need Army
and garrisons to be kept on foot? I had rather do a people
good though against their wills, than please them in show
only. . . . Let the Commonwealth have some time to take
root in the interests of men' before we risk elections.[15]
That squarely posed the problem. 'We . . . would have
enfranchised the people', declared the regicide John
Cook, looking back from 1660, 'if the nation had not been
more delighted in servitude than in freedom'.[16]

Milton in 1651 defended the republican government as
'such as our circumstances and schisms permit; it is not the
most desirable, but only as good as the stubborn struggles
of the wicked citizens allow it to be'.[17] He parted company
with Cromwell's government when it seemed to him to
be shedding its revolutionary ideals, and moved closer
to the position of Sir Henry Vane, who in 1656 declared
that 'sovereignty . . . resides . . . in the whole body of adherents to this Cause'.[18] The great difficulty is to show
'how the depraved, corrupted and self-interested will of
man, in the great body which we call the people, being
once left to its own free motion, shall be prevailed with to
espouse their true public interest'.[19] By 1660 Milton too
had despairingly decided 'more just it is, doubtless, if it
come to force, that a less number compel a greater to
retain, which can be no wrong to them, their liberty, than
that a greater number, for the pleasure of their baseness,
compel a less most injuriously to be their fellow-slaves'.[20]
The contortions of the prose reflect the reluctance of the
thought.

The Leveller answer had been the Agreement of the People, a new social contract refounding the state, acceptance of which alone should qualify for the franchise. The Rump of the Long Parliament tried to solve the problem by devising a new franchise – subsequently adopted in the Instrument of Government – which redistributed seats for the House of Commons in a way which roughly followed the distribution of taxable wealth. By disfranchising a number of smaller boroughs and substituting a new £200 county franchise for the 40s freeholder vote, it was no doubt hoped to ensure that economically independent men would prevail rather than dependents of the great. The only historian who has investigated this question concludes that this did indeed happen in Cheshire.[21] The Parliament of 1654 voted to restore the 40s freeholder franchise. Some efforts were made by Cromwell's government to remodel corporations, thought to be Presbyterian strongholds. Oliver's insistence that MPs must accept the four 'fundamentals' of the Instrument, and the written constitutions which proliferated in this period (Heads of Proposals, Agreement of the People, Instrument of Government, Petition and Advice, as well as the utopias of Winstanley, Harrington and many others) all testify to the need which was felt for placing restrictions on the newly-won sovereignty of the representatives of the propertied electorate. At no other period of English history did paper constitutions have such a vogue.

In July 1653 Cromwell told the Barebones Parliament that they existed because the majority of the electorate was not yet 'brought to own the interest of Jesus Christ,' not yet fit to call or be called. How right he was! His government could not win an election even with the Major-Generals to run it. A hundred or more members had to be excluded from each of his Parliaments before there was any hope of cooperation.

Nor was it only a matter of safeguarding the Cause. A Presbyterian in 1646 had declared: 'A tyranny is far better than an anarchy, whether in church or state:' and he defined anarchy as a condition 'where every man may say and do what is right in his own eyes'.[22] Such anti-democrats now supported the military dictatorship by asking the simple question: 'Were it not better we should have any government ... than none at all? That of the Great Turk than of the rabble rout?'[23] (This was expressed with greater theoretical sophistication by Anthony Ascham, John Dury and others.)[24] For the generals, whose illegal actions had brought the régime into existence, its preservation increasingly became a matter of self-preservation.[25] Lambert put this with brutal clarity in the House of Commons in December 1656: 'If a Parliament should be chosen according to the general spirit and temper of the nation, and if there should not be a check upon such election, there may creep into this House who may come to sit as our judges for all we have done in this Parliament, or at any other time or place.... We cannot tell what kind of Parliaments other ages may produce. We ought to take care to leave things certain'.[26] He anticipated by only four years: and then had twenty-three years in jail to reflect on the correctness of his analysis. In between the generals had desperately insisted, at every crisis of events, that there should be an Other House, or a 'select senate' (composed of themselves) which should give constitutional respectability to the Army's veto over Parliament. It is their distinctive contribution to the political thinking of the epoch.

II

One obvious difference between the English and later
revolutions is that the French revolutionaries had English experience to draw on and the Russian revolutionaries
had French experience as well, of which they were very
conscious. But the English Revolution had no predecessors. The sixteenth-century Revolt of the Netherlands
anticipated it in some respects: but that was a revolt
against alien domination, and a revolt led by protestants
against a régime trying forcibly to maintain Catholic uniformity. Both these features were lacking in England. The
English Revolution in consequence lacked a revolutionary
ideology: there was no Jean-Jacques Rousseau or Karl
Marx. There were of course many intellectual, religious
and political discontents: but before 1642 they had not
crystallized into the form of a revolutionary theory or
even an idea that fundamental change might be required.
The leaders of Parliament in the early 1640s believed
themselves to be the true conservatives and traditionalists.
They wanted to return to the days of Good Queen Bess,
if not further back.

So whereas the trinities of the later revolutions – liberty,
equality, fraternity; peace, bread and land – demanded
something *new*, something to be fought for and achieved
in the future, the trinity of the English revolutionaries –
religion, liberty and property – was intended to defend
what already existed, or was believed to exist. Get rid of
the doctrinal innovations of Laud, and the true protestant
religion would be safe: get rid of the arbitrary practices
of the eleven years' personal rule, and liberty and property would be safe. Early Parliamentarian theories were
defensive: in place of a theory of revolution was the
belief that all ills were due to evil counsellors, to papists

and Arminians in high places. Any theories which probed deeper simply looked further back. But the further back the Golden Age is placed, the more uncertain the evidence about it becomes: the greater the possibility of disagreement. The appeal to the good old days of the free Anglo-Saxons meant something very different for Levellers and Diggers from what it had meant for Sir Edward Coke;[27] Presbyterians and Quakers drew different lessons from the primitive church. Really backward-looking theory becomes forward-looking, creatively revolutionary.

So when, in the early 1640s, men found themselves unexpectedly and unwillingly facing a revolutionary situation, a situation which demanded new thinking, they were ill-equipped for the task. They had to improvise. What was to hand was the Bible, available for a century in English translation, which men had been encouraged to study as the source of all wisdom. There are dangerous doctrines in the Bible: denunciations of the rich by Old Testament prophets, suggestions of human equality in the New Testament. The Lutheran doctrine of the priesthood of all believers itself contains explosive possibilities, for there was no certain means of identifying visible saints. During the post-reformation century social stability in England had been safeguarded against the logic of protestant Christianity by the episcopal hierarchy and its courts, by ecclesiastical control of education and the censorship, and by the doctrine of the sinfulness of the mass of mankind. In the 1640s the institutional restraints collapsed with the fall of bishops, and the attempt to build up a Presbyterian disciplinary system in their place failed almost as totally. Only sin remained. But religious toleration and the lack of an effective ecclesiastical censorship allowed wholly unorthodox groups claiming to be visible saints to propagate their subversive ideas; even the fundamental doctrine of the sinfulness of the majority of men and women could be challenged. Levellers demanded a wide extension of the suffrage, regardless of whether 'the multitude' was godly or ungodly; other religious radicals – Ranters and Antinomians – were led by the spirit to reject many traditional moral restraints; Quakers saw a spark of the divine in all men, and rejected outward forms of social subordination in the name of Christian equality; Diggers demanded heaven for the poor on earth now. No wonder all conservatives rallied to oppose toleration. Thurloe differentiated sharply between 'the vile Levelling party' and 'the good and godly'.[28]

'Religion was not the thing at first contested for', Oliver rightly emphasized, 'but God brought it to that issue at last'. His belief in the necessity of toleration for all those with the root of the matter in them separated him from most of his own social class, and aligned him with the political radicals. Like Milton, he followed out the logic of the protestant doctrine of the priesthood of all believers. Since the spirit blew where it listed, it was dangerous for any mere mortal to repress those who claimed to be speaking in God's name, for thereby a truth might be suppressed. Truth had in the past appeared in unexpected places, and in forms unwelcome to authority. More practically, it was foolish when fighting a civil war to refuse the help of enthusiasts who hated the common enemy, and whose enthusiasm itself made them excellent fighting material. Disagreements would no doubt be cleared up by discussion after victory was won.

Cromwell – and it is one of his very great contributions to English history – clung tenaciously to this belief that truth was not certainly possessed by any one sect. He never expressed himself more forcefully than when he besought the Scottish Presbyterians to think it possible that they might be mistaken. This helps to explain Oliver's patience in discussions with men who profoundly disagreed with him – George Fox, John Rogers, Edmund

Ludlow. He drew the line, of course, at Catholics and
Episcopalians, for he held the Mass to be idolatrous, and
both popery and prelacy in his view were repressive
systems which might prevent Christian verity from expressing itself. But he was more tolerant to both creeds –
in England – in practice than in theory.

He also drew the line at immoral Ranters, and at religious beliefs which led to politically subversive actions –
a line which he perhaps drew at different places before
and after his was the authority in danger of subversion.
He employed Quakers in his own household, and when he
asked, apropos the sect, 'Shall I disown them because
they will not put off their hats?' he expected the answer
No.²⁹ Where Cromwell parted company from the radicals,
theologically, was in his distinction between 'the people'
and 'the people of God'. The latter were, in Biblical and
Foxean terms, conceived as a remnant. They might be
found in strange places, might know no social distinc-
tions; but they would always be a minority. The saints,
so strong in the New Model Army, were by definition set
apart from the worldly majority. 'How can the kingdom
be the saints' when the ungodly are electors and elected
to govern?' a pamphleteer had asked in 1649.³⁰ Calvinism
could not be a democratic doctrine. 'The word election
intendeth the taking out of the best not of the worst out
of things' a gentleman of Kent wrote shortly before
Cromwell was born.³¹ If Oliver was in London on 31 May
1643 he probably heard a sermon in which the Commons
were told that 'the godly part of a nation are the national
church'.³² The Protector agreed that 'the interest of honest
men is the interest of the kingdom', and that the people
should have 'what's for their good, not what pleases them'.
That was his answer to the impossibility of finding an
electorate.

After the dissolution of the Barebones Parliament, I
suggested, Oliver no longer saw himself as a Moses lead-

ing God's people to the promised land.[33] But he still enjoyed a reputation with the godly which enormously
strengthened his hand in the disputes of the period,
against Parliament, Army and republican radicals alike.
'How hard a thing it will be', wrote the Rev. Samuel
Oates in December 1654, 'for the people of God to oppose
the Lord Protector in anything, seeing he hath been so
great an instrument in many things for their good. And
all the great things which the people of God have had
done for them have been done by him'.[34] Knowledge that
men thought thus must have been a great temptation
to Oliver.

The strength of revolutionary Calvinism lay in its stress
on the godly remnant, on the solidarity against their
worldly enemies of those who recognized one another as
saints. Such a doctrine excluded by definition the possibility of democracy, which became possible only for those
who rejected Calvinism. The breakdown of Calvinism in
the mid-seventeenth century is one of the great turning
points in intellectual history. The old Arminianism of the
Laudians, tied to the sacraments of the church, was
limited by its emphasis on priestly control; the new
Arminianism of John Goodwin and Milton and the
Quakers contained the possibility of full human equality.
Mr D. P. Walker's excellent book, *The Decline of Hell*,
shows how in the seventeenth century men – and especially
the religious and political radicals – came to question the
theological assumption that God had condemned the mass
of mankind to an eternity of torment, and to assert
the right of the majority to heaven. Sin began in some
men's minds to lose its power as the great deterrent.
Theories of democracy rose as hell declined. One of the
tragedies of the old nonconformity after 1660 is that it
was clinging on to and aridly chewing over the Calvinist
dogmas which had changed the world in the preceding

century, but which had nothing to offer the post-revolutionary world.

It is time to look at the Calvinist contribution to the ideology of Cromwell and the English revolutionaries.

IX

PROVIDENCE AND OLIVER CROMWELL

I am one of those whose heart God hath drawn out to wait
for some extraordinary dispensations, according to those
promises that he hath held forth of things to be accomplished
in the later time, and I cannot but think that God is beginning of them.

CROMWELL, at Putney, 1 November 1647

An higher force him pushed
Still from behind, and it before him rushed.
MARVELL, *The First Anniversary of the
Government under O.C.*

The reference to Providence was with Cromwell an infallible
indication of a political change of front.
S. R. GARDINER, *The Great Civil War* (1894), IV, p. 288

'This doctrine of predestination is the root of puritanism,
and puritanism is the root of all rebellions and disobedient
untractableness in Parliament, etc., and of all schism and
sauciness in the country, nay in the church itself; making
many thousands of our people, and too great a part of the
gentlemen of the land, very Leightons in their hearts', – which
Leighton had published not long before a most pestilential
seditious book against the bishops, . . . in which he excited
the people to strike the bishops under the fifth rib, reviling
the Queen by the name of a daughter of Heth.

MATTHEW BROOKS, Master of Trinity College, Cambridge, to Archbishop Abbott, 12 December 1630,
quoted by P. Heylyn, *Historical and Miscellaneous
Tracts* (1681), p. 539

I

Predestination is at the heart of protestantism. Luther saw that it was the only guarantee of the Covenant. 'For if you doubt, or disdain to know that God foreknows and wills all things, not contingently but necessarily and immutably, how can you believe confidently, trust to and depend upon his promises?' Without predestination, 'Christian faith is utterly destroyed, and the promises of God and the whole Gospel entirely fall to the ground: for the greatest and only consolation of Christians in their adversities is the knowing that God lies not, but does all things immutably, and that his will cannot be resisted, changed or hindered'.[1] *Ein fester Burg ist unser Gott.* Luther declared that he would not have wanted free will, even if it could have been granted to him: only God can make salvation *certain*, for some if not for all.[2] Indeed the whole point for Luther lies in the *uniqueness* of the elect. Once touched with divine grace they are differentiated from the mass of humanity: their consciousness of salvation will make them work consciously to glorify God. The psychological effects of this *conscious* segregation of a group from the mass is enormous.

Calvin went a step further and boldly proclaimed that God was useless to humanity unless he had knowable purposes which we can trust and with which we can cooperate. 'What avails it, in short, to know a God with whom we have nothing to do? ... How can the idea of God enter your mind without instantly giving rise to the thought that since you are his workmanship, you are bound, by the very law of creation, to submit to his authority?'[3] 'Ignorance of Providence is the greatest of all miseries, and the knowledge of it the highest happiness.'[4] Faith gives us 'sure certainty and complete security of mind', of a sort that is self-evident to those who possess it and inexplicable to those who do not.[5]

Men have often commented on the apparent paradox of a predestinarian theological system producing in its adherents an emphasis on effort, on moral energy. One explanation that has been offered is that, for the Calvinist, faith revealed itself in works, and that therefore the only way in which an individual could be assured of his own salvation was by scrutinizing his behaviour carefully night and day to see whether he did in fact bring forth works worthy of salvation. It is by means of works performed through grace, in Calvin's view, that the elect 'make their calling sure, and, like trees, are judged by their fruits. . . . We dream not of a faith which is devoid of good works, nor of a justification which can exist without them.'[6] This attitude is expressed by Sir Simonds D'Ewes. After listing sixty-four signs or marks from several graces which gave him assurance to a better life, he added: 'I found much comfort and reposedness of spirit from them; being more careful than ever before to walk warily, to avoid sin and lead a godly life.' This fact convinced him that papists and Anabaptists were utterly mistaken in arguing that assurance of salvation brings forth presumption and a careless and wicked life. On the contrary, 'when a lively faith and a godly life are joined together, and are the groundwork of the signs and marks of a blessed assurance, here the very fear of losing that assurance, which is but conditional, will be a means rather to increase grace and virtue than to diminish it'.[7] 'Nothing is more industrious than saving faith', as Thomas Taylor put it.[8]

But I am not entirely convinced that this is the sole

explanation. It is highly sophisticated. Most of the evidence for it among the preachers comes from the later seventeenth century, when for other reasons works were being emphasized once more. I believe that the resolution of the paradox is psychologically simpler, if philosophically more complex. Salvation, consciousness of election, consisted of the turning of the heart towards God. A man knew that he was saved because he felt, at some stage of his life, an inner satisfaction, a glow, which told him that he was in direct communion with God. Cromwell was said to have died happy when assured that grace once known could never be lost: for once he had been in a state of grace. We are not dealing here with the mystical ecstasy of a recluse; we are dealing rather with the conscience of the average gentleman, merchant or artisan. What gave him consciousness of election was not the painful scrutiny of his works, for the preachers never tired of telling him that none could keep the commandments, that 'we cannot cooperate with any grace of God' unless there is 'a special spirit infused'.[9] It was the sense of elation and power that justified him and his worldly activities, that gave him self-confidence in a world of economic uncertainty and political hostility. The elect were those who thought they were elect, because they had an inner faith which made them feel free, whatever their external difficulties. This sense of liberation they could recognize in one another. It was natural that they should want freedom to gather in churches with others of God's people.

Philosophically the argument is circular. But Calvinism did not exist primarily as a philosophical system.[10] It gave courage and confidence to a group of those who believed themselves to be God's elect. It justified them, in this world and the next. Professor Haller seems to me to have expressed this better than anyone else when he writes that the Puritan preachers were 'dealing with the psychological problems of a dissatisfied minority'; their object was 'to inject moral purpose into men who felt lost in moral confusion'. 'Men,' he adds, 'who have assurance that they are to inherit heaven, have a way of presently taking possession of the earth.'[11] This courage and confidence enabled them to fight, with economic, political or military weapons, to create a new world worthy of the God who had so signally blessed them: a world remoulded in their image, and therefore in his. As the *Homily on the Salvation of all Mankind* put it: 'These great and merciful benefits of God, if they be well considered, do neither minister unto us occasion to be idle, and to live without doing any good works . . . but contrariwise, if we be not desperate persons, and our hearts harder than stones, they move us to render ourselves unto God wholly, with all our will, hearts, might and power to serve him in all good deeds, obeying his commandments during our lives, to seek in all things his glory.'

Those who most eagerly accepted Calvinism were men whose mode of life was active. The philosophical reconciliation of God's eternal decrees and their own inner impulse to labour for the glory of God was not a subject which occupied them overmuch. They were wise in this, for even the judicious Hooker virtually gave up the attempt at reconciliation of God's foreknowledge and man's free will, after noting that Augustine himself had changed his mind on the subject. In trying to analyse the Puritan attitude, therefore, we must not press them too hard for a philosophical consistency which they, in common with other theologians, lacked. We must consider rather how their theology helped them to live in and change the world as they found it.

Our period is one in which the literate public became increasingly conscious of scarcity.[12] Famine and starvation were as old as human history. But in the sixteenth and seventeenth centuries a growing proportion of the working population, town-dwellers and rural industrial workers, was dependent on others for its food; and an increasing proportion was literate and vocal. The traditional ruling class had no need to bother about scarcity: whoever else starved, it always had enough. The poorest peasantry and wage-labourers had no other perspective than intermittent starvation: the Land of Cockayne and even the very material advantages of heaven in *Pilgrim's Progress* testify to this. The Digger Gerrard Winstanley was less concerned with *individual* scarcity than in sharing what little there was and in increasing it for and by the community. It was the yeomanry and artisanate who stood at the margin, who could lift themselves into relative abundance by a combination of hard work and good fortune. Some may even have conceived of the possibility of total escape for society from the curse of scarcity, from the burden which had rested on humanity's back since the beginning of history. Protestantism emphasized the duty of working hard on behalf of the commonwealth, the commonwealth. But even individual escape involved tremendous effort and concentration. It might also involve breaches with what was customarily regarded as correct behaviour. It was important that men who had to follow new courses should have an inner certainty and confidence. Theories of predestination suggest the colossal power of the blind forces from which individuals were feeling the first beginnings of liberation. In folk tales men hope to overcome or outwit destiny by magic: but the prophecies on which they rely invariably turn out to be fallacious; as in *Macbeth*, destiny won by cheating.[13] But *the* book of prophecy was the Bible, and it would not deceive. If by intensive study men could master its prophecies, they would understand destiny and so become free. This was not the view only of simple-minded Bibliolaters or Fifth Monarchists; intellectuals as diverse as Joseph Mede and John Milton, John Napier and Sir Isaac Newton passionately held it: so did John Bunyan.

The 'common man's logic' of the Huguenot Peter Ramus, which so many Puritans adopted, may have helped the more philosophically-minded to feel that they had produced a system of thought,[14] or they may, with Bacon, simply have excluded the sphere of faith from rational criticism. The great scientific and political advances in our period, to which religious thought contributed so much, extended human control over the environment, and man's control over the social and political institutions under which he lived. The triumphs of Puritan thought, in the last analysis, were this-worldly. Faith was something given: if there seemed to be contradictions, that was because of the fallibility of human reason. 'Down reason then, at least vain reasonings down.' So Milton concluded, the man who of all those normally regarded as Puritans had perhaps the greatest confidence in the human intellect. There was a contradiction, but it could not be resolved within the framework of theology. We should marvel at the way in which a Bacon, a Milton, a Winstanley, tortured their Procrustean framework, rather than at their failure to break it up and start anew.

For Calvin, works are not a means whereby a man can persuade himself he is saved when he doubts it, but are the necessary and actual fruits of the faith of an honest man engaged about a worldly job. (The fact that it is necessary to explain this is evidence of the extent to which faith, in the Calvinist sense, has ceased to be regarded as a source of inner psychological strength, at least by the historians who write about it.) Must not the elect, Calvin asked, 'conceive a greater horror of sin than if it were said to be wiped off by a sprinkling of good works?'[15] A man who really believed that God had included him among the handful who were saved from eternal damnation rather naturally felt under an obligation to make some voluntary return for this voluntary grace. The price of goodness, Calvin thought, is eternal vigilance. God can preserve truth, he told Cranmer: 'Nevertheless, He would by no means have those persons inactive whom He Himself has placed on the watch.'[16] 'God crowns none but well-tried wrestlers.'[17] The Puritan Thomas Taylor neatly summed up the distinction between justification by faith and justification by works in a passage which illuminates the social context of the two doctrines: 'We teach that only Doers shall be saved, and by their doing though not for their doing. . . . Though then we cannot do so much as to *merit* heaven, yet we must by grace do so much as *keep* the way. . . . The profession of religion is no such gentlemanlike life or trade, whose rents come in by their stewards, whether they sleep or wake, work or play.'[18]

That was the distinction that mattered. Catholicism was a rentier religion. Provided the landlord performed the appropriate ceremonies on the appropriate occasions, the priestly steward brought in the rents for him to spend. But protestantism was for doers only; for those who, as Taylor goes on to explain, often look into their debt books and cast up their reckonings; 'but a bankrupt has no heart to this business'.[19] This hostility to the mere rentier lies very deep in Puritan theology, and is the basis of the 'bourgeois' doctrine of the calling. For William Perkins, 'such as live *in no calling*, but spend their time in eating, drinking, sleeping and sporting, because they have . . . lands left by their parents', are guilty of rebellion and disobedience against God.[20] Popery, Richard Sibbes thought, was 'set up by the wit of man to maintain stately idleness'.[21] There is no admission by purchase to the corporation of the godly, added John Cotton: all who hope for grace must serve an apprenticeship.[22]

Doers were saved by their doing, but not for it. The elect were active and courageous by definition, not in order to become elect. 'The thing which we mistake is the want of victory', wrote Samuel Rutherford. 'We hold that to be the mark of one that hath no grace. Nay, say I, the want of *fighting* were a mark of no grace; but I shall not say the want of *victory* is such a mark'. 'Without running, fighting, sweating, wrestling, heaven is not taken'.[23] Francis Bacon transferred this spirit – the spirit of Milton's *Areopagitica* – to science when he said: 'Not to try is a greater risk than to fail.'[24] This attitude gave the believer freedom from fear of hell or furies, courage to fight alone if need be. Samuel Butler wrote from the enemy point of view, and after the event, but he too was saying that Puritanism gives revolutionary élan, that its effects are internal and psychological. 'Ordinary wicked persons, that have any impression of human nature left, never commit any great crime without some aversion and dislike, although it be not strong enough to prevail against the present motives of utility or interest, and commonly live and die penitent for it. But the modern Saint that believes himself privileged and above nature engages himself in the most horrid of all wickednesses with so great an alacrity and assurance, and is so far from repentance, that he puts them upon the account of pious duties and good works.'[25]

The importance of being a doer is neatly brought out in one of Cromwell's letters, written to the Speaker after the fall of Bristol in September 1645. As it was brought up to him for signature, it spoke of 'the people of God with you and all England over, who have waited on God for a blessing'. As Cromwell read it through, the words did not seem to convey exactly what he wanted to say. We do not know whether his secretary had taken the letter down incorrectly, or whether the more fitting phrase came into Cromwell's mind as he read it through. He took up his pen, crossed out the words 'waited on' and altered the phrase to read 'who have *wrestled with* God for a blessing'. Passivity was intolerable even when face to face with God himself. God would allow the world to be changed only by those who helped themselves. 'Our rest we expect elsewhere', Cromwell assured St John three years later. Nor were these principles peculiar to Oliver: in 1641 Hanserd Knollys wrote in *A Glimpse of Sions Glory*: 'It is the work of the day to give God no rest till he sets up Jerusalem as the praise of the whole world.'[26] Here, as in Cromwell's letter, God is regarded almost as an impersonal force; it is like the desire of Zhelyabov, the nineteenth-century Russian conspirator, 'to give history a push'.[27] 'We cannot wait for favours from Nature', said the Soviet scientist Michurin; 'our task is to wrest them from her'.[28]

II

The Puritan integration of freedom and necessity is also an integration of the individual in the historical process. It comes at the point at which a man says: 'Trust in God and keep your powder dry.' God works through human agents. The active cooperation of the elect expedites the accomplishment of his purposes. Sloth and dishonouring God by refusing to cooperate in this way, Calvin tells us, are the greatest evils.[29] 'The work of God will go on,' Hugh Peter said in December 1648; but 'I am not in the mind we should put our hands in our pockets and wait what will come.'[30] By so cooperating we 'make our destiny our choice', as Andrew Marvell and the Matchless Orinda put it.[31]

Such an attitude demands very careful consideration of time and place, accurate assessment of each political situation. 'God permitteth not his people to fight when it seemeth good to them,' said the Geneva Bible's marginal note to Deuteronomy XX.1.[32] 'We must not put all carelessly upon a providence,' Richard Sibbes warned, 'but first consider what is our part; and, so far as God prevents [i.e. goes before] us with light, and affords us help and means, we must not be failing in our duty. We should neither outrun nor be wanting to providence. . . . When things are clear, and God's will is manifest, further deliberation is dangerous, and for the most part argues a false heart.'[33] It might be Lenin discussing on which precise day in October the Russian Revolution should take place. 'That which . . . goes nearest to my heart', cried Sir Henry Vane in the Commons in 1641, 'is the check which we seem to give to divine providence if we do not at this time pull down this [ecclesiastical] government. For hath not this Parliament been called, continued, preserved and secured by the immediate finger of God, as it were for this work?'[34] The political implications of cooperating with destiny are clear. Hooker shrewdly pointed out that 'when the minds of men are once erroneously persuaded that it is the will of God to have those things done which they fancy, their opinions are as thorns in their sides, never suffering them to take rest till they have brought their speculations into practice'.[35] Political action was thus not a thing indifferent: it might be a religious duty.

Cooperation with omnipotence was undoubtedly good for morale. 'What coward would not fight when he is sure of victory?' asked Sibbes.[36] 'The godly being in league with God,' explained Thomas Gataker, 'may have all his forces and armies for their help and assistance, whensoever need shall be.' Even when things seem to be going badly, there is consolation in the thought that 'the enemies of God's church . . . shall never be able to root it out'.[37] Cromwell's account of his feelings before Naseby is the classic exposition of this philosophy in action: 'I could not (riding alone about my business) but smile out to God in praises in assurance of victory, because God would, by things that are not, bring to naught things that are. Of which I had great assurance; and God did it.'

Yet 'the providences of God are like a two-edged sword, which may be used both ways', MPs said in 1656. 'God in his providence doth often permit of that which he doth not approve; and a thief may make as good a title to every purse which he takes by the highways. . . . If titles be measured by the sword, the Grand Turk may make a better title than any Christian princes.'[38] God spoke with different voices to different people, and problems of interpretation remained. At Putney Lieutenant-Colonel Goffe accused Cromwell of too freely and flatly declaring 'that was not the mind of God' that someone had spoken. Cromwell defended himself by saying that mistakes of fact or of logic could not be from God, for 'certainly God is not the author of contradictions'. Some might be sure that God wanted to destroy Kings and Lords, but at least, 'let them that are of that mind wait upon God for such a way where the thing may be done without sin and without scandal too.' The Levellers were more sophisticated than Cromwell, but they were no less sure that God was with them. 'God is not a God of irrationality and madness or tyranny. Therefore all his communications are reasonable and just, and what is so is of God.' Tyranny is irrational and therefore ungodly.[39] Wildman appealed to the Army Council 'to consider what is justice and what is mercy and what is good, and I cannot but conclude that that is of God. Otherwise I cannot think that anyone doth speak from God when he says that what he speaks is of God.'[40] There is still room for discussion, and a way can be won through to arguments based on reason and humanitarianism; but only by postulating that these are in accordance with God's will. They cannot be justified in themselves.

Now it is clear that at any time in history the convic-

tion that God is on your side in a struggle of cosmic
dimensions is a powerful asset: the churches in all
ages and all wars have tried to give men just that conviction. But there is a very real sense in which the Puritans
were *right* in their conviction – more right than the many
no less sincere churchmen who believed that God was
on the other side in the civil war. If for 'God' we sub-
stitute some such phrase as 'historical development' or
'the logic of events', as the Puritans almost did, then
there can be no doubt that powerful impersonal forces,
beyond the control of any individual will, were working
for Cromwell and his army. The evidence for this is not
merely that Parliament won the civil war: it is also the
complete inability of the old government to rule in the
old way which had been revealed in 1640, its financial
and moral bankruptcy. John Owen spoke in 1651 of 'the
constant appearing of God against every party that . . .
have lifted up themselves for the reinforcement of things
as in former days.'[41] Not even 1660 brought back 'things
as in former days'. The future lay with the causes supported by the Puritans and Parliamentarians. In that sense
they were cooperating with history, with God. And this is
true of the nobler as well as of the less noble aspects of
the cause. When Milton wrote on Cromwell's behalf to
the Landgrave of Hesse, advocating religious toleration
on grounds of Christian charity, he concluded with a
lofty confidence justified by the event: 'With inculcat-
ing and persuading these things we shall never be
wearied; beyond that there is nothing allowed to human
force or counsels; God will accomplish his own work
in his own time.' God and the Cause would triumph in
the end; but they would triumph the faster, and both
God's glory and England's welfare would be the greater,
the more convinced Christians fought the good fight
here and now.

Sustained, then, by an outlook on life which helped

them in the daily needs of economic existence; conscious of a bond of unity with others who shared their convictions; aware of themselves as an aristocracy of the spirit against which aristocracies of this world were as nought; fortified by the earthly victories which this morale helped to bring about: how should the hard core of convinced Puritans not have believed that God was with them and they with him? Believing this, how should they not have striven with all their might? 'The greater the trust, the greater the account,' Cromwell told Hammond; 'there is not rejoicing simply in a low or high estate, in riches or poverty, but only in the Lord.' In this sainthood of all believers the saints were perforce doers, not (for the best of them) in any calculation of reward for action, but simply because that was what being a saint meant. At Doomsday, Bunyan said, men will be asked not 'Did you believe?' but 'Were you doers, or talkers only?'[42] To be convinced that one was a soldier in God's army and to stand back from the fighting would have been a contradiction far less tolerable than that which philosophers have detected between individual freedom and divine predestination. Previous theologians had explained the world: for Puritans the point was to change it.

Hence followed what appears the irrational conviction that God will look after the ends if we, according to our lights, attend to the means. 'Duties are ours, events are the Lord's,' said Samuel Rutherford.[43] This line of argument seems to have played no inconsiderable part in bringing about the moral conviction that Charles I must be executed; both Ireton and Cromwell used it in that context. Ireton in the Whitehall Debates of December 1648 declared that 'Men as men are corrupt and will be so.' This however was not an argument for inaction (because the ungodly would pervert even good actions to evil ends) but for confidence that God will use our actions for his ends, provided we enter into them with integrity of heart. 'We cannot limit God to this or that . . . but certainly if we take the most probable way according to the light we have, God gives those things' their success. It is therefore a duty to God far more than to ourselves to keep our powder dry and follow the sensible, prudent course. 'Neglect not walls and bulwarks and fortifications for your own defence,' wrote John Cotton about 1630; 'but ever let the name of the Lord be your strong tower.'[44] Oliver, writing to St John, said of Sir Henry Vane, 'I pray he make not too little, nor I too much, of outward dispensations. God preserve us all, that we, in the simplicity of our spirits, may patiently attend upon them. Let us all not be careful what use men will make of these actings. They shall, will they, nill they, fulfil the good pleasure of God, and we shall serve our generations.'

To Hammond on 25 November 1648 Oliver wrote: 'If thou wilt seek to know the mind of God in all that chain of providence whereby God brought thee thither and that person [Charles 1] to thee; how, before and since, God has ordered him, and affairs concerning him; and then tell me whether there be not some glorious and high meaning in all this, above what thou hast yet attained? And, laying aside thy fleshly reason, seek of the Lord to teach thee what that is; and he will do it.' Again, after a more or less rational discussion of the nature of authority, Cromwell added: 'But truly these kind of reasonings may be but fleshly, either with or against: only it is good to try what truth may be in them. And the Lord teach us. My dear friend, let us look into providences.' 'Reasonings' for Oliver clearly stand in the same relation to providences as theory to fact. ('We are very apt, all of us, to call that faith that perhaps may be but carnal imagination and carnal reasonings.') To Hammond Cromwell concluded:

Let us beware lest fleshy reasoning see more safety in making use of this principle [of suffering passively, Vane's principle] than in acting. . . . Our hearts are very deceitful, on the right and on the left. What think you of providence disposing the hearts of so many of God's people this way, especially in this poor Army? . . . The encountering difficulties therefore makes us not to tempt God, but acting before and without faith. . . . Ask we our hearts, whether we think that, after all, these dispensations, the like to which many generations cannot afford, should end in so corrupt reasonings of good men, and should so hit the designings of bad? Thinkest thou, in thy heart, that the glorious dispensations of God point but to this? Or to teach his people to trust in him and to wait for better things, when, it may be, better are sealed to many of their spirits? And, as a poor looker-on, I had rather live in the hope of that spirit, and take my share with them, expecting a good issue, than be led away with the other.[45]

The line of thought is identical in Ireton and Cromwell. Clement Walker – not always good evidence – fits into the general picture sufficiently well to be worth quoting here. 'When it was first moved in the House of Commons to proceed capitally against the King, Cromwell stood up and told them "that if any man moved this upon design, he should think him the greatest traitor in the world; but since providence and necessity had cast them upon it, he should pray God to bless their counsels, though he were not provided on the sudden to give them counsel".' (Another report of the same speech has it 'Since the providence of God hath cast this upon us, I cannot but submit to providence, though I am not yet provided to give you my advice'.) Such arguments from such men on such a subject at such a time deserve the closest attention: so they steeled themselves to one of the boldest and most epoch-making gestures in history – the public execution of a king by his subjects, for the first time in modern Europe. The arguments were not invented for the occasion: they were part of the

normal apparatus of thought of the fighting Puritans – of
Oliver's beloved schoolmaster, Thomas Beard, from whom
he no doubt first learnt them;[46] of Hugh Peter, who
wrote in 1646: 'Our work will be only to look to the duty
which is ours, and leave events to God, which are his.'[47]

For Oliver 'waiting on providences' meant making absolutely sure that the political situation was ripe before
taking drastic action – ensuring that the Army and its
leaders were with him, that the City would acquiesce,
etc., etc. One can see how all this to the ungodly eye
could look like waiting on events, waiting to see which
way the cat would jump – often indeed encouraging the
cat to jump in the desired direction at the proper time.
Alternatively it could be described retrospectively as making necessities in order to plead them. ('Necessity, the
tyrant's plea', his Secretary for Foreign Languages was
to call it.) The royalist Joseph Beaumont may have been
referring obliquely to Cromwell in *Psyche* (1648):

> When this more than brutish General once
> In lawless gulfs himself had plunged, he
> Prints on his mad adventure's exigence
> The specious title of Necessity;
>   To which he blushes not to count the law,
>   Whether of earth or heaven, oblig'd to bow.
> (Canto xi, stanza 32).

This suggestion roused Oliver to fury. To his first
Parliament he declared 'Feigned necessities, imaginary
necessities, are the greatest cozenage that men can put
upon the providence of God, and make pretences to
break down rules by. But it is as legal and as carnal and
as stupid to think that there are no necessities that are
manifest necessities because necessities may be abused
and feigned.' 'God knoweth,' Oliver threatened, 'what he
will do with men when they shall call his revolutions
human designs, and so detract from his glory. . . . It is an
honour to God to acknowledge the necessities to have

been of God's imposing when truly they have been so. . . . It was, say some, the cunning of the Lord Protector; . . . it was the craft of such a man and his plot that hath brought it about. . . . Oh, what blasphemy is this! . . . Therefore, whatsoever you may judge men for, and say this man is cunning and politic and subtle, take heed, again I say, how you judge of his revolutions as the products of men's inventions!'

This relation between means and ends, the duty of keeping our powder dry until the time came to commit the Lord's forces, was a Puritan commonplace. It was indeed, it has been argued, a natural consequence of Ramus's logic so favoured by the Puritans: none could know in advance how God would choose to work his effect in any particular case.[48] 'The Lord is on our side,' said a preacher at Paul's Cross in the year of the Armada; 'but I beseech you to consider powder and shot for our great ordnance.'[49] God 'doth not always deliver his people by miracles', Oliver Cromwell's grandfather told the Huntingdonshire trained bands next year; 'it behoveth us to reform ourselves'.[50] The end of prayer and fasting, Richard Greenham told his congregation, is not 'the neglect of the ordinary means, but the pulling away of our confidence in them; that we might rest in the only power and goodness of God.'[51] Thomas Taylor perhaps expressed it most clearly: 'Neglect of means ordained by God' is equivalent to presumption against God's power, leaving it to him to help us when we refuse to help ourselves. 'For God, who hath not tied himself, hath tied us unto these [means], as these to his own ends.' God can work his purpose a myriad ways, at any time: we have only the opportunities that offer themselves to us here and now. Those men sin 'that presume of his power to convert and save them, but reject and despise the means. It is a foolish presumption to say, God can preserve my life without meat and drink, and therefore I will not eat nor drink'.[52] As an example of such foolish presumption and neglect of means we may cite the Scottish clergy, who in February 1649 were reported as proclaiming 'that God is powerful enough of himself to punish the Independents, without requiring help from man'. Perhaps Oliver and his régime erred in this way in the inadequacy of their preparations for the Western Design of 1655: 'God has not brought us hither,' Oliver told his Council in July 1654, 'but to consider the work that we may do in the world as well as at home.'

Puritanism roused men from the passivity which, as Oliver shrewdly pointed out to Hammond, might be a cover for cowardice. 'As if God should say, "Up and be doing, and I will help you and stand by you",' he wrote to the Deputy-Lieutenants of Suffolk at the end of July 1643; 'There is nothing to be feared but our own sin and sloth'. Puritanism did not plunge men into fatalism. It taught courage, the victory of mind over matter, of reason over superstition: and trust in God was essential to this victory.

> Give me the man, that with a quaking arm
> Walks with a stedfast mind through greatest harm;
> And though his flesh doth tremble, makes it stand
> To execute what reason doth command.[53]

Wither's lines are entirely within the Puritan tradition. Freedom was action taken in conformity with the will of God.

On the other hand passivity, lack of personal initiative, might in some circumstances be evidence that a man or men was being used by God: that he was not self-seeking.[54] The Barebones Parliament was called by God (as well as by the Lord General) in consequence of 'as wonderful providences as ever passed upon the sons of man in so short a time. . . . Neither directly nor indirectly did you seek to come hither.' 'I called not myself to this place', Oliver in his turn claimed of the Protectorate. 'I should be false to the trust that God hath placed upon me', he told his first Parliament, if he should consent to 'the wilful throwing away of this government' which he had not sought. He would 'sooner be willing to be rolled into my grave and buried with infamy'. At the dissolution he added: if the cause 'be of God, he will bear it up. If it be of man, it will tumble, as everything that hath been of man, since the world began, hath done.' A major argument against accepting the crown in 1657 was that 'at the best I should do it doubtingly. And certainly what is so done is not of faith,' and consequently is 'sin to him that doth it'.[55]

In discussing the Puritan theory of providence, it is important to compare it with ideas and social attitudes prevalent before it, rather than with what came later. Puritanism overthrew the doctrine of passive obedience to divinely constituted authority. The Puritan theory appeals to human will-power and to some degree to human reason; not to arbitrary divine intervention from outside. We are still dealing, we must always remember, with a pre-industrial age; an age when man's ability to control his environment was still undemonstrated, when only a Bacon dreamed that science might be 'the instigator of man's domination of the universe', and thus 'the conqueror of need'; when only a few like Bacon himself and George Hakewill were beginning to challenge the intellectual superiority of the ancient world, and the dogma of progressive cultural decay. In such an age confidence in man could be built up only slowly: activity on God's behalf was a necessary transitional concept between passivity in obedience to irresistible providence (tempered by magic) and activity for the relief of man's estate.

In this century man's age-old helplessness in the face of hostile nature was being broken down; ordinary men (as opposed to lords of serfs) could begin to envisage the

possibility of controlling their environment, including
their social environment. This is reflected in the growth
of social contract theories, the new insistence on the
rights of bourgeois communities.[56] Puritanism aided
science by its abolition of mystery, its emphasis on law, its
insistence on direct personal relationship to God and cooperation with him. For in order to cooperate with God's
purposes one must first understand them: the more historical and scientific knowledge one possessed, the
more capable one was of *active* cooperation. Science was
for action, not contemplation: here Bacon, Hakewill and
Calvinist theologians were at one. The scientific approach
to God's works in the universe was a way of getting to
know him. The world glorifies God because of what it is:
God himself pronounced it good. Hence the importance
of studying it scientifically so as to read its lessons aright.
But 'Knowledge without practice is no knowledge', wrote
the Puritan author of the marginal headings to Greenham's *Works*.[57] 'The soul of religion is the practical
part', Christian was still assuring Faithful a century
later.[58]

The desire to grasp God's purposes drove the Puritan
to science and to history; and the object of the new
Ramean logic was described by a Puritan as being 'to
direct men to see the wisdom of God'. These studies no
less than divinity helped to build up that cosmic optimism
and self-confidence which is the common faith of seventeenth-century Puritans and scientists. Their religion is
of this world. A heavier emphasis on the consolations of
the next world comes only after 1660, after the defeat of
the radical Puritans.[59]

In this age of the accumulation of capital, then, little
groups of men were very slowly pulling themselves up
by their own bootstraps, intellectually and morally as
well as economically. This is brought out very clearly
in one of the Duchess of Newcastle's letters, in which

she described a mock sermon preached at a Puritan service by an anti-Puritan. 'There are some men,' the pretended preacher is supposed to have said, 'that believe
they are or at least may be so pure in spirit by saving
grace as to be sanctified, and to be so much filled with
the Holy Ghost as to have spiritual visions, and ordinarily to have conversation with God, believing God to be
a common companion to their idle imaginations. But this
opinion proceeds from an extraordinary self-love, self-
pride and self-ambition, as to believe they are the only
fit companions for God himself and that not any of God's
creatures are or were worthy to be favoured but they,
much less to be made of God's privy council, as they
believe they are – as to know his will and pleasure, his
decrees and destinies, which indeed are not to be known,
for the Creator is too mighty for a creature to comprehend him.'[60] This is caricature, and our sympathies are
with the caricaturist. Yet if there is any validity in the
equation of God's purposes, in the Puritan's mind, with
the historical process, then the last sentence is especially
relevant, and provides food for thought.

The Duchess's preacher (like Hakewill's opponent,
Bishop Goodman) is advocating the passivity, the acceptance of the *status quo*, which we know the Duke of
Newcastle favoured. The universe and its laws are incomprehensible: therefore neither scientific nor political
action can change existing conditions. The 'self-love, self-
pride and self-ambition', unpleasant though they are, may
have been the necessary price to pay for a Luther, destroying belief in magical religion, a Bacon, planning for
the relief of man's estate, and a Cromwell, aspiring to
carry out God's will on earth. We must set the theorists
of passivity against their social background of economic
stagnation, social inequality and religious and political
tyranny. Coleridge 'could never read Bishop [Jeremy]
Taylor's tract on *The Doctrine and Practice of Repentance*

without being tempted to characterize High Calvinism as (comparatively) a lamb in wolf's skin, and strict Arminianism as approaching the reverse'.[61]

The novelty lay in Puritanism's combination of a deep sense of God as law, of the universe as rational, with an equally deep sense of change, of God working through individuals to bring his purposes to perfection. 'We do not imagine God to be lawless,' Calvin had proclaimed. 'He is a law to himself.'[62] God's seeming arbitrariness (e.g. in his choice of the elect) is simply our failure to comprehend. It is 'from the feebleness of our intellect,' Calvin explained, that 'we cannot comprehend how, though after a different manner, he [God] wills and wills not the very same thing'.[63] Part of God's covenant, Hakewill thought, is the orderly and perpetual working of the universe, the fact that 'God alters no law of nature', as John Preston put it. Hakewill's (and Bacon's) starting point was human activity, man's endeavour to discover the world in order to change it.[64] This emphasis on the rationality and law-abidingness of the universe greatly expedited the long task of expelling magic from everyday life: miracles were driven back to the epoch of the primitive church. It prepared for the Newtonian conception of God the great watch-maker, and of a universe first set in motion by external compulsion but then going by its own momentum.

But Newton's conception, though it derives logically enough from Calvinism, is the static view of a post-revolutionary civilization. Hakewill's more agreeably active image is of 'a great chess-board'.[65] For the sixteenth-century protestant and the early seventeenth-century Puritan liberty and necessity, predestination and free will, were still dialectically fused: and God is their point of union. In God 'we see the highest contradictions reconciled', Bunyan believed.[66] God was needed to bring change into what would otherwise have been a static mechanical universe.[67] In the seventeenth century materialists were political conservatives: God was the principle of change. For the Puritan it was important to study history, no less than science, since it was the story of God in action. History, properly understood, was a rational process, revealing God's purposes. It had a meaning, and an ascertainable meaning. 'Indeed there are [hi]stories that do ... give you narratives of matters of fact,' Cromwell told the Barebones Parliament, but what mattered was 'those things wherein the life and power of them lay; those strong windings and turnings of providence, those very great appearances of God in crossing and thwarting the purposes of men ... by his using of the most improbable and the most contemptible and despicable means'. There is no such thing as chance: what appears fortuitous to us does so only because we are ignorant of the grand design. The significance of this conception for the development of a more scientific approach to history needs no emphasis.[68]

III

The sense of sin, of guilt, is I suppose always especially intense in an age of economic and social revolution. Yet it may be true to suggest that it was more intense during our period than in any earlier or later crisis. This period sees the beginning of mankind's leap from the realm of magic to the realm of science. I am speaking now not of the advanced thinkers, but of the masses of the population. For them, throughout the Middle Ages and for countless centuries earlier, the real world had not been something external which men controlled: there was no subject-object relationship. One might influence external reality by magic (black or white, witchcraft or Catholicism), or one might fail to influence it; but there was no question of ordinary human beings understanding and mastering laws to which nature conformed. Traditional techniques and lore were learned by rote; but for ordinary men and women the goings-on of the universe were mysterious and undiscernible. When a natural catastrophe affected them, they had recourse to the intercession, by prayers and ceremonies, of the priest or the magician: the relationship was vicarious, second-hand. (Though in the sixteenth century the great magi, like Bruno or Dr Faustus, hoped to attain a more direct and personal control.)

If we turn to the present day, the change is obvious. After two centuries of industrial civilization, most men and women accept the existence of scientific laws, even when they do not understand them. They expect uniformities: the surviving superstitions and magical practices are only semi-serious. How did mankind move from the one attitude to the other?

It moved, I believe, through protestantism: through the direct relationship of the individual to God, the conception of God as law, order and purpose, and of the duty of the individual to grasp and cooperate with these purposes. It was a terrible burden for the individual conscience to bear. Cut off from the social aids and supports of Catholicism (confession, absolution), as from the stable certainties of the medieval village, each individual had to make his own terms with the world and with God. We think of the protestant bourgeois in the words of Tyndale's Bible which Professor Tawney made famous: 'The Lord was with Joseph and he was a lucky fellow.'[69] But it was very far from being as simple as that. Hundreds of Josephs were unlucky; but they had to wrestle on all through the night. Steady concentration, continuous trial and error, hopeless fighting in isolated corners – such was the lot of the protagonist of the new values as he slowly built up his certainties, and with

them, accidentally, the scientific attitude. Things were
always going wrong, but it was the duty of the godly
to make them go right, to snatch impossible victory to
the greater glory of God. It was *in defeat* that Milton
set about justifying the ways of God to men. Both the
sense of sin, and the feeling of justification, came, ultimately, from readiness to break with tradition, to obey
the internal voice of God even when it revealed new
tasks, suggested untraditional courses of action. Problems
had to be solved within one's own conscience, in isolation
from society. As the hymn puts it,

> Not the labours of my hands
> Can fulfil thy law's demands.

The metaphor is that of the small craftsman in his work-
shop, 'for ever in my great Taskmaster's eye'. It was impossible to fulfil the law, and yet one must continually
strive for an elusive perfection, which from time to time
suffuses one's whole being with a happiness and confidence more than human, and makes mere legal
righteousness seem petty and irrelevant. Hence the tense
effort, the self-confident elation when things were going
well, the desperate feelings of guilt in defeat. (We recall
Cromwell's early sense of sin.) The nonconformist conscience as we know it today, the deep sense of guilt, is
the product of an epoch in which Joseph has ceased to be
a lucky fellow, and the Lord has ceased to intervene on
his behalf. For the world of scientific certainties has now
been built. The desperate search for God has ended by
squeezing him right out of the universe. And science is a
collective activity: knowledge is pooled. Man can again
share his certainties with a community, and he is now no
longer passively at the mercy of a hostile material and
social environment: he can control them both, within
extensible limits. The individual need no longer bear the
sky on a single pair of shoulders. An approach to the

world which in our period produced a Luther, a Descartes, a Milton, a Bunyan, today produces psychiatric cases.

God, then, is the principle of change, his will the justification of action. Yet God works through individuals, and the success of a virtuous human being is at once his victory and the victory of divine grace working in him. The question whether one or other of these, grace and the human will, may be the *causa causans* is not one which would occur to the Puritan to ask. Joseph Caryl in 1643 preached before the Lord Mayor, Aldermen and City companies a sermon which the House of Commons ordered to be printed. 'When God makes a change in times', he told his auditors, 'it becomes us to make a change also.'[70] God makes the change, and we cooperate: such is the historical process. In November 1640 Stephen Marshall had preached to the House of Commons on 2 Chronicles 15.2. 'The Lord is with you while ye be with him, and if ye seek him he will be found of you.' They must be up and doing if God is to continue to favour England.[71]

'God is beginning to stir in the world,' Hanserd Knollys wrote in 1641. 'God uses the common people and the multitude to proclaim that the Lord God Omnipotent reigneth.' 'You that are of meaner rank, common people, be not discouraged: for God intends to make use of the common people in the great work of proclaiming the kingdom of his son.'[72] That was to put the theory to unorthodox uses, calling the lower classes into politics as God's agents: yet the theory is the same. God works through human agents: men cooperate with God, some consciously, some unconsciously ('will they, nill they', in Cromwell's words[73]). For those who consciously work with and for God, this is a two-way process. They, the elect, are free: the rest are God's pawns. God normally worked through kings, his lieutenants on earth, Thomas

Scott wrote in 1623: but he might on exceptional occasions raise up a David to quicken Saul's zeal. 'In the case of necessity, God himself dispenseth with his written law; because the law of nature, which he hath written in every man's heart, subjects him thereunto.' Scott was going no further than to urge Prince Charles and Buckingham to oppose James I's foreign policy;[74] but 26 years later Milton used this traditional line of thought to answer those royalists who argued that wicked kings should be left to God to punish. 'Why may not the people's act of rejection be as well pleaded by the people as the act of God, and the most just reason to depose him?[75]

God worked through men: human beings were the agents of God. Thus the cause was infinitely greater than the man, and criticism of the failings of individuals was beside the point. Cromwell wrote to Wharton, on 1 January 1650: 'I do not condemn your reasonings; I doubt them. It's easy to object to the glorious actings of God, if we look too much upon instruments. I have had computation made of the members in Parliament – good kept out, most bad remaining; it has been so these nine years, yet what has God wrought! The greatest works last, and still is at work. . . . How hard a thing is it to reason ourselves up to the Lord's service, though it be so honourable, how easy to put ourselves out of it, when the flesh has so many advantages!' Three years later Oliver himself made computations of members of Parliament, for then God spoke with a different voice. But in either case, confidence in the Cause enabled him to transcend mere human reasonings. Such reasonings, where God is concerned, may miss the main point.

IV

A natural tendency of the theory of the cooperation of
the elect with God was to claim that worldly success was
in itself evidence of divine approbation. There is, of
course, nothing specifically Puritan in this attitude of
mind. The doctrine that might is right is at least
as old as ordeal by battle, and corresponds to a primitive view of society in which each tribe has its own God.
The faithful reflection of such a stage of society in the
Old Testament helped to perpetuate the attitude of mind,
and to justify the more sophisticated version of the theory
which the Puritans evolved.

The outbreak of actual fighting in the civil war
naturally gave a great fillip to the argument from success.
'Where is your Roundheads' God now?' asked a triumph-
ant royalist in 1644. 'Hath he forsaken you Roundheads
of Bolton now? Sure he is turned Cavalier.'[76] But soon the
God of Battles revealed himself consistently on the side
of the New Model Army. After the second civil war
Cromwell explained to the Speaker the exception of
Poyer, Laugharne and Powell from mercy in the terms
for the surrender of Pembroke on the ground that 'they
have sinned against so much light, and against so many
evidences of Divine Providence going along with and
prospering a righteous cause, in the management of which
themselves had a share'. The fact of military victories,
'continued seven or eight years together' allowed a
pamphleteer of 1648 to argue that: 'In such cases successes are to be looked upon as clear evidence of the truth,
righteousness and equity of our cause.'[77] When the Army
decided to march on London at the end of November
in the same year, its generals declared: 'We are now
drawing up with the Army to London, there to follow

providence as God shall clear our way.'[78] God cleared
their way to the execution of the King, 'a path', Milton
thought, 'not dark but bright, and by his guidance shown
and opened to us.' The justice of the sentence on
Charles was confirmed by 'the powerful and miraculous
might of God's manifest arm'. 'The hand of God appeared
so evidently on our side' that the disapproval of man
was, for the poet, irrelevant. The ability to wield 'the
sword of God' came from heaven. If asked how he knew
this, Milton replied that, on this occasion at least, the
exceptional quality of the successful event carried its
own stamp of divine approval. 'Justice and victory,' he
added, are 'the only warrants through all ages, next under
immediate revelation, to exercise supreme power.'[79]

I have already quoted many of Cromwell's references
to 'the providences of God in that which is falsely called
the chances of war'.[80] 'How dangerous a thing it is . . . to
appeal to God the righteous judge,' he told the Scots
in September 1648. 'You have appealed to the judgment
of heaven', he told the Dutch Ambassadors in June 1653.
'The Lord has declared against you.' And in 1655, speaking to his first Parliament, Oliver generalized. 'What are
all our histories and other traditions of nations in former
times but God manifesting himself that he hath shaken
and tumbled down and trampled upon everything that
he hath not planted? . . . Let men take heed and be twice
advised, how they call his revolutions, the things of
God and his working of things from one period to another, how, I say, they call them necessities of men's
creations.' Oliver had no doubts when he dissolved his
last Parliament with the words: 'Let God judge between
you and me'.

The argument from success proved convincing, or
convenient, for many royalists and Presbyterians when it
came to accepting the Commonwealth. The plea that
de facto power *ought* to be obeyed was used on behalf

of the Commonwealth by Anthony Ascham, John Dury, John Wilkins and Marchamont Nedham. The success of the new régime helped to persuade Hobbes to return to England from exile, even if he did not regard the victories of the Parliamentary armies as providential. He claimed that his *Leviathan* helped to persuade royalists to submit to the Protectorate.[81]

If success justified, did failure condemn? Richard Cromwell decided in May 1659, logically, to acquiesce in 'the late providences that have fallen out among us', and not to resist his overthrow.[82] The Restoration was, in Burnet's words, 'an instance much more extraordinary than any of those were upon which they had built so much'.[83] 'The Lord had ... spit in their faces', complained Fleetwood in December 1659. The restoration forced Puritans to rethink their whole position. Had they been wrong in believing their cause to be the Lord's? Or had they pursued it by the wrong means? The Scot Johnston of Warriston confided to his *Diary* in January 1660: 'And whereas I thought I was following the call of God's providence [in cooperating with Cromwell] ... the truth is I followed the call of providence when it agreed with my humour ... and seemed to tend to honour and advantage; but if that same providence had called me to quit my better places and take me to meaner places or none at all, I had not so hastily and contentedly followed it.'[84] Not all were as honest as Warriston, who was to be executed three years after writing those lines. Some, happy in the occasion of their death, were able to preserve their faith because they did not realize the completeness of their failure. Thus Major-General Harrison, taunted before his execution by 'one telling him that he did not know how to understand the mind of God in such a dispensation as this', could still reply, 'Wait upon the Lord, for you know not what the Lord is leading to, and what the end of the Lord will be.' 'Though we may suffer hard things,' he proclaimed from the scaffold, 'yet he hath a gracious end, and will make for his own glory and the good end of his people.'[85]

But as the years rolled by it became clear that God's end was not that which the radicals had taken it to be. The problem of justifying the ways of God to men obsessed the more serious-minded among the Puritans. Most took the line of concluding that Christ's kingdom was not of this world, of accepting the nonconformists' exclusion from politics, and turned their attention to business and quietist religion. In *Pilgrim's Progress* it was Mr By-ends and Mr Money-love who preached that worldly success justified.[86] In 1655 Milton had written on behalf of the people of England: 'A cause is neither proved good by success, nor shown to be evil. We insist, not that our cause be judged by the outcome, but that the outcome be judged by the cause.'[87] Nevertheless the collapse of all his hopes, the rejection of all his sacrifices, forced him to wrestle with God as perhaps no man had wrestled before. The fruits of this anguish were *Paradise Lost, Paradise Regained* and *Samson Agonistes*. But even in *Samson Agonistes*, Milton could envisage victory for his cause only by a divine miracle of destruction, something like that with which the Fifth Monarchists had consoled themselves after the defeat of the Levellers and Diggers in 1647-9.

The post-Restoration passivity of most nonconformists was matched by a unanimity in deploring revolution, to which the ex-revolutionaries contributed loudly. Thus the historian of the Royal Society, eight years after his eulogistic poem upon the death of Oliver Cromwell, wrote that: 'this wild amazing men's minds with prodigies and conceits of providences has been one of the most considerable causes of those spiritual distractions of which our country has long been the theatre.'[88] In 1685 Sprat used the providential argument on behalf of James II against the defeated Whigs; after 1688 Ascham's 'whatever is, is divine' was employed to defend the new *de facto* regime of William III.[89] What had been a revolutionary theory was transformed into a banal conservatism.

We can see perhaps a more significant outcome of the restoration in theories of history. Charles II's return in 1660, so totally unexpected until a few months before it actually happened, suggested once more the workings of an inscrutable providence, bringing about results which no man had willed. Clarendon, one of the few faithful old Cavaliers who had willed it, did more than anyone to propagate this mystifying view, from which he no doubt thought the monarchy would benefit. This could be part of the explanation of the eclipse for a century of the dangerous aspect of Harrington's theory of history, that changes in the balance of property must lead to political change unless legislative action not in conflict with economic tendencies modified this determinism. The aspect of Harringtonianism which was orthodox for the later seventeenth and eighteenth centuries was the static conviction that property must rule. After 1688 property became the *deus ex machina* inscrutably and ineluctably achieving its ends, whatever unpropertied men might will. Divine providence yielded place to the iron laws, not to be challenged until the revival of political radicalism in the later eighteenth century. God, who had been so close to Oliver Cromwell, withdrew into the vast recesses of Newtonian space.

X

OLIVER CROMWELL
AND ENGLISH HISTORY

The Lord hath done such things amongst us as have not been
known in the world these thousand years.

CROMWELL, Speech at dissolution of his first Parliament,
27 January 1654

Nations stumble upon establishments which are indeed the
result of human action, but not the execution of any human
design. If Cromwell said that a man never mounts higher
than when he knows not whither he is going, it may with
more reason be affirmed of communities, that they admit of
the greatest revolutions where no change is intended, and
that the most refined politicians do not always know whither
they are leading the state by their projects.

ADAM FERGUSON, *An Essay on the History of
Civil Society* (Edinburgh, 1767), p. 187

Oliver Cromwell lay buried and dead,
　　Heigho! buried and dead!
There grew a green apple-tree over his head,
　　Heigho! over his head!
The apples were ripe and all ready to drop,
　　Heigho! ready to drop!
Then came an old woman to gather the crop,
　　Heigho! gather the crop!

Oliver rose and gave her a crack,
　　Heigho! gave her a crack!
That knocked the old woman flat down on her back,
　　Heigho! down on her back!
The apples are dried and they lie on the shelf,
　　Heigho! lie on the shelf!
If you want e'er a one you must get it yourself,
　　Heigho! get it yourself!

Old rhyme

I

Twenty months after Oliver Cromwell's death Charles II
sat once more on his father's throne. The intervening
period had shown that no settlement was possible until
the Army was disbanded. Richard Cromwell lacked the
prestige with the soldiers necessary if he was to prolong
his father's balancing trick; but after his fall no Army
leader proved capable of restoring the old radical alliance,
and nothing but social revolution could have thwarted the
'natural rulers'' determination to get rid of military rule.
Taxes could be collected only by force: the men of
property refused to advance money to any government
they did not control. The foreign situation helped to
make Charles's restoration technically unconditional:
there was a general fear that the peace of November 1659
which ended 24 years of war between France and Spain
would be followed by an alliance of the two countries
to restore the Stuarts.[1] Once it seemed likely that Charles
would return, most of those who had fought against his
father hastened to show their loyalty to the son. Not
only the King came back but the House of Lords and
ultimately the bishops too. Sectaries and Presbyterians
were excluded from the church and persecuted at the
instance of the House of Commons. Regicides were
hanged, drawn and quartered. Milton barely escaped
with his life. Oliver's corpse was dug up and hanged at
Tyburn. Godliness was at a discount at the court of the
merry monarch, but the cult of King Charles the Martyr

prospered. Defeat for everything that Cromwell stood for could hardly have been more complete.

But the appearances were deceptive, the cheering which greeted Charles ᴨ factitious. Within a few years not only Bristol Baptists were looking back nostalgically to 'those halcyon days of prosperity, liberty and peace, . . . those Oliverian days of liberty'.[2] An unsentimental civil servant like Samuel Pepys, soon to be accused of papist leanings, recorded in July 1667 that: 'Everybody do now-a-days reflect upon Oliver and commend him, what brave things he did and made all the neighbour princes fear him.'[3] Cromwell's former ambassador to France, Lockhart, whom Charles ᴨ also employed, 'found he had nothing of that regard that was paid him in Cromwell's time'. George Downing made a similar remark about the attitude of the Dutch to him, and the Ambassador of the Netherlands in 1672 told Charles ᴨ to his face that of course his country treated him differently from the Protector, for 'Cromwell was a great man, who made himself feared by land and by sea'.[4] The common people were muttering similar things. 'Was not Oliver's name dreadful to neighbour nations?' Lodowick Muggleton asked in 1665. Four years later an apothecary of Wolverhampton was in trouble for contrasting Cromwell's successful Dutch policy with Charles ᴨ's bungling.[5] Nor was it only in foreign affairs that such contrasts could be made. Roger Boyle's biographer points out that the inefficiency of Charles ᴨ's government was such that 'despite the king's frequent efforts to reward him, Orrery was a richer man in the service of Cromwell than in the service of Charles ᴨ'.[6] It is the sort of thing men notice. The odious comparisons had become so frequent that French and Italian visitors commented on them.

And if we look on another 20 years, it becomes clear that the reigns of Charles ᴨ and James ᴨ were only an interlude. In 1660 the old order had not been restored:

neither prerogative courts nor the Court of Wards nor feudal tenures. Royal interference in economic affairs did not return, nor (despite James II's attempts) royal interference with control of their localities by the 'natural rulers'. After 1688 the policies of the 1650s were picked up again. The revolution of 1688 itself was so easily successful because James II remembered all too clearly that he had a joint in his neck. The lesson of January 1649 for the kings of Europe did not need repeating for another 144 years. The follies of James, and William III's own semilegitimate claim to royalist loyalty, meant that the Liberator did not need to retain the large army which brought him to power: a settlement very like that which Oliver sought in vain was arrived at, with a strong executive but ultimate control by Parliament and the taxpayers. Parliament became again a permanent part of the constitution. Taxes could not be levied without the approval of the representatives of the men of property in the House of Commons; they could not be anticipated without the goodwill of bankers and the moneyed interest. All attempts to build up an independent central executive, with its own judicial system or subservient judges, strong enough to coerce the 'natural rulers' had failed – Laud's and James II's no less than the Major-Generals'. In 1649 and again in 1653 London juries acquitted John Lilburne against all the authority of the central government: in. 1656 the republican Bradshaw demanded trial by a jury of 'men of value', and Cromwell, 'seeming to slight that', spoke against juries.[7] By the end of the century juries were no longer accountable to the government for their verdicts; judges had become independent of the crown, dependent on Parliament. There was to be no administrative law in England, no more torture. The gentry and town oligarchies henceforth dominated local government, Parliamentary elections and juries.

For James I customs had been one of many sources of

revenue; by the end of the century customs dues were raised or lowered in the interests of the national economic policy which the commercial classes now dictated. At the restoration the Navigation Act had been re-enacted, and the power of the East India Company confirmed: imperial trade, and especially re-exports, were expanding rapidly. Sprat in 1667 could assume as a truism learnt in the preceding twenty years that 'the English greatness will never be supported or increased . . . by any other wars but those at sea'.[8] But it was only after 1688 that governments came to assume that 'trade must be the principal interest of England' – as the old Rumper Slingsby Bethel had vainly tried to convince Charles II in 1680.[9]

Parliament now determined foreign policy, and used the newly-mobilized financial resources of the country, through an aggressive use of sea power, to protect and expand the trade of a unified empire. England itself had by then been united under the dominance of the London market; separate courts no longer governed Wales and the North, 'cantonization' was no longer a danger. William III's political and economic subjugation of Ireland was thoroughly Cromwellian: the Union with Scotland in 1707 was on the same lines as that of 1652–60. By the end of the century industrial freedom had been won, monopolies had been overthrown, government interference with the market, including the labour market, had ended. The anti-Dutch policy was sponsored by the republicans of the City and the Rump, and later by the Stuart Kings, who had their own reasons for disliking the Dutch republic. The policy of colonial expansion into the western hemisphere, first against Spain, then against France, enjoyed more support among the gentry, and gradually won over a majority in the House of Commons as Dutch and Spanish power declined and French increased. After 1688 there was no opposition between the two policies, for the Netherlands had been effectively subordinated to England, and all the power of the English state could be concentrated on the battle with France for the Spanish empire and the trade of the world. The two foreign policies fused as the landed and moneyed interests fused. England emerged from the seventeenth-century crisis geared to the new world of capitalism and colonial empire.[10]

The control which the Parliamentary class won extended to the church too. The destruction of the Laudian bureaucracy in the church, as of Charles I's bureaucracy in the state, made inevitable the domination of the gentry over church and state alike. *Cuius regio eius religio*: Cromwell had used the phrase to justify him in following his own conscience and permitting toleration. But in the long run the region belonged to the gentry rather than to the Lord Protector, whose title, as he himself declared, implied that the office was held on behalf of others. The failure in 1660 to restore the High Commission meant that the bishops could not prevent the squire's domination of the parson, just as the failure to restore Star Chamber deprived the central government of any effective control over the squire in his capacity as Justice of the Peace. The hierarchy could no longer control the religious views of clergy and laity, as before 1640 in alliance with the crown it had been able to do. Church courts, which were still handing men over to be burned when Cromwell was born, had virtually ceased to function by the end of the century. JPs had succeeded to many of their functions. Apart from a brief interlude in James II's reign, no one after Cromwell's Triers ever again attempted to interfere with the patronage rights of the gentry. The monopoly of the national church had been broken. The House of Commons remained hostile to the idea of religious toleration; but nonconformity in the reigns of Charles II and James II both showed under persecution that it had come to stay, and shook off its revolutionary political associations. The Toleration Act of 1689 recognized these facts. Presbyterians and Congregationalists were not comprehended in the national church, but the Church of England was subordinated to Parliament, the parson to the squire. The high-flying clergy, the Non-jurors, were excluded as the Laudians had been under Cromwell. The Puritan Revolution was defeated in 1660; but Great Britain in the eighteenth and nineteenth centuries was unique among the great powers of Europe for the strength of its evangelical tradition. It was also more tolerant than most European countries.

During the seventeenth century an intellectual revolution had taken place. The second wife of Oliver's grandfather, Sir Henry Cromwell, was alleged to have been killed by witchcraft, and in 1593 a woman was hanged for the crime. Sir Henry endowed a sermon against witchcraft, to be preached at Huntingdon annually for all time. Oliver must have heard many such sermons. Yet the occupation of Scotland by English troops under Cromwell's command led to a virtual cessation of witch persecution there. In England the burning of witches was coming to an end, and educated men were ceasing to believe in their existence. It may be a tribute to Sir Henry's lectureship that Huntingdon was one of the last places in England to see a witch executed, early in the eighteenth century. By that time the Royal Society had made science respectable.

Science had entered Oxford behind the Parliamentary armies, and in 1669 the turncoat Robert South used an official Oxford occasion to attack, in one breath, 'Cromwell, fanatics, the Royal Society and the new philosophy'.[11] But science and the new philosophy survived Oliver. The nucleus of the Royal Society was the group which had been installed in Oxford by the Parliamentary Commissioners, including John Wallis, the Long Parliament's cryptographer, Jonathan Goddard, physician to Cromwell's armies in Ireland and Scotland, Thomas Sydenham, former Cromwellian officer, Sir William Petty, a surveyor of Ireland for the Protector; its leading figure was John Wilkins, Oliver's brother-in-law, first secretary of the Royal Society. The Society's second secretary was Henry Oldenburg, also associated with the Oxford group, who in 1654 had described Cromwell as 'the greatest hero of the century'.[12] It would be absurd to link Cromwell too closely with the scientific movement. But as we have seen he was interested in mathematics, and many scientists emerged under his patronage. It is said to have been 'through the favour and power of Cromwell' that Goddard became Professor of Physic at Gresham College in 1655.[13] In the following year the Protector interested himself in the chair of geometry at the same college, to which Laurence Rooke was elected in 1657. Both were excellent appointments. The history of science in England would be very different but for the Revolution which Oliver led. In consequence of the intellectual ferment of the Revolution, divine right in all spheres was in decline by the end of the century. Political discussion was no longer conducted by swapping Biblical texts or Anglo-Saxon precedents, but in rational and utilitarian terms. The concept of scientific law had evolved: God, like the King, was bound by law. By 1712, when Richard Cromwell died, the world into which Oliver was born in 1599 had been modernized out of all recognition.[14]

The 'natural rulers' had also successfully resisted all attempts from below to circumscribe their authority, whether by an extension of the Parliamentary franchise or by a written constitution. Here too Cromwell played a prominent part, in outmanoeuvring and then suppressing the Levellers, in defeating the religious radicals who at one time, however wrongly, had thought of him as their leader. The abolition of tithes, extension and redistribution of the suffrage, and serious reform of the law, all had to wait until the nineteenth century. Ireton told the Agitators at Putney, 'Liberty cannot be provided for in a general sense if property be preserved.' 'Liberty and property', the royalist Sir Robert Filmer confirmed, 'are as contrary as fire to water'.[15]

In the great seventeenth-century struggle to decide who was to benefit from the extension of cultivation which was necessary to feed the growing cities,[16] the common people were defeated no less decisively than was the crown. The abolition of the Court of Wards and of feudal tenures was a great relief for the gentry, but only for them; the acts of 1656 and 1660 specifically retained copyhold unchanged. The radical movements to win security of tenure for copyholders were defeated. Squatters and cottagers who had no written title to their holdings could be evicted. The Barebones Parliament was the last to contemplate legislation against depopulating enclosures. In 1654, for the first time, Parliament authorized the export of corn when prices were low; by 1700 England had solved its own food problems and was regularly exporting corn. Fen drainage alone extended the country's arable area by 10%. Expensive clover and root crops enabled cattle to be kept alive through the winter, thus not only increasing the meat supply but also at last breaking the manure barrier which for so long had held back agricultural expansion. But smaller cultivators did not benefit by this agricultural revolution. Commons, wastes and fens, like royal forests, were enclosed and cultivated by the private enterprise of capitalist farmers and improving landlords. 'I know several that did remember the going of a cow for 4d. per annum. The pigs did cost nothing', wrote John Aubrey in the 1680s, looking back to the disafforestation of earlier decades. 'Now the highways are encumbered with cottages, and travellers with the beggars that dwell in them.'[17] The yeomen, who had formed the backbone of Cromwell's army, lost their hold on the land. Enclosure and eviction helped first to create and then to feed a proletariat for the eighteenth-century industrial revolution, and to create a market for its products. The French Revolution guaranteed the survival of the peasantry in France: the English Revolution ensured its disappearance in England.

In the 1630s Oliver Cromwell had defended the rights of the inhabitants of Huntingdon in their common lands: as Lord of the Fens he had protected commoners against the court-supported great capitalist fen-drainers; in 1641 he got a clause put into the Grand Remonstrance on their behalf. But in May 1649, less than a fortnight after the suppression of the Leveller regiments at Burford, Cromwell was named as one of fifty-odd commissioners joined with the Earl of Bedford, and the adventurers' authority to drain the Fens – formerly challenged by Oliver Cromwell – was renewed. Three days after Oliver had dissolved the Rump, he sent a major of his own regiment to suppress commoners who were opposing the adventurers. In 1654 he issued an ordinance to protect Bedford and his works, and to lay the cost of the upkeep of the work upon the inhabitants of the area. Oliver himself received 200 acres of the drained lands. In this symbolic reversal – and in his alleged somersault over tithes[18] – we see the reason for the hatred which the religious and political radicals felt for the leader who had betrayed their cause.

So, for good and for evil, Oliver Cromwell presided over the great decisions which determined the future course of English and world history. Marston Moor, Naseby, Preston, Worcester – and regicide[19] – ensured that England was to be ruled by Parliaments and not by absolute kings: and this remains true despite the Protector's personal failure to get on with his Parliaments.

Cromwell foreshadows the great commoners who were to rise by merit to rule England in the eighteenth century. The man who in the 1630s fought the Huntingdon oligarchy and the government of Charles which backed it up ultimately made England safe for its 'natural rulers', despite his own unsuccessful attempt to coerce them through the Major-Generals. The man whose first Parliamentary speech was against the 'popery' of the Arminian bishops and their protégés, who collaborated with Londoners to get evangelical preaching in his locality (and who besought Scottish Presbyterians 'in the bowels of Christ' to think it possible they might be mistaken) ensured that England should never again be ruled by high-flying bishops or persecuting presbyteries, that it should be a relatively tolerant country, and that the 'natural rulers' should control the church both centrally and locally. The man who almost emigrated to New England in despair of old England lived to set his country on the path of empire, of economic aggression, of naval war. He ruthlessly broke the resistance not only of the backward-looking royalists but also of those radicals whose programme for extending the franchise would have ended the exclusive political sway of Cromwell's class, whose agrarian programme would have undermined that class's economic power, and whose religious programme would have left no national church to control – even though half at least of Oliver sympathized with the last demand. The dreams of a Milton, a Winstanley, a George Fox, a Bunyan, were not realized; nor indeed were those of Oliver himself: 'Would that we were all saints'. The sons of Zeruiah proved too strong for the ideals which had animated the New Model Army. If Cromwell had not shot down the Levellers, someone else would no doubt have done it. But in fact it was Oliver who did: it is part of his historical achievement.

The British Empire, the colonial wars which built it up,

the slave trade based on Oliver's conquest of Jamaica, the plunder of India resulting from his restitution and backing of the East India Company, the exploitation of Ireland; a free market, free from government interference and from government protection of the poor; Parliamentary government, the local supremacy of JPs, the Union of England and Scotland; religious toleration, the nonconformist conscience, relative freedom of the press, an attitude favourable to science; a country of landlords, capitalist farmers and agricultural labourers, the only country in Europe with no peasantry: none of these would have come about in quite the same way without the English Revolution, without Oliver Cromwell.

If we see this revolution as a turning point in English history comparable with the French and Russian Revolutions in the history of their countries, then we can agree with those historians who see Cromwell in his Revolution combining the roles of Robespierre and Napoleon, of Lenin and Stalin, in theirs. Oliver was no conscious revolutionary like Robespierre or Lenin: the achievements of the English Revolution were not the result of his deliberate design. But it would not have astonished Oliver or his contemporaries to be told that the consequences of men's actions were not always those which the protagonists intended. 'This kind of government of the church', wrote one of the New Model Army's chaplains in 1651, 'God doth not manage according to the wisdom and thoughts, no not of his very people, but wholly according to the counsel of his own will and the thoughts of his own heart: doing things that they must not know yet but must know afterwards; yea, such things as for the present seem absurd and absolutely destructive.'[20] Another of Oliver's close associates, in the same year, declared that 'the actings of God's providence in carrying on the interest of Christ are and shall be exceedingly unsuited to the reasonings and expectations of the most

of men', who 'expect that nothing must be done but
what suits unto . . . their principles; and if anything contrary be wrought, even of God himself, how deceived and
how disappointed are they!'[21] On one occasion, perhaps
in 1636, Cromwell took a heavy dose of mithridate as a
precaution against plague infection: he was surprised
to find it had the effect of curing his pimples.[22] He
would have been no less surprised if he could have known
that his heroic struggles to build God's kingdom in England had as their lasting consequence the removal of
obstacles to the development of English capitalism. 'From
plague to pimples' would be an unfair summary of the
great Protector's career: but it contains a thought.

Remembering Pepys, we may perhaps think Oliver's
most important contribution was to the formation of a
popular national consciousness. His assertion, more effectively than ever since the fifteenth century, of England's
power in Europe, was strongly emphasized by contemporary poetical eulogists. Oliver 'showed/ The ancient
way of conquering abroad', said Waller; he 'once more
joined us to the continent', Marvell agreed. 'He made us
freemen of the continent', Dryden echoed, and taught the
English lion to roar. Thomas Sprat thought Oliver restored the 'subdued courage' of this lion, and sharpened
its claws. It may be observed that none of these four poets
had been supporters of the Parliamentary cause during
the civil war. But some republicans shared the enthusiasm
too: the anonymous editor of *Milton's Republican Letters*
(1682 – probably printed in Holland) contrasted Cromwell's attitude to Louis xiv's France with that of Charles
ii. This emphasis survived into the eighteenth century.
'He supported his state and terrified all Europe, as well
as the three nations, by the grandeur of his courage and
the spirit of his army:' the praise, rather unexpectedly,
comes from Jonathan Swift. Cromwell, said Henry Field-
ing, 'carried the reputation of England higher than it

ever was at any time,' in addition to promoting men by merit. Chatham eulogized Cromwell's 'sagacious mind'. It has been argued that it was during the revolutionary decades that a consciousness of nationality embraced the whole English people.[23] This is not an easy proposition to prove, or to disprove. A cursory reading of Shakespeare and other Elizabethans shows that strong patriotic, not to say jingoistic, feelings already existed in England. Foxe and Milton had identified Englishmen with the chosen people.[24] What Oliver Cromwell did was to popularize in action this identification, and to link it to an aggressive foreign policy. But just because more people were drawn into political action during the revolutionary forties and fifties, and brought under the more direct dominance of London, it may well be that national consciousness was extended to new geographical areas and lower social levels.

The transition from divine right of monarchy to the divine right of the nation had lasting consequences. The new English patriotism was closely associated with religion, with liberty and with the rise of the middle class. Its symbol in the eighteenth century was to be the unattractive figure of John Bull – Oliver Cromwell minus ideology.

II

Historians have given us many Cromwells, created if not after their own image at least as a vehicle for their own prejudices. Immediate post-restoration descriptions were naturally almost wholly hostile, though men like Bate and Carrington did emphasize the Protector's interest in England's trade and the navy. Clarendon saw Cromwell as Machiavelli's Prince in action, regarding him with a mixture of repulsion and admiration. 'Cromwell, though the greatest dissembler living, always made his hypocrisy of singular use and benefit to him, and never did anything, how ungracious or imprudent soever it seemed to be, but what was necessary to the design.'[25] Ludlow's *Memoirs,* written from a republican standpoint, laid equal stress on ambition and hypocrisy. Algernon Sidney in his *Discourses concerning Government* (not published until 1698, though Sidney was executed in 1683) pilloried Cromwell as the betrayer of the republic. A first attempt to redress the balance, brought out shortly after the revolution of 1688, was Nathaniel Crouch's *History of Oliver Cromwell. A Brief Character of the Protector Oliver Cromwell,* published in 1692, noted the changed atmosphere: 'Many in our times . . . have a great reverence for the memory of Oliver Cromwell, Protector; as being a man of piety and a great champion for the liberties of the nation'. Thirty years later Isaac Kimber, a Baptist minister, wrote a life which was on the whole favourable; as was that of John Banks in 1739. Laurence Echard in 1718 had depicted Cromwell as an honest patriot, and Rapin in 1723–7, though critical, thought him 'one of the greatest men of his age'. Gilbert Burnet saw him as both enthusiast and dissembler, but 'when his own designs did not lead him out of the way', a lover of justice, virtue and learning.[26]

But for most respectable historians Cromwell fell between two stools. Tories denounced the revolutionary and regicide, Whigs the wrecker of the Good Old Cause. The Tory David Hume saw Oliver as a 'frantic enthusiast', and the radical Mrs Catherine Macaulay thought him 'the most corrupt and selfish being that ever disgraced a human form'. John Millar agreed that Oliver was 'one of the most notorious tyrants and usurpers that the world ever beheld'. Goldsmith claimed that he was himself named after and indeed related to Cromwell. Burke once said that Goldsmith should have been called Oliver Cromwell, not Oliver Goldsmith. Goldsmith in his *History of England* was in fact not too severe on the Protector.[27] The radical William Godwin thought that Cromwell 'became the chief magistrate solely through his apostacy and by basely deceiving and deserting the illustrious band of patriots with whom he had till that time been associated in the cause of liberty'. Nevertheless, Godwin admitted, 'the government of England had never been so completely freed from the fear of all enemies, both from without and within, as at the period of the death of Cromwell.' Hallam repeated the charge of fanaticism, which led Macaulay to retort with a Cromwell who revealed most of the qualities of the nineteenth-century English middle class. 'No sovereign ever carried to the throne so large a portion of the best qualities of the middling orders, so strong a sympathy with the feelings and interests of his people. . . . He had a high, stout, honest English heart.'

It was Carlyle's *Letters and Speeches of Oliver Cromwell,* published in 1845, which finally allowed Cromwell to speak for himself – though not without irritating Carlylean asides and interjections. Carlyle's edition established for all time and beyond dispute that Cromwell was not the ambitious hypocrite of the traditional legend. Carlyle praised Cromwell for some of the reasons which led eighteenth-century radicals to reject him. Cromwell the God-sent Hero reflected Carlyle's own view of what was needed in mid-nineteenth-century England, trembling on the brink of Chartism, democracy and other evils. Even more conservative was the French statesman, François Guizot. Exiled himself by the revolution of 1848, he knew better than nineteenth-century Englishmen what revolutions were like. His *Histoire de la République d'Angleterre et de Cromwell,* published in the 1850s, laid a stress on the social and class forces at work in the English Revolution which had not been heard since the seventeenth century. But Guizot rather naturally disapproved of popular revolutions, and was horrified at the 'excesses' to which 'religious fanaticism' gave rise in England. He gave Cromwell qualified praise as a despot who restored order at the expense of liberty, but his moral was stern: 'God does not grant to those great men who have laid the foundations of their greatness amidst disorder and revolution the power of regulating at their pleasure, and for succeeding ages, the government of nations.' (God, it seems to be implied, should by these standards have been kinder to Guizot.)

After Carlyle, the main formative influence in the nineteenth century was Samuel Rawson Gardiner, whose *History* of England from 1603 to 1656 was published between 1863 and 1901, and *Cromwell's Place in History* in 1902. Masterly in detail, irreplaceable in learning, perfect in literary sense and knack of apt quotation, the work of Gardiner (himself a descendant of Cromwell) was also responsible for inventing the idea that the seventeenth century had seen a 'Puritan Revolution'. Gardiner's Cromwell was a sophisticated and liberalized version of Carlyle's Puritan Hero, a man whose ideal was constitutional monarchy; who wished for bit-by-bit reform, and opposed 'the exaggerations of Puritanism': something like a nineteenth-century liberal in advance of his time. That was why he had become, in Gardiner's phrase, 'the national hero of the nineteenth century', 'the greatest because the most typical Englishman of all time'. There is of course far more to Gardiner than that: his was the first serious professional history of the English Revolution, and we all stand on his shoulders. Nevertheless, 'the Puritan Revolution' was an unfortunate concept. It suffered both from exaggeration by Gardiner's epigones and from an equally exaggerated reaction away from it by some twentieth-century historians.

Gardiner's liberal prepossessions were attacked by implication in Sir John Seeley's *The Growth of British*

Policy, published in 1895. In keeping with the spirit of his age, Seeley stressed Cromwell the imperialist. Hilaire Belloc among others recalled Cromwell's hostility to democracy, which seemed more reprehensible in the twentieth century than it had done in the nineteenth. The weaknesses of the English liberal attitude were revealed in a conversation held in Moscow in 1934 between H. G. Wells and Stalin. 'Take the history of England in the seventeenth century', Stalin suggested. 'Did not many people say that the old social order was rotten? Yet nevertheless, was not a Cromwell needed to overthrow it by force?' Wells replied, conventionally enough, 'Cromwell acted in accordance with the constitution and in the name of constitutional order.' 'In the name of the constitution,' retorted Stalin, 'he took up arms, executed the king, dissolved Parliament, imprisoned some and beheaded others.' Stalin had his own axe to grind; but it is difficult not to think that he had the last word.

Nevertheless, Gardiner's liberal prepossessions were less distorting than the late W. C. Abbott's laboured comparisons between Cromwell and Hitler in his indispensable *Writings and Speeches of Oliver Cromwell*, published from 1937 to 1947. Some historians have even extended to the 1650s the word 'totalitarian', already overworked and almost meaningless in its twentieth-century applications. Oliver has never failed to appeal to eccentrics. Mr Trevor Davies accused him of fighting the civil war in order to be able to persecute witches.[28] On the other hand a writer in the *Occult Review* of 1936 – apparently in all seriousness – repeated contemporary charges that Oliver owed his success to black magic, witchcraft and compacts with the devil. Professor Trevor-Roper has fitted Cromwell into his own patterns by describing him as a 'country-house radical' and 'natural backbencher', who could lead a revolution of destruction but had no positive ideals or abilities. The professor's view that only 'a little parliamentary management by the executive' was needed to solve the political problems of the 1650s would have surprised the men of the seventeenth century no less than his dismissal of the Protector's foreign policy as 'futile', 'thirty years out of date', prepared 'to surrender all English interests in Asia to the Dutch.'

The best biography of Cromwell still remains that by Sir Charles Firth, first published in 1900. It is completely in the Gardiner tradition, with little attempt to relate Cromwell to the social and economic problems of his time; but within its limits it is first-class. Mr Maurice Ashley wrote three studies of Cromwell which seem to illustrate their author's preoccupations. That of the 1930s is sub-titled *The Conservative Dictator;* those of the 1950s depict Oliver as a constitutional liberal manqué. The influence of contemporary problems can also be seen in Dr R. S. Paul's *The Lord Protector* (1955), with its stress on Oliver the oecumenicist; but his is the best life in English since Firth's.[29] Readers will no doubt have decided for themselves by this time how far this book has been written to air my own prejudices and distortions of history.

III

In folk memory, so apt to embody causes in individuals, Oliver Cromwell came to personify the English Revolution, particularly its more destructive and violent aspects. Cromwell the destroyer of castles and manor-houses, the desecrator of churches, has a place in folklore whose inaccuracy does not make it any the less interesting for the historian. As we have seen,[30] Oliver has been blamed for far more iconoclasm than he was guilty of: his reputation as a desecrator of sacred places has probably incorporated some of that of his kinsman, Thomas Cromwell. But there is a validity in the image of Cromwell blowing up the strongholds of the king, the aristocracy and the church: that, after all, is what the Revolution had achieved.[31]

But some more positive aspects of Oliver and his revolution lived on in popular memory. However we interpret the old rhyme quoted at the head of this chapter, it suggests that those who recalled Oliver did not easily acquiesce in others gathering the fruits of his labours. Self-help is the moral, but not for everyone. Men long remembered Oliver's concern for the career open to the talents (in which too he was anticipated by men around Thomas Cromwell[32]), for religious toleration, for trade, for national unity, for the greatness of England. It is possible that his popular reputation stood the higher just because he was rejected by Tories and aristocratic republicans alike. Seventeenth-century Baptists recalled 'Oliverian days of liberty'.[33] In 1716 a Yorkshire parish remembered that the glebe had been enclosed by freeholders 'in Oliver's time'.[34] In the West Riding of Yorkshire the phrase 'in Oliver's days' was still in common use in the early nineteenth century to describe a time of unusual prosperity.[35] The poet George Crabbe in 1812 described in moving lines:

> ...a remnant of that crew
> Who, as their foes maintain, their sovereign slew;
> An independent race, precise, correct,
> Who ever married in the kindred sect:
> No son or daughter of their order wed
> A friend to England's king who lost his head;
> Cromwell was still their saint, and when they met,
> They mourned that saints were not our rulers yet.
>   Fixed were their habits; they arose betimes,
> Then prayed their hour, and sang their party-rhymes:
> Their meals were plenteous, regular and plain;
> The trade of Jonas brought him constant gain;
> Vender of hops and malt, of coals and corn –

And, like his father, he was merchant born:
Neat was their house; each table, chair and stool
Stood in its place, or moving moved by rule;
No lively print or picture graced the room;
A plain brown paper lent it decent gloom;
But here the eye, in glancing round, surveyed
A small recess, that seemed for china made;
Such pleasing pictures seemed this pencilled ware
That few would search for nobler objects there –
Yet, turned by chosen friends, and there appeared
His stern strong features whom they all revered;
For there in lofty air was seen to stand
The bold protector of the conquered land;
Drawn in that look with which he wept and swore,
Turned out the members and made fast the door,
Ridding the House of every knave and drone,
Forced, though it grieved his soul, to rule alone.
The stern still smile each friend approving gave,
Then turned the view, and all again were grave.[36]

It is hard to believe that Crabbe was inventing. *The Examiner* for 25 January 1711, just a century before Crabbe wrote, tells us that Whigs had portraits of Cromwell. So did John Bowring, a radical fuller of Exeter, grandfather of the biographer of Jeremy Bentham; so too did the father of Ebenezer Elliott, the Chartist poet.[37]

The American and French Revolutions, and the revival of radicalism in England, brought a new interest in seventeenth-century politics, and an occasional good word for Cromwell. The Instrument of Government's franchise deserved consideration, Earl Fauconberg suggested in 1785.[38] Shelburne thought that Cromwell, 'while he had power .. did set more things forward than all the kings who reigned during the century, King William included. England was never so much respected abroad, while at home ... talents of every kind began to show themselves, which were immediately crushed or put to sleep at the restoration.'[39] In America John Adams described Oliver's government as 'infinitely more glorious and happy than that of his Stuart predecessor'. Patrick Henry invoked the spirit of Cromwell, and Ezra Styles in 1794 cried: 'There must and will arise new Cromwells . . . to . . . resume the work which Oliver and the judges once achieved.'[40] But in post-revolutionary America more emphasis was laid on the dangers of a Cromwellian tyranny. The same was true of France. St Just indeed in December 1792 quoted the precedent of Oliver and the trial of Charles I. But both Danton and Robespierre were accused by their enemies of aiming at a Cromwellian dictatorship, and Charles-Philippe Ronsin was alleged to aspire to become the French Cromwell, rather surprisingly as a result of reading Hume's *History of England*.[41]

In England men on whom Home Office spies were keeping a watch in 1812 were calling for 'a second Oliver . . . to cleanse the Augean stable'.[42] Jeremy Bentham five years later regretted that the English Revolution had produced no Code Cromwell, and highly praised Oliver's interest in law reform.[43] When Samuel Bamford visited the House of Commons at about the same time he reflected (or so he tells us) 'Oh! for the stamp of stern old Oliver on this floor . . . and his voice to arise above this babel howl . . . "Begone; give place to honest men".'[44] 'Even to this day,' testified Macaulay in 1828, Oliver's 'character, though constantly attacked and scarcely ever defended, is popular with the great body of our countrymen'.[45] This suggests that Carlyle did not so much create a more sympathetic version of Oliver Cromwell as give expression to something which already existed below the level of polite letters. In 1836 *The Political Penny Magazine* had defended Cromwell.[46] *The Bradford Observer* in 1849 thought Oliver incarnated 'the genius of genuine Saxon liberty'.[47] The Chartist leader Ernest Jones wrote *A Song of Cromwell's Time,* and in 1850 George Harney's *The Red Republican* hailed 'a spirit of Cromwellian might . . . stirring at this hour'. 'Where Cromwell dared to

lead, we dare to follow now.' England's sons should 'swear
by the strength of Cromwell's soul to win their freedom
yet'.[48] So it was not quite so surprising as Carlyle thought
when, on inspecting the battlefield of Worcester, he met
a labourer who wished to God 'we had another Oliver,
sir, times is dreadful bad'.[49]

Both Alton Locke and Joseph Arch recalled ancestors
who had fought for Cromwell. Mrs Gaskell praised his
'admirable commercial policy'. The American Civil War
brought new references to the seventeenth century. The
name of Cromwell brought cheers, in Manchester at
least. 'The party of Cromwell and Milton still lives', declared Goldwin Smith; and it supported the North.[50]
Cromwell was T. H. Green's 'particular hero', whom he
regarded as an unselfish character, though admitting that
he had been accused of unscrupulousness, violence, simu-
lation, dissimulation and other vices, as was inevitable in
a revolutionary leader.[51] In 1873 the Nottingham branch
of the First International used to meet at a public house
called the Oliver Cromwell.[52] Even in the 1890s, the
proposal to raise a statue to Oliver at Westminster roused
a storm, and led Swinburne to write his 'Cromwell's
Statue':

> How should Cromwell stand
> With knights and with queenlings hewn in stone?

As late as the 1950s the suggestion that a college at
Durham University might be named after the man who
created a University at Durham three hundred years
earlier met with astonishingly fierce opposition. The name
finally accepted, by an appropriately drab compromise,
was Grey College.

But quarrels rage not merely between royalists and
Parliamentarians over the memory of the Protector. The
reactions of radical posterity to Oliver have been as
mixed as those of his radical contemporaries. Mrs

Catherine Macaulay could not abide him. William Cobbett recalled Cromwell's share in abolishing the feudal tenures of the gentry at the expense of the common people.⁵³ Nineteenth-century radicals and socialists were divided over him. The dispute was summed up after a speech made not so long ago by an eminent Liberal member of the Cromwell Association. 'The question we must all ask ourselves', he thundered as he reached his peroration, 'is, On which side would I have stood at Naseby?' 'Yes,' said a voice from the audience; 'and on which side would you have stood at Burford?'

If we emphasize the 1640s we can with Marvell see Oliver Cromwell as 'the force of angry heaven's flame', an elemental power cleaving its way through all opposition

> To ruin the great work of time,
> And cast the kingdom old
> Into another mould.

Or we can see him as the fiery protagonist of greater liberty of thought and opportunity, hostile to dogmatism, privilege and shams. If on the other hand we dwell on Cromwell's suppression of the Levellers and his subsequent uneasy career, he appears an all-too-human class-conscious conservative, a wily politician using all his arts to preserve a hated military régime – and as the founder of the British Empire. We can no doubt find threads of continuity in Oliver's personality, his religion, his social prejudices, as I have tried to do in this book.⁵⁴. I sympathize with the ageing, disillusioned man who struggled on under the burden of the protectorate, knowing that without him worse would befall: who wanted to be painted 'warts and all'. But it is the boisterous and confident leader of the 1640s who holds my imagination, and whose pungent, earthy truths echo down the centuries. So long as men and women 'with the root of the matter in them' call in question those values of their society which deny our common humanity, so long indeed as the great issues of liberty and equality which Oliver raised remain unresolved, so long will he continue to fascinate, and the debate over him will continue.

I conclude with another passage from Andrew Marvell – Cromwell's coolest contemporary admirer, and the least corruptible of all the politicians who survived from the Oliverian age into that of the Cavalier Parliament:

> And well he therefore does, and well has guessed,
> Who in his age has always forward pressed:
> And, knowing not where heaven's choice may light,
> Girds yet his sword, and ready stands to fight. . . .
> If these the times, then this must be the man.
>   (*The First Anniversary of the Government under O.C.*)

Notes

I OLIVER CROMWELL AND THE ENGLISH REVOLUTION

1 In what follows I am summarizing points made more fully in my *The Century of Revolution* (1961) and *Reformation to Industrial Revolution* (1967).

2 Ed. T. H. Aston, *Crisis in Europe, 1560–1660* (1965), *passim*.

3 A. D. Lublinskaya, *French Absolutism: the crucial phase, 1620–1629* (Cambridge University Press, 1968), *passim*.

4 G. R. Elton, *The Tudor Constitution* (1960), p. 285.

5 J. Hurtsfield, *The Queen's Wards* (1958), *passim*.

6 F. J. Fisher, 'Tawney's Century', in *Essays in the Economic and Social History of Tudor and Stuart England, in Honour of R. H. Tawney* (ed. F. J. Fisher, Cambridge University Press, 1961); J. Thirsk (ed.), *The Agrarian History of England and Wales*, IV, 1500–1640 (Cambridge University Press, 1967), *passim*.

7 G. Winstanley, *A New-Year's Gift for the Parliament and Armie* (1650), p. 24, in *The Works of Gerrard Winstanley* (ed. G. H. Sabine, Cornell University Press, 1941), pp. 373–4.

8 See pp. 23–4 below.

9 I have discussed these matters at some length in my *Economic Problems of the Church* (1956), *passim*.

10 I have discussed these and similar problems in my *Society and Puritanism in pre-Revolutionary England* (1964), *passim*.

11 See my *Intellectual Origins of the English Revolution* (1965) for documentation.

12 Sir J. E. Neale, 'The Elizabethan Political Scene', in *Essays in Elizabethan History* (1958), pp. 59–84; J. Hurstfield, 'The Succession Struggle in Late Elizabethan England', in *Elizabethan Government and Society: Essays presented to Sir John Neale* (ed. S. T. Bindoff, J. Hurstfield and C. H. Williams, 1961), pp. 369–96.

13 P. Collinson, 'John Field and Elizabethan Puritanism', in *Elizabethan Government and Society*, p. 159.

14 P. Collinson, *The Elizabethan Puritan Movement* (1967), especially Part IV, Chapter 4.

15 In this phrase from his speech of September 1656 Oliver may have been echoing the opening words of Tom May's *The History of the Parliament* (1647), which referred to 'Queen Elizabeth of glorious memory' (p. 1), or Sir Anthony Weldon's reference to 'Queen Elizabeth of happy memory', in *The Court and Character of King James* (1651), pp. 1–2. Cf. the laudatory poems to Queen Elizabeth published in 1650 by Mistress Anne Bradstreet.

16 Ed. M. A. E. Green, *Diary of John Rous* (Camden Soc., 1856), p. 19.

17 See p. 45 below.

18 R. Ashton, *The Crown and the Money Market, 1603–40* (Oxford, 1960), *passim*.

19 John Bradshaw, President of the Court which tried Charles ɪ in 1649, quoted the precedent of Mary.

20 See p. 46 below.

21 Ed. J. Bruce and D. Masson, *The Quarrel between the Earl of Manchester and Oliver Cromwell* (Camden Soc., 1875), p. 72.

II FROM COUNTRY GENTLEMAN TO LORD OF THE FENS: 1599–1640

1 A fourth edition appeared in 1648. Bunyan was still using the book in 1680 (*Works*, ed. G. Offor, 1860, III, p. 587).

2 *Op. cit.* (1597 ed.), pp. 460, 462, 471, 13, 386. Beard also influenced William Prynne (see W. Lamont, *Marginal Prynne*, 1963, p. 31).

3 See p. 198 below.

4 See pp. 33–4 above.

5 Ed. R. Davies, *The Life of Marmaduke Rawsdon of York* (Camden Soc., 1863), pp. 112–13.

6 Ed. J. Thirsk, *The Agrarian History of England and Wales*, IV, 1500–1640, pp. 242–3; *Victoria County History of Huntingdonshire*, II, pp. 89–91.

7 'Dr Alablaster' is William Alabaster the poet, chaplain to James ɪ. Alabaster had earlier been a papist for fifteen or more years. The sermon in question seems to have been preached in 1617. Cf. pp. 30–2 above.

8 L. Stone, *The Crisis of the Aristocracy, 1558–1641* (Oxford University Press, 1965), Chapter III.

9 Ed. F. N. L. Poynter and W. J. Bishop, *A Seventeenth-Century Doctor and his Patients: John Symcotts 1592?–1662* (Bedfordshire Historical Record Soc., XXXI, 1961), pp. xx–xxiii.

10 For reasons see my *Economic Problems of the Church*, Chapters V and VI.

11 See my *Society and Puritanism in Pre-Revolutionary England*, pp. 93–4, and references there cited.

12 See pp. 17–18 above.

13 Arise Evans, *A Rule from Heaven: or Wholsom Counsel to the Distracted State: Wherein is discovered The onely Way for settling the Good Old Cause* (1659), p. 22.

14 *Calendar of State Papers, Domestic, 1631–3*, p. 501; Sir W. Dugdale, *A Short View of the Late Troubles in England* (1681), p. 460.

15 The Duke of Manchester, *Court and Society from Elizabeth to Anne* (1864), II, p. 51.

III FROM CAPTAIN TO LIEUTENANT-GENERAL: 1640–46

1 J. Rushworth, *Historical Collections* (1680), III, p. 1381.

2 T. Sprat, *The History of the Royal Society of London* (1667), p. 73.

3 D. H. Pennington, 'County and Country: Staffordshire in Civil War Politics, 1640–44', *North Staffordshire Journal of Field Studies*, V (1966), pp. 16, 19.

4 W. Lilly, *The True History of King James I and Charles I* (1715), p. 64.

5 See p. 76 below and pp. 46–8 above.

6 Sir Philip Warwick, *Memoirs of the Reign of King Charles the First* (1813), pp. 193–4, 275.

7 T. May, *History of the Parliament* (1647), III, pp. 78–9.

8 T. Tany, *Theaureaujohn High Priest to the Jewes, His Disputive Challenge to the Universities of Oxford and Cambridge, and the whole Hirarch of Roms Clargical Priests* (1651 (–2)), p. 6.

9 B. Whitelocke, *Memorials of the English Affairs* (1702), p. 72.

10 Cromwell's words so closely recall Falstaff's (*Henry IV*, Part I, Act iv, scene 2) as to suggest to Mr A. L. Morton that 'Cromwell in his unregenerate days at the Inns of Court may have seen a performance of *Henry IV*' (A. L. Morton, *The Matter of Britain*, 1966, p. 48). Another famous Cromwellian phrase was anticipated in *Henry V*, when Exeter bids the King of France 'in the bowels of the Lord, deliver up the crown' (Act ii, scene 4). The phrase of course was biblical (Philippians, I-8); it had been

used by John Aylmer in 1559 (*An Harborowe for Faithful and trewe Subjectes*, Sig. R 2v); and by Cromwell in a letter of 11 January 1635.

11 Whitelocke, *loc. cit.*

12 Sir Philip Warwick, *Memoirs*, p. 279.

13 See p. 58 above.

14 *Historical MSS. Commission, Portland MSS.*, I, p. 87. Hotham and his father were executed as traitors in January 1645, Cromwell twice acting as teller in the Commons against motions for clemency to Sir John.

15 *The Quarrel between Manchester and Cromwell*, pp. 72, 74.

16 See pp. 59–60 above.

17 The distinction was familiar to contemporaries. The Elizabethan *Homilies* contrasted those who 'wear a russet coat' with the man who 'ruffleth in silk and velvets'. William Kempe on his famous dance to Norwich in 1600 was accompanied part of the way by a village maiden in 'her russet petticoat'. The jester Richard Tarleton wore russet on the stage to establish his links with the groundlings. The poets Samuel Rowlands and George Wither sang of rustics 'in homespun russet', 'plain in russet clad'. In Cheshire in the 1620s the richest yeomen 'went but in russet coats' (S. Clarke, *The Lives of sundry Eminent Persons*, 1683, p. 4). At Newcastle 'thick grey russets' were provided as 'the most suitable and warm kind of wearing for the poor', though after 1646 they were given better clothes (R. Howell, *Newcastle upon Tyne and the Puritan Revolution*, 1967, p. 316). Cf. Bishop Hall, quoted on p. 53 above. Nicholas Breton had contrasted 'russet jerkins' with 'velvet gowns' (*The Pilgrimage to Paradise*, 1592).

18 He made the same point to Sir Thomas Barrington on 6 October 1643.

19 *Historical MSS. Commission, Portland MSS.*, I, p. 87.

20 This man, Edward Stone, later showed great initiative in cooperating with Cromwell against the Scottish invasion in 1648.

21 D. Underdown, 'The Ilchester Election, February 1646', *Proceedings of the Somerset Archaeological and Natural History Society*, Vol. 110 (1966), p. 41. After the war was over, in Glamorganshire 'men of no social standing had been placed on the County Committee, while baronets, knights and other gentlemen had been passed over', Sir J. F. Rees, 'Politics and Religion in the Vale of Glamorgan during the Civil War', in *Glamorgan History* (ed. S. Wilkins, 1963), p. 192; cf. A. H. Dodd, *Studies in*

Stuart Wales (Cardiff, 1962), pp. 110-76, for other Welsh counties.

22 J. Vicars, *Jehovah-Jireh* (1644), p. 367
23 Clarendon, *History of the Rebellion* (1888), IV, p. 305.
24 *The Quarrel between Manchester and Cromwell*, p. 75.
25 *Calendar of State Papers, Venetian, 1643–47*, p. 162.
26 Cf. a character in Massinger's *The Duke of Milan:* 'Now speak / Or be for ever silent' (*Plays*, 1897, p. 89). First printed 1623.
27 Ed. M. Sylvester, *Reliquiae Baxterianae* (1696), I, p. 49.
28 Ed. H. G. Tibbutt, *The Letter-Books of Sir Samuel Luke* (1963). p. 420.
29 See pp. 46–8 above.
30 G. F. Nuttall, 'Was Cromwell an Iconoclast?', *Trans. Congregational History Soc.*, XII, pp. 51–66. See pp. 197–9 below.
31 *Reliquiae Baxterianae*, I, p. 51.
32 See pp. 66–8 above.
33 Cf. the advice given by John Pym to the Governor of Providence Island towards the end of 1638: 'God makes no difference between them that do faithfully and heartily seek him, though there be in the appearance of men some difference between them in opinion and practice concerning outward things', quoted by A. P. Newton, *Colonizing Activities of the Early Puritans* (Yale University Press, 1914), p. 256.
34 R. W(illiams), *The Fourth Paper by Major Butler* (1652), Preface.
35 See pp. 66–8 above, pp. 212–13 below.
36 See p. 71 above.
37 Cromwell also patronized Major Henry Lilburne, of a very different political outlook, who in 1648 was killed by his own soldiers as a royalist sympathizer.
38 Abbott, *op. cit.*, III, p. 13; IV, p. 274. See pp. 122–3, 125–6, 133–5, 170–1, 187 below.
39 See M. Roberts, *Gustavus Adolphus, II, 1626–32* (1958), pp. 182–9.
40 Clarendon, *History of the Rebellion*, IV, pp. 45–6.
41 G. Wither, *Carmen Eucharisticon* (1649), quoted by C. V. Wedgwood, *Poetry and Politics under the Stuarts* (Cambridge, 1960), p. 114.
42 *Letter-Books of Sir Samuel Luke*, pp. 304, 309-10.
43 I. Roy, 'The Royalist Council of War, 1642–46', *Bulletin of the Institute of Historical Research*, XXV (1962); J. Engberg, 'Royalist Finances during the English Civil War, 1642–46', *Scandinavian Economic History Review*, XIV (1966).

IV   FROM SOLDIER TO POLITICIAN:
1647–49

1 See Chapter IX below.

2 One possible explanation is that Joyce *had* a commission to take the King into custody, but not to remove him from Holmby House—which is what Joyce was proposing to do when Charles asked for his commission. Cromwell and Fairfax told the King that Joyce had no commission from them to remove him; 'he was removed from Holdenby without their privity, knowledge or consent' (*Clarke Papers,* Camden Soc., I, p. 125; Warwick, *Memoirs of the Reign of King Charles I,* p. 331).

3 Cf. the Leveller John Wildman: 'The constant importunity and solicitation of many friends could not prevail with Cromwell to appear until the danger of imprisonment forced him to fly to the Army (the day after the first rendez-vous) for shelter' (*Putney Projects,* 1647, p. 7).

4 *Thurloe State Papers,* (1742), V, p. 674.

5 *Thurloe State Papers,* I, pp. 94–5.

6 J. Lilburne, *Jonahs Cry out of the Whales Belly* (1647), p. 5.

7 Denzil Lord Holles, *Memoirs,* in F. Maseres, *Select Tracts* (1815), I, p. 240.

8 *A Declaration, or Representation* (1647) in *The Leveller Tracts, 1647–53* (ed. W. Haller and G. Davies, Columbia University Press, 1944), p. 55.

9 This refers to the fact that many unpopular officers had been driven out of the Army.

10 Clarendon, *History of the Rebellion,* IV, p. 261. For the Army in 1647 see especially H. N. Brailsford, *The Levellers and the English Revolution* (1961), Chapters X–XIV.

11 *Clarke Papers,* I, pp. 440–2; D. E. Underdown, 'The Parliamentary Diary of John Boys, 1647–8', *Bulletin of the Institute of Historical Research,* XXXIX (1966), pp. 152–3.

12 Clarendon, *History of the Rebellion,* IV, p. 271.

13 (J. Wildman), *Putney Projects* (1647), p. 27. Ware had been the scene of the rendezvous on 15 November.

14 See p. 246 below.

15 C. V. Wedgwood, *The Trial of Charles I* (1964), pp. 43, 233.

16 See pp. 232–3 below. One possible explanation of the correspondence is that when Hammond was appointed to command the Isle of Wight he and Oliver were agreed in wanting to save the King's life; and that Hammond, away from the main body

of the Army, had not followed the changing mood of the lower officers and rank and file as his cousin had done.

17 *Reliquiae Baxterianae*, I, pp. 50–1.

18 G. Burnet, *History of My Own Time* (ed. O. Airy, 1897), I, p. 79.

19 There were ultimately 59 signatures to the death warrant – the same number as those who had voted against Strafford's attainder in May 1641.

20 J. E. Farnell, 'The Usurpation of Honest London Householders: Barebones Parliament', *English Historical Review*, LXXXII (1967), pp. 24–5.

V THE LORD GENERAL: 1649–53

1 *The Hunting of the Foxes by Five Small Beagles* (1649), in *Leveller Manifestoes of the Puritan Revolution* (ed. D. M. Wolfe, New York, 1944), pp. 370, 366.

2 P. Gregg, *Free-born John* (1967), p. 269; Brailsford, *The Levellers and the English Revolution*, chapter 23.

3 See p. 110 below.

4 O. Lutaud, 'Le parti politique "Niveleur" et la première Révolution anglaise', *Revue Historique*, fascicule 46 (1962), p. 86.

5 P. W. Thomas, *Sir John Berkenhead, 1617–1679* (Oxford University Press, 1969), p. 122; *Mr. Peters Last Report of the English Wars* (1646), pp. 9–10; *Memoirs of Sir Andrew Melvill* (1918), pp. 92, 99–100; ed. J. Mayer, 'Inedited Letters of Cromwell, Colonel Jones, Bradshaw and Other Regicides', *Transactions of the Historical Soc. of Lancashire and Cheshire*, New Series I, p. 195; Abbott, *op. cit.*, II, p. 254.

6 *Walwyns Wiles* (1649), in *The Leveller Tracts, 1647–53*, ed. W. Haller and G. Davies, p. 310. The Levellers also protested that the Irish expedition was a violation of the Army's Solemn Engagement of 5 June 1647, not to disband or divide until the liberties of Englishmen were secure.

7 See pp. 144, 151 below.

8 *The Essayes of Michael Lord of Montaigne* (trans. J. Florio, World's Classics), I, p. 56.

9 R. S. Paul, *The Lord Protector* (1955), p. 218.

10 R. P. Stearns, *The Strenuous Puritan: Hugh Peter, 1598–1660* (Illinois University Press, 1954), p. 356.

11 In fact it was announced on 16 February 1650, that in the past year £715,000 had been spent on the army in Ireland.

12 Cromwell was paraphrasing a resolution discussed in the Commons on 8 December 1641 but not accepted by the King (Ed.

W. H. Coates, *Journal of Sir Simonds D'Ewes,* New Haven, 1942, pp. 254, 305, 311–12). I owe this reference to the kindness of Dr Robin Clifton.

13 R. Clifton, 'An Examination of the fear of Catholics and of Catholic plots in England, 1637–1645, with principal reference to central sources' (Oxford D. Phil. Thesis, 1967).

14 E. Ludlow, *Memoirs* (ed. C. H. Firth, 1894), I, pp. 246–7. We may compare the similar attempt later in Scotland to appeal to the common people by offering them legal protection against their landlords and great men (See pp. 125–30 below.)

15 Dodd, *Studies in Stuart Wales,* p. 106.

16 Whitelocke, *op. cit.,* p. 416. In 1656 the Protector knighted James Whitelocke, by then a colonel.

17 See p. 133 below.

18 This striking phrase was not Oliver's. It had been used before him by Robert Burton in 1621 (*Anatomy of Melancholy,* Everyman ed., II, p. 84), by Milton in 1645 (*Tetrachordon, Prose Works,* Yale ed., II, pp. 634–5) and by Henry Denne, *The Man of Sin Discovered* (1646, p. 30). Denne was a leader of the mutinous regiments at Burford, though he recanted to save his life.

19 Ed. C. S. Terry, *The Cromwellian Union* (Scottish History Soc., 1902), p. xxiii.

20 Cf. p. 123 above.

21 J. Salmon, *A Rout, A Rout* (1649), pp. 15–21. But cf. pp. 131, 206 below.

22 See p. 80 above.

23 Mayer, *op. cit.,* p. 192.

24 Ed. J. T. Rutt, *Diary of Thomas Burton* (1828), I, p. xxv.

25 C. H. Firth and R. S. Rait, *Acts and Ordinances of the Interregnum* (1911), II, pp. 403–6.

26 J. E. Farnell, 'The Navigation Act of 1651, the First Dutch War and the London Merchant Community', *Economic History Review,* Second Series, XVI, pp. 441–2.

27 *Calendar of State Papers, Venetian, 1647–52,* p. 188.

28 Farnell, *op. cit.,* p. 445.

29 *Calendar of State Papers, Venetian, 1643–7,* p. 129.

30 Ed. J. J. Jusserand, *Recueil des Instructions données aux Ambassadeurs et Ministres de France,* XXIV, *Angleterre,* I, *1648–65* (1929), p. 35.

31 S. R. Gardiner, *History of the Commonwealth and Protectorate* (1903), I, pp. 312–13.

32 Farnell, *op. cit.,* p. 443.

33 S. von Bischoffshausen, *Die Politik des Protectors Oliver Cromwell* (Innsbruck, 1899), p. 221.
34 Ludlow, *op. cit.*, I, pp. 244–8. See pp. 125–6 above.
35 Ed. S. M. Ffarington, *The Farington Papers* (Chetham Soc., 1856), p. 168.
36 See pp. 206–10 below.
37 Ed. C. H. Josten, *Elias Ashmole (1617–1692)* (1966), II, p. 591.
38 Whitelocke, *op. cit.*, pp. 548–51.
39 Cf. p. 209 below.
40 Ludlow, *op cit.*, I, pp. 352–4.
41 See Chapter IX below.
42 J. Nickolls, *Original Letters and Papers of State Addressed to Oliver Cromwell* (1743), p. 26.
43 Clarendon, *History of the Rebellion*, V, p. 282.
44 Farnell, 'The Usurpation of Honest London Householders: Barebone's Parliament', p. 44.
45 *Burton's Diary*, I, p. 1.
46 William Hickman to Oliver Cromwell, in Nickoll's *Original Letters*, p. 31.
47 G. E. Aylmer, 'Office Holding as a Factor in English History, 1625–42', *History*, XLIV, p. 240. I have benefited from hearing Professor Aylmer talk about English administration in the 1650s.
48 *Thurloe State Papers*, I, p. 747.
49 R. Howell, *Newcastle upon Tyne and the Puritan Revolution*, pp. 308–13.
50 See p. 187 below.

VI   THE LORD PROTECTOR: 1653–55

1 Bischoffshausen, *Die Politik des Protectors Oliver Cromwell*, pp. 148, 153, 155.
2 Ed. T. Carte, *A Collection of Original Letters and Papers* (1739), II, pp. 92, 95, 103; ed. J. R. Powell, *The Letters of Robert Blake* (Navy Records Soc., 1937), pp. 322–4, 393–6.
3 *Thurloe State Papers*, I, pp. 591–2; Nedham, *A True State of the Case of the Commonwealth* (1653), p. 37. I owe this reference to Mr I. A. McCalman.
4 G. Burnet, *The Life and Death of Sir Matthew Hale* (1774), p. 18.
5 Ed. Sir G. Isham, *The Correspondence of Bishop Brian Duppa and Sir Justinian Isham, 1650–60* (Northants. Record Soc., 1955), p. 94.
6 E. Waller, *Poems* (Muses Library), II, p. 15.

7 The betrayal of the Bordelais rebels by Irish troops employed by Spain had inflamed anti-Irish feelings in England (P. A. Knachel, *England and the Fronde,* Cornell University Press, 1967, pp. 242–7), as did the use of Irish troops in the massacre of the Vaudois, celebrated in Milton's sonnet.

8 R. Baillie, *Letters and Journals* (1775), II, p. 411.

9 (E. Sexby), *Killing No Murder* (1657), Preface.

10 *Reliquiae Baxterianae,* p. 70.

11 Ed. C. Severn, *Diary of the Rev. John Ward, Vicar of Stratford-upon-Avon* (1839), p. 138.

12 Quoted by W. C. Braithwaite, *The Beginnings of Quakerism* (1912), p. 440.

13 See 'The English Revolution and the Brotherhood of Man', in my *Puritanism and Revolution* (1958) pp. 123–52. Sources of some of the quotations in the above paragraph will be found there.

14 See pp. 33–4, 42 above.

15 *Thurloe State Papers,* I, p. 438.

16 Samuel Pepys, *Diary,* 8 September, 1667.

17 *Thurloe State Papers,* V, p. 286.

18 Ed. A. R. and M. B. Hall, *The Correspondence of Henry Oldenburg* (Wisconsin University Press, 1965—), I, p. 57.

19 Thurloe to Montagu, 25 October 1656, in Carte, *A Collection of Original Letters and Papers,* II, p. 115.

20 Sir Charles Firth, *Oliver Cromwell and the Rule of the Puritans in England* (World's Classics), p. 400.

21 See my *Intellectual Origins of the English Revolution,* pp. 164–65.

22 Petition of Sir John Barrington to the House of Commons, 24 July 1645, in *Proceedings and Debates of the British Parliaments respecting North America* (ed. L. F. Stock, Washington), I, (1924), p. 167.

23 See pp. 33–4, 42 above.

24 *Calendar of State Papers, Colonial, 1574–1660,* pp. 294, 296, 309, 316–19; Newton, *Colonizing Activities of the Early Puritans,* p. 315.

25 H. F. Kearney, *The Eleven Years' Tyranny of Charles I* (Historical Association Aids for Teachers Series, 1962), p. 10.

26 Richelieu's *Testament Politique,* quoted by H. Hauser, *La pensée et l'action économiques du Cardinal de Richelieu* (Paris, 1944), p. 138.

27 W. D. Jordan, *White over Black: American Attitudes towards the Negro* (Chapel Hill, 1968), pp. 63–4.

28 Ed. E. B. Sainsbury, *A Calendar of the Court Minutes of the East India Company* (1913), pp. xxiii, 335–7, 374.

29 See my *Puritanism and Revolution*, p. 143; also Knachel, *England and the Fronde*, pp. 163, 206–9; cf. p. 269.

30 *Puritanism and Revolution*, p. 144.

31 Knachel, op. cit., p. 272 and Chapter IX, *passim*. Professor Knachel seems to miss the point that French hostility towards England declined at the same time as and probably because of the growing conservatism of the English government.

32 *The Correspondence of Henry Oldenburg*, I, pp. 53, 57, 37.

33 Folke Dahl, 'King Charles Gustavus of Sweden and the English Astrologers William Lilly and John Gadbury', *Lychnos* (1937), p. 180. The source of the story is Lilly.

34 See my *Intellectual Origins of the English Revolution*, p. 103 and references there cited.

35 *Calendar of State Papers, Venetian, 1657–9*, p. 137. Professor Michael Roberts explains Cromwell's Baltic policy in terms of secular national interest in 'Cromwell and the Baltic', *English Historical Review*, LXXVI, pp. 402–46. For a vigorous and effective defence of Cromwell's foreign policy in non-religious terms see Roger Crabtree, 'The Idea of a Protestant Foreign Policy', in *Cromwell Association Handbook* (1968–9), pp. 2–19.

36 *Calendar of State Papers, Venetian, 1636–9*, pp. 421–2; *1640–2*, pp. 77–8.

37 Slingsby Bethel, *The World's Mistake in Oliver Cromwell, Harleian Miscellany* (1744–52), I, pp. 280–8.

38 Now is the time to admit that the quotation on the title-page of this book omits three words. Milton actually wrote 'God is decreeing to begin some new and great period *in his church*'. The last three words convey to a modern reader something quite different from what Milton intended. 'God's church' was for him roughly what we mean by 'mankind', 'humanity'. Milton was certainly not referring to one church among many, or to a building open on Sundays only: he was referring to all mankind, though no doubt to the elect in particular. So I felt that the passage would be better understood without the words which I now reveal. For God's historical purposes see Chapter IX below

39 *Calendar of State Papers, Venetian, 1632–6*, p. 110.

40 Z. I. Roginsky, 'Iz Istorii Anglo-Russkikh Otnosheniy v pervoy Protektorata Kromvelya', *Novaya i Noveyshaya Istoriya* (No. 5, 1958), pp. 75–8; cf. my *Puritanism and Revolution*, p. 133.

41 See pp. 160–1 above.

42 Clarendon, *History of the Rebellion,* VI, p. 92.
43 *Burton's Diary,* I, p. lxxxv.
44 Ludlow, *Memoirs,* I, p. 365.
45 J. Bentham, *Works* (ed. J. Bowring, 1843), IV, p. 501.

VII KING? 1656–58

1 I owe this point to the unpublished Welsh M.A. Thesis of Mr. A. M. Johnson, 'Buckinghamshire, 1640–60: A Study in County Politics'. Mr Johnson suggests that as the county families re-established themselves economically, Cromwellian rule (at any rate in Buckinghamshire) was based on a party which found itself increasingly isolated.

2 In May 1648 Cromwell had given orders for the suppression of a hunting meeting in Gloucestershire which was to be used as a cover for a seditious assembly.

3 P. J. Pinckney, 'Bradshaw and Cromwell in 1656', *Huntington Library Quarterly,* XXX, p. 236.

4 T. Adams, *Works* (1629), pp. 1008–9; Rushworth, *Historical Collections,* II, p. 163.

5 Cf. H. R. Trevor-Roper, 'The Union of Britain', in *Religion, the Reformation and Social Change* (1967), pp. 445–67.

6 Joshuah Sylvester, *The Complete Works* (ed. A. B. Grosart, 1880), I, p. 240; Sir W. Ralegh, *Works* (1751), I, p. 184; Fulke Greville, *Life of Sir Philip Sidney* (Oxford, 1907), p. 81; A. D. Lublinskaya, *French Absolutism: the crucial phase,* p. 166.

7 Henry King, 'An Elegy on Sir Charles Lucas and Sir George Lisle'; *Burton's Diary,* I, pp. 315–16.

8 Ludlow, *Memoirs,* I, pp. 405–6; Clarendon, *History of the Rebellion,* VI, p. 17. Milton referred both to the Dutch federal constitution and to the 'cantonization of England' in *The Readie and Easie Way* (1660).

9 Carte, *Original Letters and Papers,* I, p. 78; J. R. Jones, 'Booth's Rising of 1659', *Bulletin of the John Rylands Library,* XXXIX, p. 423.

10 Cf. H. Parker, *Of a Free Trade* (1648)—merchants cantonizing world trade; Francis Beaumont, *Psyche* (1648), Canto X, stanza 281—'Satan here cants out his provinces'; M. Purver, *The Royal Society: Concept and Creation,* p. 121—Sir William Petty to Samuel Hartlib; S. Butler, *Hudibras,* Part III, Canto ii, line 243—'spiritual cantons'.

11 (Anon.), *The Second Part of Englands New-Chains Discovered* (1649), p. 15.

12 Burnet, *History of My Own Time*, I, pp. 127–8; K. H. D. Haley, *The First Earl of Shaftesbury* (Oxford, 1968), p. 669, quoting Ashley Cooper.

13 G. P. Gooch, *The History of English Democratic Ideas in the Seventeenth Century* (Cambridge University Press, 1898), p. 263.

14 J. Collop, *Poems* (ed. C. Hilberry, Wisconsin University Press, 1962), p. 75.

15 *Burton's Diary*, I, p. 378.

16 I owe this suggestion to discussions with my former pupils Ceri Jones and John Ward.

17 Speaker Onslow, quoted in Burnet, *History of My Own Time*, I, pp. 126–7.

18 David Underdown, 'Cromwell and the Officers, February 1658', *E.H.R.*, LXXXIII, p. 106.

19 Nickolls, *op. cit.*, pp. 141–2; cf the passage from John Goodwin quoted at the head of this chapter.

20 Ed. A. L. Sells, *The Memoirs of James II, 1652–60* (1962), p. 281.

21 R. Parr, *Life of . . . James Ussher* (1686), p. 75.

22 J. Owen, *Works* (1850–3), VI, p. 112.

23 Collinson, *The Elizabethan Puritan Movement*, p. 285; cf. p. 187.

24 F. Osborn, *Letters . . . to Colonel William Draper*, p. 7, in *Miscellaneous Works* (1722), II. 'O.P.'='Oliver Protector'.

25 *Burton's Diary*, IV, p. 73.

26 Ed. R. Vaughan, *The Protectorate of Oliver Cromwell* (1839), I, p. 70.

27 *A Second Narrative of the Late Parliament* (1658), in *Harleian Miscellany* (1744–56), III, p. 467. Oliver claimed in this too to have been overruled by his Council. Cf. pp. 125–6 above.

28 Baillie, *Letters and Journals*, II, p. 423.

29 Firth and Rait, *Acts and Ordinances of the Interregnum*, II, p. 1168. I owe the reference to the proclamation to my former pupil, Mr J. F. MacGregor of the University of Adelaide.

30 Sir Henry Vane, *A Healing Question* (1656), in *Somers Tracts* (1809–15), VI, p. 307.

31 *Burton's Diary*, I, p. 408.

32 R. Baxter, *A Sermon of Repentance* (1660), p. 43.

33 R. P. Stearns, *The Strenuous Puritan* (Urbana, 1954), p. 394. Cf. Milton: such men's knowledge of what awaited them added to the bitterness of their position as they waited and watched.

34 D. Underdown, 'Cromwell and the Officers, 1658', *English Historical Review*, LXXXIII, pp. 104, 107.

35 Samuel Butler, *Hudibras*, Part III, Canto ii, line 215.

36 *Burton's Diary*, III, p. 160; Ludlow, *Memoirs*, II, p. 436; Burnet, *History of My Own Time*, I, p. 147; *Thurloe State Papers*, VII, pp. 365–75.

37 E. Burroughs, *The Memorable Works of a Son of Thunder and Consolation* (1672), pp. 458–60.

38 See p. 267 below.

39 W. W. Cooper, *Historical Notes concerning the Disease, Death and Disinterment of Oliver Cromwell* (Dublin, 1848), p. 5; cf. p. 24.

40 *Reliquiae Baxterianae*, p. 57.

41 Pinckney, 'Bradshaw and Cromwell in 1656', p. 240.

42 Robert Blair, *Autobiography* (1848), p. 210.

43 See pp. 38, 40, 43–5, 50–1, 61 above.

44 *Calendar of State Papers, Domestic, 1657–8*, p. 9. The letter-book of a merchant of Lucca sold at Sotheby's in 1960 contained a bill of lading for 25 bales of silks sent to the Protector on 30 August 1658.

45 'L'on ne montait jamais si haut, que quand on ne sait où l'on va', Cardinal de Retz, *Mémoires*.

46 G. F. Nuttall, 'Was Cromwell an Iconoclast?' *Transactions of the Congregational Historical Soc.*, XII (1933–6), pp. 51–66.

47 See my *Intellectual Origins of the English Revolution*, especially the Appendix.

48 See pp. 40–1 above.

49 P. Scholes, *The Puritans and Music* (1934), especially Chapter IX.

50 G. E. Aylmer, 'Britain Transformed: Crown, Conscience and Commonwealth', in *The Age of Expansion: Europe and the World, 1559–1660* (ed. H. Trevor-Roper, 1968), p. 240.

VIII THE PEOPLE OF ENGLAND AND THE PEOPLE OF GOD

1 Warwick, *Memoirs*, pp. 193–4.

2 See p. 95 above.

3 Robert Huntington, *Sundry Reasons inducing Major Robert Huntington to lay down his Commission* (1648), p. 3.

4 See Chapter IX below.

5 D. E. Underdown, 'The Parliamentary Diary of John Boys, 1647–8', pp. 152–3.

6 See p. 93 above.

7 M. E. James, 'Obedience and Dissent in Henrician England: the Lincolnshire Rebellion, 1536', *Past and Present*, No. 46.

8 Cf. pp. 127–8, 131 above.

9 See my *Society and Puritanism in pre-Revolutionary England*, p. 414.

10 R. Baxter, *The Holy Commonwealth* (1659), p. 243.

11 (Anon.), *Salus Populi Solus Rex* (1648), quoted by Brailsford, *The Levellers in the English Revolution*, pp. 345–6.

12 Milton, *Complete Prose Works* (Yale), IV, p. 635.

13 *Mr. Peters Last Report of the English Warres* (1646), p. 6.

14 J. Nickolls, *Original Letters*, p. 28. My italics.

15 J. Mayer, 'Inedited Letters of Cromwell, Col. Jones, Bradshaw and Other Regicides', pp. 190–1.

16 (Anon.), *A Complete Collection of the Lives and Speeches of those persons lately executed*, p. 49.

17 Milton, *Complete Prose Works* (Yale), IV, pp. 316–17.

18 Vane, *A Healing Question* (1656), in *Somers Tracts* (1809–15), VI, p. 311.

19 Vane, *A Needful Corrective or Ballance in Popular Government* (May, 1659), quoted by A. H. Woolrych, 'The Good Old Cause and the Fall of the Protectorate', *Cambridge Historical Journal*, XIII (1057), p. 154.

20 Milton, *The Readie and Easy Waie to Establish a Free Commonwealth*, in *Works* (Columbia University Press), VI, pp. 140–1.

21 P. J. Pinckney, 'The Cheshire Election of 1656', *Bulletin of the John Rylands Library*, XLIX (1967), pp. 418–19.

22 (Anon.), *Anti-Toleration* (1646), p. 33.

23 John Price, *The Cloudie Clergy* (1650), p. 18. I owe this reference to the Oxford B.Litt. Thesis of Mr D. A. Kirby.

24 This school of very pragmatic thinkers seems to me to have been taken a little portentously of late: see Irene Coltman, *Private Men and Public Causes* (1962), Part III; J. M. Wallace, *Destiny His Choice: the Loyalism of Andrew Marvell* (1968), Chapter I. The best study still remains that of Perez Zagorin, *A History of Political Thought in the English Revolution* (1954), Chapter V. See pp. 247–8 below.

25 See p. 134 above.

26 *Burton's Diary*, I, pp. 281–2.

27 I have discussed this at length in my *Puritanism and Revolution*, pp. 50–122.

28 *Clarke Papers*, II, p. 245.

29 G. Fox, *Journal* (ed. N. Penney, Cambridge University Press, 1911), I, pp. 400, 427.

30 Woodhouse, *Puritanism and Liberty*, p. 246.

31 Ed. D. M. Loades, *The Papers of George Wyatt, Esquire* (Camden Fourth Series, V), p. 71.

32 Francis Cheynell, *Sions Memento and Gods Alarm* (1643), p. 38. Printed by order of the House of Commons.

33 Mr W. M. Lamont argues that the abandonment by Oliver Cromwell and his government of the ideal of a single religious community, co-extensive with the state, which had been shared by Laud and the Presbyterians, was a major turning-point in English history, after which 'nothing could be the same again'. (*Godly Rule*, 1969, pp. 138–44. This stimulating book appeared after mine was in proof.)

34 Quoted by L. F. Brown, *Baptists and Fifth Monarchy Men* (New York, 1911), p. 72. The writer is best known to history as the father of Titus Oates, of Popish Plot fame.

IX PROVIDENCE AND OLIVER CROMWELL

1 Luther, *The Bondage of the Will* (trans. H. Cole, 1823), pp. 31–2.

2 *Ibid.*, pp. 369–70.

3 J. Calvin, *The Institutes of the Christian Religion* (trans. H. Beveridge, 1949), I, p. 41; cf. p. 47.

4 *Ibid.*, p. 134.

5 *Ibid.*, II, pp. 70, 157.

6 *Ibid.*, II, pp. 97–8.

7 Sir S. D'Ewes, *Autobiography and Correspondence* (ed. J. O. Halliwell, 1845), I, p. 369.

8 T. Taylor, *Works* (1653), pp. 178–9.

9 D. Rogers, *A Practicall Catechisme* (3rd ed., 1640), p. 253.

10 For Calvin's attempts at reconciliation, see especially *Institutes*, I, pp. 187, 202–5, 229, 241, 254, 264; cf. Bunyan, *Works*, I, p. 299, II, pp. 123, 312.

11 W. Haller, *The Rise of Puritanism* (Columbia University Press, 1938), pp. 141, 162.

12 Cf. C. B. MacPherson, 'The Maximization of Democracy', in *Philosophy, Politics and Society*, 3rd Series (ed. P. Laslett and W. G. Runciman), pp. 97–100.

13 *Moby Dick* is a relatively late example.

14 See my *Intellectual Origins of the English Revolution*, pp. 291–3, and references there cited.

15 Calvin, *Institutes*, II, p. 102.

16 Ed. H. Robinson, *Original Letters relative to the English Reformation* (Parker Soc.), II (1847), p. 712. Cf. Calvin, *Institutes*, II, p. 5.

17 Calvin, *Commentary on Genesis* (trans. J. King, 1965), I, p. 171.

18 T. Taylor, *Works*, pp. 166–7.

19 *Ibid.*, p. 172.

20 W. Perkins, *A Clowd of Faithfull Witnesses*, pp. 63–4, in *Works* (1616–18), III.

21 R. Sibbes, *Works* (Edinburgh, 1862–64), I, p. 91; cf. p. 88.

22 J. Cotton, *The Covenant of Gods Free Grace* (1645), pp. 19–20.

23 Ed. A. A. Bonar, *Letters of Samuel Rutherford* (1894), p. 399.

24 F. Bacon, *Works* (ed. J. Spedding, R. L. Ellis and D. D. Heath, 1862–74), III, p. 617.

25 S. Butler, *Characters and Passages from Notebooks* (Cambridge University Press, 1908), p. 307. Butler was referring primarily no doubt to the more radical sectaries. But he would have said (and I agree) that their actions were justified by principles put forward earlier by more conservative Puritans.

26 H. Knollys, *A Glimpse of Sions Glory* (1641), in Woodhouse, *Puritanism and Liberty*, p. 233.

27 D. Footman, *Red Prelude* (1944), title page.

28 *Soviet News*, 8 June 1951.

29 Calvin, *Institutes*, I, pp. 192, 223–5, 231; cf. pp. 212–13.

30 *Clarke Papers*, II, p. 90.

31 A. Marvell, *Upon Appleton House*; K. Philips, *L'Accord du Bien*, in *Minor Poets of the Caroline Period* (ed. G. Saintsbury, Oxford, 1905), I, p. 564; cf. p. 599.

32 'When thou goest out to battle against thine enemies, and seest horses, and chariots, and a people more than thou, be not afraid of them: for the Lord thy God is with thee, which brought thee up out of the land of Egypt'.

33 Sibbes, *Works*, I, p. 209; cf. p. 211.

34 Sir H. Vane, *Speech in the House of Commons* (1641), pp. 8–9.

35 R. Hooker, *Of the Laws of Ecclesiastical Polity* (Everyman ed.), I, p. 139.

36 Sibbes, *Works*, I, p. 98; cf. John Downame, *A Guide to Godlynesse* (1622), Book I, p. 52.

37 T. Gataker, *An Anniversarie Memoriall of Englands Delivery from Spanish Invasion* (1626), pp. 10, 20.

38 *Burton's Diary*, I, p. xxx. The Great Turk often appeared in this context: see *Anglia Liberata*, p. 6.

39 R. Overton, *An Appeale* (1647), in Wolfe, *Leveller Manifestoes*, pp. 158–9.
40 *Clarke Papers*, I, p. 384.
41 J. Owen, *Works*, VIII, p. 336.
42 Bunyan, *Works*, III, p. 123.
43 *Letters of Samuel Rutherford*, p. 238; cf. my *Puritanism and Revolution*, p. 265.
44 L. Ziff, *The Career of John Cotton* (Princeton, 1962), p. 62.
45 Cf. p. 101 above. The whole letter deserves careful study as the *locus classicus* of the theory expounded by a man in the process of acting upon it to transform history.
46 See pp. 39–40 above.
47 H. Peter, *Gods Doings and Mans Duty* (1646), p. 6.
48 L. Howard, ' "The Invention" of Milton's "Great Argument": A Study of the Logic of "God's Ways to Man".' *Huntington Library Quarterly*, IX (1946), p. 172. See p. 224 above.
49 M. Maclure, *The Paul's Cross Sermons* (Toronto University Press, 1958), p. 71.
50 W. M. Noble, *Huntingdonshire and the Spanish Armada* (1896), pp. 54–5.
51 R. Greenham, *Works* (1612), p. 212. Cf. John Preston, quoted in my *Puritanism and Revolution*, p. 265.
52 T. Taylor, *Works*, p. 101.
53 G. Wither, *Brittans Remembrancer* (Spencer Soc., 1880), I, p. 125. First published 1628.
54 See pp. 137, 139, 143 above.
55 See my 'Protestantism and the Rise of Capitalism', in *Essays in the Economic and Social History of Tudor and Stuart England, in Honour of R. H. Tawney*, pp. 15–39.
56 Cf. Perry Miller, *The New England Mind: the 17th Century* (New York, 1939), Chapter XIV.
57 R. Greenham, *Works*, p. 196; cf. p. 343.
58 Bunyan, *Works*, III, p. 122.
59 Perry Miller, *op. cit.*, pp. 160, 37–8; see also pp. 147–82 *passim*.
60 Margaret, Duchess of Newcastle, *CCXI Sociable Letters* (1664), p. 159. The great Puritan, John Preston, it was remarked by a bishop, 'talked like one that was familiar with God Almighty' (T. Ball, *Life of the renowned Dr Preston*, 1885, p. 159). Bunyan often wrote as though he enjoyed the confidence of God (e.g. *Works*, I, p. 524).
61 S. Coleridge, *The Friend* (1865), p. 289.
62 Calvin, *Institutes*, II, p. 227; cf. p. 577.

63 *Ibid.,* I, p. 202; cf. pp. 187, 205, 254, 264. Cf. J. Owen, *Works,* XI, pp. 140–204: *The Immutability of the Purposes of God.*

64 See my *Intellectual Origins of the English Revolution,* pp. 200, 268, 291; *Puritanism and Revolution,* p. 273.

65 G. Hakewill, *An Apologie or Declaration of the Power and Providence of God in the Government of the World* (third ed., 1635), Book V, p. 252.

66 Bunyan, *Works,* I, p. 431; cf. p. 434.

67 C. Caudwell, *The Crisis in Physics* (1949), *passim;* Perry Miller, *op. cit.,* pp. 227–31.

68 Cf. P. Miller and T. H. Johnson, *The Puritans* (New York, 1938), pp. 81–6, 362.

69 R. H. Tawney, *Religion and the Rise of Capitalism* (Penguin ed.), p. 179.

70 J. Caryl, *Davids Prayer for Solomon* (1643), p. 36.

71 E. Kirby, 'Sermons before the Commons, 1640–2', in *American Historical Review,* XLIV.

72 Woodhouse, *Puritanism and Liberty,* p. 234.

73 See p. 232 above.

74 T. Scott, *Vox Dei* (1623), p. 16.

75 Milton, *The Tenure of Kings and Magistrates* (1649), in *Complete Prose Works* (Yale), III, p. 211. Milton refers to the orthodox Calvinist theory of the concurrence of first and second causes in the social contract, thus expressed by John Davenport: 'In regular actings of the creature, God is the first agent; there are not two several and distinct actings, one of God, another of the people: but in one and the same action God, by the people's suffrages, makes such an one governor or magistrate, and not another' (J. Davenport, *A Sermon,* 1669, in *Publications of the Colonial Soc. of Massachusetts,* X, p. 6).

76 Ed. G. Ormerod, *Tracts relating to Military Proceedings in Lancashire during the Great Civil War,* (Chetham Soc., II, 1849), p. 193. I owe this reference to my former pupil, Mr R. Allan.

77 (Anon.), *Salus Populi Solus Rex* (17 October, 1648), quoted by Brailsford, *The Levellers and the English Revolution,* p. 346.

78 Woodhouse, *Puritanism and Liberty,* p. 467.

79 Milton, *Complete Prose Works* (Yale), III, p. 191. The self-validating quality of remarkable events was of course a familiar argument to demonstrate the historical accuracy of the Bible.

80 See pp. 137–8, 232–5 above.

81 T. Hobbes, *English Works* (ed. Sir W. Molesworth, 1839–45), VII, p. 336

82 D. Masson, *Life of John Milton*, V (1877), pp. 450–1.

83 Burnet, *The Life and Death of Sir Matthew Hale* (1774), p. 26. It is perhaps worth recording that Burnet nevertheless still regarded it as 'the safest rule for the conduct of one's life', which he 'ever endeavoured to follow, ... that from first to last it seemed to be carried on by a series of providences' (ed. H. C. Foxcroft, *A Supplement to Burnet's History of My Own Time*, 1902, p. 89).

84 *Diary of Sir Archibald Johnston of Warriston* (Scottish History Soc.), III, p. 167.

85 *A Complete Collection of the Lives and Speeches of those persons lately executed*, pp. 6, 10.

86 Bunyan, *Works*, III, pp. 134–5.

87 Milton, *Complete Prose Works* (Yale), IV, p. 652.

88 Sprat, *The History of the Royal Society of London*, p. 362.

89 Sprat, *A True Account and Declaration of the Horrid Conspiracy against the Late King* (second ed., 1685), p. 159; G. Straka, 'The Final Phase of Divine Right Theory in England, 1688–1702', *English Historical Review*, LXXVII, pp. 638–58.

X   OLIVER CROMWELL AND ENGLISH HISTORY

1 *Clarke Papers*, IV, pp. 143–6; G. Davies, *The Restoration of Charles II, 1658–60* (San Marino, 1955), p. 174.

2 Ed. E. B. Underhill, *The Records of the Church of Christ meeting in Broadmead, Bristol, 1640–87* (Hanserd Knollys Soc., 1847), pp. 39, 45. Cf. L. F. Brown, *Baptists and Fifth Monarchy Men*, p. 76.

3 Ed. H. B. Wheatley, *The Diary of Samuel Pepys* (1946), VII, p. 17, cf. II, p. 191, IV, pp. 43–4, 222, 287, 366, VI, pp. 157–8, VII, p. 97.

4 *History of My Own Time*, I, pp. 139, 145; Pepys, *Diary*, II, p. 191.

5 *Reliquiae Baxterianae*, II, p. 48; L. Muggleton, *A True Interpretation .... of the whole Book of the Revelation of St. John* (1665), p. 106.

6 K. M. Lynch, *Roger Boyle, First Earl of Orrery* (Tennessee University Press, 1965), p. 127. Orrery is our old friend Lord Broghill.

7 P. J. Pinckney, 'Bradshaw and Cromwell in 1656', p. 236.

8 Sprat, *The History of the Royal Society of London*, p. 404.

9 S. Bethel, *The Interest of Princes and States* (1680), p. 2, and chapter I *passim*.

10 See pp. 13–14, 55–7, 130–2, 155–68 above.

11 South had published a panegyric on the Lord Protector in April 1654.

12 *The Correspondence of Henry Oldenburg*, I, pp. xxxiv–vi, 37.

13 Ed. Sir H. Hartley, *The Royal Society: Its Origins and Founders* (*Notes and Records of the Royal Society*, XV, 1960), p. 72.

14 See my *Intellectual Origins of the English Revolution*, Chapter II and *passim*.

15 Sir R. Filmer, *Observations Upon Aristotles Politics* (1652), in *Patriarcha and other Political Works* (ed. P. Laslett, Oxford, 1949), p. 225.

16 See pp. 17–18, 48–9 above.

17 J. Aubrey, *Remaines of Gentilisme and Judaisme* (ed. J. Britten, 1881), pp. 247–8.

18 See pp. 125–6, 145, 187 above.

19 'The question had been judged in the field at Naseby before it was tried in Westminster Hall' said Gibbon, in the year of the execution of Louis XVI (*Miscellaneous Works*, Dublin, 1796, II, p. 232).

20 W. Dell, *Several Sermons and Discourses* (1709), pp. 225–6. It was a familiar protestant point; Dell went on to quote Luther to illustrate it.

21 J. Owen, *Works* VIII, pp. 327–9.

22 Ed. F. N. L. Poynter and W. J. Bishop, *A Seventeenth-century Doctor and his Patients: John Symcotts, 1592?–1662* (Bedfordshire Historic Record Soc., XXXI, 1961), p. 76.

23 H. Kohn, 'The Genesis and Character of English Nationalism', *Journal of the History of Ideas*, I, pp. 79–93.

24 See quotations from Milton and Cromwell on my title-page.

25 Quoted by F. Raab, *The English Face of Machiavelli* (1964), p. 152. The whole section of this stimulating book devoted to Cromwell is well worth reading (pp. 130–54).

26 Burnet, *History of My Own Time*, I, p. 142.

27 James Prior, *The Life of Oliver Goldsmith* (1837), I, p. 6.

28 R. Trevor Davies, *Four Centuries of Witch Beliefs* (1947), Chapter IX.

29 There is an excellent study in Russian by M. A. Barg, *Cromwell and His Time* (Moscow, 1952), though the author lacks Dr Paul's sensitivity to Cromwell's religious beliefs. Unfortunately I cannot read the biographies in Hungarian and Czech, by L. Makkai and M. Hroch respectively.

30 See p. 197 above.

31 Alan Smith, 'The Image of Cromwell in Folklore and Tradition',

Folklore, Vol. 79 (1968), pp. 17–39, on which the above paragraph is based.

32 W. G. Zeeveld, *The Foundations of Tudor Policy* (Harvard University Press, 1948), esp. pp. 160, 194, 209–11.

33 See p. 254 above.

34 M. W. Beresford, 'Glebe Terriers and Open Field, Yorkshire', *Yorkshire Archaeological Journal,* XXXVII, p. 330.

35 Mrs Gaskell, *Life of Charlotte Bronte* (World's Classics), p. 12.

36 G. Crabbe, *Tales* (1812), Tale VI, 'The Frank Courtship'.

37 *Autobiographical Recollections of Sir John Bowring* (1877), pp. 31–2; E. Elliott, *More Verses* (1850), II, p. 161.

38 The Rev. Christopher Wyvill, *Political Papers chiefly respecting the reform of the Parliament of Great Britain* (n.d.), II, p. 363.

39 Lord Edmond Fitzmaurice, *Life of William, Earl of Shelburne* (1875), I, p. 23 (an autobiographical fragment written in 1802–3). I owe this reference to the kindness of my friend Mr Peter Brown.

40 H. Trevor Colbourn, *The Lamp of Experience: Whig History and the Intellectual Origins of the American Revolution* (North Carolina University Press, 1965), p. 95; E. Styles, *A History of Three of the Judges of King Charles I* (1794), quoted by E. S. Morgan (ed.), *Puritan Political Ideas, 1558–1794* (New York, 1965), pp. 391–2.

41 A. Soboul, *Les Sans-Culottes Parisiens en l'an II* (Paris, 1958), pp. 341, 745, 804; R. C. Cobb, *Les Armées Révolutionnaires,* II (Paris, 1963), pp. 813–14, 824. There were similar references in the Russian Revolution, though by then the analogy usually drawn upon—and warned against—was that of Napoleon (see especially I. Deutscher, *The Prophet Unarmed: Trotsky, 1921–29,* Oxford, 1959, *passim*).

42 P.R.O., H.O. 42/123. I owe this reference to the kindness of Mr Raphael Samuel, one of a group of historians associated with *Past and Present* which is investigating Cromwell's reputation in nineteenth-century England, with special reference to the radical and working-class movements (*Past and Present,* No. 40, pp. 187–190).

43 See p. 171 above.

44 S. Bamford, *Passages in the Life of a Radical* (ed. T. Hilton, 1967), p. 27. First published 1844—before Carlyle.

45 T. B. Macaulay, *Critical and Historical Essays* (1854), I, pp. 177–8.

46 No. 2, 10 September, 1836; No. 3, 17 September, 1836.

47 Quoted by Asa Briggs, *Saxons, Normans and Victorians* (Hast-

ings and Bexhill Branch of the Historical Association, 1966), p. 25.

48 *Op. cit.*, I, pp. ii, 48, 72, 111.

49 J. A. Froude, *Thomas Carlyle a History of his Life in London, 1834–81* (1890), I, p. 336.

50 Goldwin Smith, *England and America* (1865), pp. 8–10. I am grateful to Professor Peter Marshall for drawing my attention to this book.

51 Melvin Richter, *The Politics of Conscience: T. H. Green and his Age* (1964), pp. 47, 246–7.

52 I owe this information to Mr Raphael Samuel.

53 W. Cobbett, *Legacy to Labourers*, Letter II.

54 For a fresh interpretation, which appeared too late for me to use, see Lamont, *Godly Rule*, Chapter VI.

Bibliography

I ON OLIVER CROMWELL

The essential reference book is W. C. Abbott's edition of *The Writings and Speeches of Oliver Cromwell* (Harvard University Press, 1937–47), in four volumes. Far and away the best biography is Sir Charles Firth, *Oliver Cromwell* (World's Classics). The following are some books, pamphlets and articles dealing with Cromwell published during the last twelve years:

Roger Crabtree, 'The Idea of a Protestant Foreign Policy', in *Cromwell Association Handbook* (1968–9).

Christopher Hill, *Oliver Cromwell, 1658–1958* (Historical Association pamphlet, 1958).

P. J. Pinckney, 'Bradshaw and Cromwell in 1656', *Huntington Library Quarterly*, XXX.
'The Cheshire Election of 1656', *Bulletin of the John Rylands Library*, XLIX.

Ed. F. N. L. Poynter and W. J. Bishop, *A Seventeenth-Century Doctor and his Patients: John Symcotts, 1592?–1662* (Bedfordshire Historical Record Soc., XXXI).

M. Roberts, 'Cromwell and the Baltic', *English Historical Review*, LXXVI.

A. Smith, 'The Image of Cromwell in Folklore and Tradition', *Folklore*, Vol. 79.

D. E. Underdown, 'The Parliamentary Diary of John Boys, 1647–8', *Bulletin of the Institute of Historical Research*, XXXIX.
'Cromwell and the Officers, 1658', *English Historical Review*, LXXXIII.

II BACKGROUND

Here are a number of books and articles which may be useful for background reading, published during the same period.

R. Ashton, 'Cavaliers and Capitalists', *Renaissance and Modern Studies*, V.

Ed. T. Aston, *Crisis in Europe, 1560–1660* (Routledge & Kegan Paul, 1965).

G. E. Aylmer, *The Struggle for the Constitution, 1603–1689* (Blandford Press, 1963).

Ed. H. E. Bell and R. L. Ollard, *Historical Essays, 1600–1750, presented to David Ogg* (A & C Black, 1963).

H. N. Brailsford, *The Levellers and the English Revolution* (Cresset Press, 1961).

Ed. C. H. Carter, *From the Renaissance to the Counter Reformation: Essays in Honor of Garrett Mattingly* (New York, 1965; Cape, 1966).

R. Davis, *A Commercial Revolution* (Historical Association pamphlet, 1967).

J. E. Farnell, 'The Navigation Act of 1651, the First Dutch War and the London Merchant Community', *Economic History Review*, Second Series, XVI.

'The Usurpation of Honest London Householders: Barebones Parliament', *English Historical Review*, LXXXII.

Ed. F. J. Fisher, *Essays in the Economic and Social History of Tudor and Stuart England, in Honour of R. H. Tawney* (Cambridge University Press, 1961).

H. J. Habakkuk, 'Public Finance and the Sale of Confiscated Property during the Interregnum', *Economic History Review*, Second Series, XV.

'Landowners and the Civil War', *ibid.*, Second Series, XVIII.

W. Haller, *Foxe's Book of Martyrs and the Elect Nation* (Cape, 1963).

C. Hill, *Puritanism and Revolution* (Panther History, 1968).
The Century of Revolution, 1603–1714 (Sphere Books, 1969).
Society and Puritanism in Pre-Revolutionary England (Panther History, 1969).
Intellectual Origins of the English Revolution (Oxford, 1965).
Reformation to Industrial Revolution (Penguin Books, 1969).

Ed. E. W. Ives, *The English Revolution, 1600–1660* (Edward Arnold, 1968).

Ed. J. P. Kenyon, *The Stuart Constitution* (Cambridge University Press, 1966).

W. Lamont, *Godly Rule* (Macmillan, 1969).

C. B. Macpherson, *The Political Theory of Possessive Individualism* (Clarendon Press, 1962).

R. Nevo, *The Dial of Virtue: A Study of Poems on Affairs of State in the Seventeenth Century* (Princeton University Press, 1963).

V. Pearl, 'The "Royal Independents" in the English Civil War', *Transactions of the Royal Historical Soc.*, 1968.

F. Raab, *The English Face of Machiavelli* (Routledge & Kegan Paul, 1964).

I. Roots, *The Great Rebellion, 1642–1660* (Batsford, 1968).

L. Stone, *The Crisis of the Aristocracy, 1558–1641* (Clarendon Press, 1965).

Ed. J. Thirsk, *The Agrarian History of England and Wales,* IV, 1500–1640 (Cambridge University Press, 1967).

J. Thirsk, 'Younger Sons in the Seventeenth Century', *History, LIV.*

H. R. Trevor-Roper, *Religion, the Reformation and Social Change* (Macmillan, 1967).

D. E. Underdown, *Royalist Conspiracy in England, 1649–1660* (Yale University Press, 1960).

M. Walzer, *The Revolution of the Saints* (Harvard University Press, 1965).

C. V. Wedgwood, *The Trial of Charles I* (Collins, 1964).

C. Wilson, *England's Apprenticeship, 1603–1763* (Longmans, 1965).

A. H. Woolrych, 'The Calling of Barebone's Parliament', *English Historical Review*, LXXX.

P. Zagorin, 'The Social Interpretation of the English Revolution', *Journal of Economic History*, September 1959.

Index

73 74   12 11 10 9 8 7 6 5 4 3 2